Real-Resumes For Nursing Jobs

...including real resumes used to change careers
and resumes used to gain federal employment

Anne McKinney, Editor

PREP PUBLISHING

FAYETTEVILLE, NC

PREP Publishing
1110 ½ Hay Street
Fayetteville, NC 28305
(910) 483-6611

Library of Congress Cataloging-in-Publication Data

McKinney, Anne, 1948–
Real resumes for nursing jobs : including real resumes used to change careers and resumes used to gain federal employment / Anne McKinney.
     p. cm. -- (Real-resumes series)
  ISBN 978-1475093834; 1475093837;
  1. Nurses--Employment. 2. Resumes (Employment) 3. Nursing--Vocational guidance. I. Title.
II. Series.

  RT86.7.M425 2003
  610.73'06'9-dc21   2003042948

Printed in the United States of America

By PREP Publishing

Business and Career Series:

RESUMES AND COVER LETTERS THAT HAVE WORKED

RESUMES AND COVER LETTERS THAT HAVE WORKED FOR MILITARY PROFESSIONALS

GOVERNMENT JOB APPLICATIONS AND FEDERAL RESUMES

COVER LETTERS THAT BLOW DOORS OPEN

LETTERS FOR SPECIAL SITUATIONS

RESUMES AND COVER LETTERS FOR MANAGERS

REAL-RESUMES FOR COMPUTER JOBS

REAL-RESUMES FOR MEDICAL JOBS

REAL-RESUMES FOR FINANCIAL JOBS

REAL-RESUMES FOR TEACHERS

REAL-RESUMES FOR STUDENTS

REAL-RESUMES FOR CAREER CHANGERS

REAL-RESUMES FOR SALES

REAL ESSAYS FOR COLLEGE & GRADUATE SCHOOL

REAL-RESUMES FOR AVIATION & TRAVEL JOBS

REAL-RESUMES FOR POLICE, LAW ENFORCEMENT & SECURITY JOBS

REAL-RESUMES FOR SOCIAL WORK & COUNSELING JOBS

REAL-RESUMES FOR CONSTRUCTION JOBS

REAL-RESUMES FOR MANUFACTURING JOBS

REAL-RESUMES FOR RESTAURANT, FOOD SERVICE & HOTEL JOBS

REAL-RESUMES FOR MEDIA, NEWSPAPER, BROADCASTING & PUBLIC AFFAIRS JOBS

REAL-RESUMES FOR RETAILING, MODELING, FASHION & BEAUTY JOBS

REAL-RESUMES FOR HUMAN RESOURCES & PERSONNEL JOBS

REAL-RESUMES FOR NURSING JOBS

REAL-RESUMES FOR AUTO INDUSTRY JOBS

REAL RESUMIX AND OTHER RESUMES FOR FEDERAL GOVERNMENT JOBS

REAL KSAS--KNOWLEDGE, SKILLS & ABILITIES--FOR GOVERNMENT JOBS

REAL BUSINESS PLANS AND MARKETING TOOLS

Judeo-Christian Ethics Series:

SECOND TIME AROUND

BACK IN TIME

WHAT THE BIBLE SAYS ABOUT...Words that can lead to success and happiness

A GENTLE BREEZE FROM GOSSAMER WINGS

BIBLE STORIES FROM THE OLD TESTAMENT

Contents

Real-Resumes For Nursing Jobs

...including real resumes used to change careers
and resumes used to gain federal employment

Anne McKinney, Editor

PREP PUBLISHING

As the editor of this book, I would like to give you some tips on how to make the best use of the information you will find here. Because you are considering a career change, you already understand the concept of managing your career for maximum enjoyment and self-fulfillment. The purpose of this book is to provide expert tools and advice so that you *can* manage your career. Inside these pages you will find resumes and cover letters that will help you find not just a job but the type of work you want to do.

Overview of the Book

Every resume and cover letter in this book actually worked. And most of the resumes and cover letters have common features: most are one-page, most are in the chronological format, and most resumes are accompanied by a companion cover letter. In this section you will find helpful advice about job hunting. Step One begins with a discussion of why employers prefer the one-page, chronological resume. In Step Two you are introduced to the direct approach and to the proper format for a cover letter. In Step Three you learn the 14 main reasons why job hunters are not offered the jobs they want, and you learn the six key areas employers focus on when they interview you. Step Four gives nuts-and-bolts advice on how to handle the interview, send a follow-up letter after an interview, and negotiate your salary.

The cover letter plays such a critical role in a career change. You will learn from the experts how to format your cover letters and you will see suggested language to use in particular career-change situations. It has been said that "A picture is worth a thousand words" and, for that reason, you will see numerous examples of effective cover letters used by real individuals to change fields, functions, and industries.

The most important part of the book is the Real-Resumes section. Some of the individuals whose resumes and cover letters you see spent a lengthy career in an industry they loved. Then there are resumes and cover letters of people who wanted a change but who probably wanted to remain in their industry. Many of you will be especially interested by the resumes and cover letters of individuals who knew they definitely wanted a career change but had no idea what they wanted to do next. Other resumes and cover letters show individuals who knew they wanted to change fields and had a pretty good idea of what they wanted to do next.

Whatever your field, and whatever your circumstances, you'll find resumes and cover letters that will "show you the ropes" in terms of successfully changing jobs and switching careers.

Before you proceed further, think about why you picked up this book.
- Are you dissatisfied with the type of work you are now doing?
- Would you like to change careers, change companies, or change industries?
- Are you satisfied with your industry but not with your niche or function within it?
- Do you want to transfer your skills to a new product or service?
- Even if you have excelled in your field, have you "had enough"? Would you like the stimulation of a new challenge?
- Are you aware of the importance of a great cover letter but unsure of how to write one?
- Are you preparing to launch a second career after retirement?
- Have you been downsized, or do you anticipate becoming a victim of downsizing?
- Do you need expert advice on how to plan and implement a job campaign that will open the maximum number of doors?
- Do you want to make sure you handle an interview to your maximum advantage?

**Introduction:
The Art of
Changing
Jobs...
and Finding
New Careers**

- Would you like to master the techniques of negotiating salary and benefits?
- Do you want to learn the secrets and shortcuts of professional resume writers?

Using the Direct Approach

As you consider the possibility of a job hunt or career change, you need to be aware that most people end up having at least three distinctly different careers in their working lifetimes, and often those careers are different from each other. Yet people usually stumble through each job campaign, unsure of what they should be doing. Whether you find yourself voluntarily or unexpectedly in a job hunt, the direct approach is the job hunting strategy most likely to yield a full-time permanent job. The direct approach is an active, take-the-initiative style of job hunting in which you choose your next employer rather than relying on responding to ads, using employment agencies, or depending on other methods of finding jobs. You will learn how to use the direct approach in this book, and you will see that an effective cover letter is a critical ingredient in using the direct approach.

Lack of Industry Experience Not a Major Barrier to Entering New Field

"Lack of experience" is often the last reason people are not offered jobs, according to the companies who do the hiring. If you are changing careers, you will be glad to learn that experienced professionals often are selling "potential" rather than experience in a job hunt. Companies look for personal qualities that they know tend to be present in their most effective professionals, such as communication skills, initiative, persistence, organizational and time management skills, and creativity. Frequently companies are trying to discover "personality type," "talent," "ability," "aptitude," and "potential" rather than seeking actual hands-on experience, so your resume should be designed to aggressively present your accomplishments. Attitude, enthusiasm, personality, and a track record of achievements in any type of work are the primary "indicators of success" which employers are seeking, and you will see numerous examples in this book of resumes written in an all-purpose fashion so that the professional can approach various industries and companies.

The Art of Using References in a Job Hunt

You probably already know that you need to provide references during a job hunt, but you may not be sure of how and when to use references for maximum advantage. You can use references very creatively during a job hunt to call attention to your strengths and make yourself "stand out." Your references will rarely get you a job, no matter how impressive the names, but the way you use references can boost the employer's confidence in you and lead to a job offer in the least time.

You should ask from three to five people, including people who have supervised you, if you can use them as a reference during your job hunt. You may not be able to ask your current boss since your job hunt is probably confidential.

A common question in resume preparation is: "Do I need to put my references on my resume?" No, you don't. Even if you create a references page at the same time you prepare your resume, you don't need to mail, e-mail, or fax your references page with the resume and cover letter. Usually the potential employer is not interested in references until he meets you, so the earliest you need to have references ready is at the first interview. Obviously there are exceptions to this standard rule of thumb; sometimes an ad will ask you to send references with your first response. Wait until the employer requests references before providing them.

An excellent attention-getting technique is to take to the first interview not just a page of references (giving names, addresses, and telephone numbers) but an actual letter of reference written by someone who knows you well and who preferably has supervised or employed you. A professional way to close the first interview is to thank the interviewer, shake his or her hand, and then say you'd like to give him or her a copy of a letter of reference from a previous employer. Hopefully you already made a good impression during the interview, but you'll "close the sale" in a dynamic fashion if you leave a letter praising you and your accomplishments. For that reason, it's a good idea to ask supervisors during your final weeks in a job if they will provide you with a written letter of recommendation which you can use in future job hunts. Most employers will oblige, and you will have a letter that has a useful "shelf life" of many years. Such a letter often gives the prospective employer enough confidence in his opinion of you that he may forego checking out other references and decide to offer you the job on the spot or in the next few days.

With regard to references, it's best to provide the names and addresses of people who have supervised you or observed you in a work situation.

Whom should you ask to serve as references? References should be people who have known or supervised you in a professional, academic, or work situation. References with big titles, like school superintendent or congressman, are fine, but remind busy people when you get to the interview stage that they may be contacted soon. Make sure the busy official recognizes your name and has instant positive recall of you! If you're asked to provide references on a formal company application, you can simply transcribe names from your references list. In summary, follow this rule in using references: If you've got them, flaunt them! If you've obtained well-written letters of reference, make sure you find a polite way to push those references under the nose of the interviewer so he or she can hear someone other than you describing your strengths. Your references probably won't ever get you a job, but glowing letters of reference can give you credibility and visibility that can make you stand out among candidates with similar credentials and potential!

The approach taken by this book is to (1) help you master the proven best techniques of conducting a job hunt and (2) show you how to stand out in a job hunt through your resume, cover letter, interviewing skills, as well as the way in which you present your references and follow up on interviews. Now, the best way to "get in the mood" for writing your own resume and cover letter is to select samples from the Table of Contents that interest you and then read them. A great resume is a "photograph," usually on one page, of an individual. If you wish to seek professional advice in preparing your resume, you may contact one of the professional writers at Professional Resume & Employment Publishing (PREP) for a brief free consultation by calling 1-910-483-6611.

Part One: Some Advice About Your Job Hunt

What if you don't know what you want to do?

Your job hunt will be more comfortable if you can figure out what type of work you want to do. But you are not alone if you have no idea what you want to do next! You may have knowledge and skills in certain areas but want to get into another type of work. What *The Wall Street Journal* has discovered in its research on careers is that most of us end up having at least three distinctly different careers in our working lives; it seems that, even if we really like a particular kind of activity, twenty years of doing it is enough for most of us and we want to move on to something else!

That's why we strongly believe that you need to spend some time figuring out *what interests you* rather than taking an inventory of the skills you have. You may have skills that you simply don't want to use, but if you can build your career on the things that interest you, you will be more likely to be happy and satisfied in your job. Realize, too, that interests can change over time; the activities that interest you now may not be the ones that interested you years ago. For example, some professionals may decide that they've had enough of retail sales and want a job selling another product or service, even though they have earned a reputation for being an excellent retail manager. We strongly believe that interests rather than skills should be the determining factor in deciding what types of jobs you want to apply for and what directions you explore in your job hunt. Obviously one cannot be a lawyer without a law degree or a secretary without secretarial skills; but a professional can embark on a next career as a financial consultant, property manager, plant manager, production supervisor, retail manager, or other occupation if he/she has a strong interest in that type of work and can provide a resume that clearly demonstrates past excellent performance in *any* field and *potential* to excel in another field. As you will see later in this book, "lack of exact experience" is the last reason why people are turned down for the jobs they apply for.

How can you have a resume prepared if you don't know what you want to do?

You may be wondering how you can have a resume prepared if you don't know what you want to do next. The approach to resume writing which PREP, the country's oldest resume-preparation company, has used successfully for many years is to develop an "all-purpose" resume that translates your skills, experience, and accomplishments into language employers can understand. What most people need in a job hunt is a versatile resume that will allow them to apply for numerous types of jobs. For example, you may want to apply for a job in pharmaceutical sales but you may also want to have a resume that will be versatile enough for you to apply for jobs in the construction, financial services, or automotive industries.

Based on more than 20 years of serving job hunters, we at PREP have found that your best approach to job hunting is **an all-purpose resume** and **specific cover letters tailored to specific fields** rather than using the approach of trying to create different resumes for every job. If you are remaining in your field, you may not even need more than one "all-purpose" cover letter, although the cover letter rather than the resume is the place to communicate your interest in a narrow or specific field. An all-purpose resume and cover letter that translate your experience and accomplishments into plain English are the tools that will maximize the number of doors which open for you while permitting you to "fish" in the widest range of job areas.

Figure out what interests you and you will hold the key to a successful job hunt and working career. (And be prepared for your interests to change over time!)

"Lack of exact experience" is the last reason people are turned down for the jobs for which they apply.

Your resume will provide the script for your job interview.

When you get down to it, your resume has a simple job to do: Its purpose is to blow as many doors open as possible and to make as many people as possible want to meet you. So a well-written resume that really "sells" you is a key that will create opportunities for you in a job hunt.

This statistic explains why: The typical newspaper advertisement for a job opening receives more than 245 replies. And normally only 10 or 12 will be invited to an interview.

But here's another purpose of the resume: it provides the "script" the employer uses when he interviews you. If your resume has been written in such a way that your strengths and achievements are revealed, that's what you'll end up talking about at the job interview. Since the resume will govern what you get asked about at your interviews, you can't overestimate the importance of making sure your resume makes you look and sound as good as you are.

Your resume is the "script" for your job interviews. Make sure you put on your resume what you want to talk about or be asked about at the job interview.

So what is a "good" resume?

Very literally, your resume should motivate the person reading it to dial the phone number or e-mail the screen name you have put on the resume. When you are relocating, you should put a local phone number on your resume if your physical address is several states away; employers are more likely to dial a local telephone number than a long-distance number when they're looking for potential employees.

If you have a resume already, look at it objectively. Is it a limp, colorless "laundry list" of your job titles and duties? Or does it "paint a picture" of your skills, abilities, and accomplishments in a way that would make someone want to meet you? Can people understand what you're saying? If you are attempting to change fields or industries, can potential employers see that your skills and knowledge are transferable to other environments? For example, have you described accomplishments which reveal your problem-solving abilities or communication skills?

The one-page resume in chronological format is the format preferred by most employers.

How long should your resume be?

One page, maybe two. Usually only people in the academic community have a resume (which they usually call a *curriculum vitae*) longer than one or two pages. Remember that your resume is almost always accompanied by a cover letter, and a potential employer does not want to read more than two or three pages about a total stranger in order to decide if he wants to meet that person! Besides, don't forget that the more you tell someone about yourself, the more opportunity you are providing for the employer to screen you out at the "first-cut" stage. A resume should be concise and exciting and designed to make the reader want to meet you in person!

Should resumes be functional or chronological?

Employers almost always prefer a chronological resume; in other words, an employer will find a resume easier to read if it is immediately apparent what your current or most recent job is, what you did before that, and so forth, in reverse chronological order. A resume that goes back in detail for the last ten years of employment will generally satisfy the employer's curiosity about your background. Employment more than ten years old can be shown even more briefly in an "Other Experience" section at the end of your "Experience" section. Remember that your intention is not to tell everything you've done but to "hit the high points" and especially impress the employer with what you learned, contributed, or accomplished in each job you describe.

Once you get your resume, what do you do with it?
You will be using your resume to answer ads, as a tool to use in talking with friends and relatives about your job search, and, most importantly, in using the "direct approach" described in this book.

When you mail your resume, always send a "cover letter."
A "cover letter," sometimes called a "resume letter" or "letter of interest," is a letter that accompanies and introduces your resume. Your cover letter is a way of personalizing the resume by sending it to the specific person you think you might want to work for at each company. Your cover letter should contain a few highlights from your resume—just enough to make someone want to meet you. Cover letters should always be typed or word processed on a computer—never handwritten.

1. Learn the art of answering ads.
There is an "art," part of which can be learned, in using your "bestselling" resume to reply to advertisements.

Sometimes an exciting job lurks behind a boring ad that someone dictated in a hurry, so reply to any ad that interests you. Don't worry that you aren't "25 years old with an MBA" like the ad asks for. Employers will always make compromises in their requirements if they think you're the "best fit" overall.

What about ads that ask for "salary requirements?"
What if the ad you're answering asks for "salary requirements?" The first rule is to avoid committing yourself in writing at that point to a specific salary. You don't want to "lock yourself in."

There are two ways to handle the ad that asks for "salary requirements."
First, you can ignore that part of the ad and accompany your resume with a cover letter that focuses on "selling" you, your abilities, and even some of your philosophy about work or your field. You may include a sentence in your cover letter like this: "I can provide excellent personal and professional references at your request, and I would be delighted to share the private details of my salary history with you in person."

Second, if you feel you must give some kind of number, just state a range in your cover letter that includes your medical, dental, other benefits, and expected bonuses. You might state, for example, "My current compensation, including benefits and bonuses, is in the range of $30,000-$40,000."

Analyze the ad and "tailor" yourself to it.
When you're replying to ads, a finely tailored cover letter is an important tool in getting your resume noticed and read. On the next page is a cover letter which has been "tailored to fit" a specific ad. Notice the "art" used by PREP writers of analyzing the ad's main requirements and then writing the letter so that the person's background, work habits, and interests seem "tailor-made" to the company's needs. Use this cover letter as a model when you prepare your own reply to ads.

Side notes:

Never mail or fax your resume without a cover letter.

What if the ad asks for your "salary requirements?"

Date

Exact Name of Person
Title or Position
Name of Company
Address (number and street)
Address (city, state, and zip)

Dear Exact Name of Person: (or Sir or Madam if answering a blind ad.)

With the enclosed resume, I would like to express my interest in exploring employment opportunities with your organization.

As you will see, I offer nursing skills honed in medical clinic and coronary step-down unit environments. Presently working as the Charge Nurse and Clinical Coordinator for a busy local clinic, I supervise two Licensed Practical Nurses and a Phlebotomist while overseeing support activities ranging from controlling inventory, to providing triage for patients being admitted, to assisting in patient and family education efforts. My daily activities include assisting in minor procedures and administration of medications as well as in phlebotomy, PFTs, nebulizer treatments, oxygen therapy, vital signs, and EKGs. I also handle administrative functions such as scheduling, providing referrals to specialists, completing insurance authorizations, filing, and operating computer systems for record keeping.

Employers are trying to identify the individual who wants the job they are filling. Don't be afraid to express your enthusiasm in the cover letter!

In an earlier job as a Charge Nurse and Preceptor for a coronary step-down unit, I supervised 11 people providing total patient care in a 32-bed unit. In that capacity, I personally provided and supervised others in providing the full range of pre- and post-operative care for coronary patients. I received cross -training in open-heart and medical-surgical step down, CCU, and nephrology care while also participating in educating patients and family members on all aspects of disease management including proper aftercare, dietary issues, and medication and possible drug interactions.

My education and training include an Associate Degree in Nursing and the completion of Basic and Advanced Cardiac Life Support (BCLS and ACLS) certification training.

If you can use an articulate and enthusiastic nursing professional with excellent organizational skills, I hope you will contact me to suggest a time when we might meet to discuss your needs. I can provide outstanding references at the appropriate time.

Sincerely,

Sherry Stevens

2. Talk to friends and relatives.

Don't be shy about telling your friends and relatives the kind of job you're looking for. Looking for the job you want involves using your network of contacts, so tell people what you're looking for. They may be able to make introductions and help set up interviews.

About 25% of all interviews are set up through "who you know," so don't ignore this approach.

3. Finally, and most importantly, use the "direct approach."

The "direct approach" is a strategy in which you choose your next employer.

More than 50% of all job interviews are set up by the "direct approach." That means you actually mail, e-mail, or fax a resume and a cover letter to a company you think might be interesting to work for.

To whom do you write?

In general, you should write directly to the *exact name* of the person who would be hiring you: say, the vice-president of marketing or data processing. If you're in doubt about to whom to address the letter, address it to the president by name and he or she will make sure it gets forwarded to the right person within the company who has hiring authority in your area.

How do you find the names of potential employers?

You're not alone if you feel that the biggest problem in your job search is finding the right names at the companies you want to contact. But you can usually figure out the names of companies you want to approach by deciding first if your job hunt is primarily geography-driven or industry-driven.

In a **geography-driven job hunt,** you could select a list of, say, 50 companies you want to contact **by location** from the lists that the U.S. Chambers of Commerce publish yearly of their "major area employers." There are hundreds of local Chambers of Commerce across America, and most of them will have an 800 number which you can find through 1-800-555-1212. If you and your family think Atlanta, Dallas, Ft. Lauderdale, and Virginia Beach might be nice places to live, for example, you could contact the Chamber of Commerce in those cities and ask how you can obtain a copy of their list of major employers. Your nearest library will have the book which lists the addresses of all chambers.

In an **industry-driven job hunt,** and if you are willing to relocate, you will be identifying the companies which you find most attractive in the industry in which you want to work. When you select a list of companies to contact **by industry,** you can find the right person to write and the address of firms by industrial category in *Standard and Poor's, Moody's,* and other excellent books in public libraries. Many Web sites also provide contact information.

Many people feel it's a good investment to actually call the company to either find out or double-check the name of the person to whom they want to send a resume and cover letter. It's important to do as much as you feasibly can to assure that the letter gets to the right person in the company.

On-line research will be the best way for many people to locate organizations to which they wish to send their resume. It is outside the scope of this book to teach Internet research skills, but librarians are often useful in this area.

What's the correct way to follow up on a resume you send?

There is a polite way to be aggressively interested in a company during your job hunt. It is ideal to end the cover letter accompanying your resume by saying, "I hope you'll welcome my call next week when I try to arrange a brief meeting at your convenience to discuss your current and future needs and how I might serve them." Keep it low key, and just ask for a "brief meeting," not an interview. Employers want people who show a determined interest in working with them, so don't be shy about following up on the resume and cover letter you've mailed.

It pays to be aware of the 14 most common pitfalls for job hunters.

STEP THREE: Preparing for Interviews

But a resume and cover letter by themselves can't get you the job you want. You need to "prep" yourself before the interview. Step Three in your job campaign is "Preparing for Interviews." First, let's look at interviewing from the hiring organization's point of view.

What are the biggest "turnoffs" for potential employers?

One of the ways to help yourself perform well at an interview is to look at the main reasons why organizations *don't* hire the people they interview, according to those who do the interviewing.

Notice that "lack of appropriate background" (or lack of experience) is the *last* reason for not being offered the job.

The 14 Most Common Reasons Job Hunters Are Not Offered Jobs (according to the companies who do the interviewing and hiring):

1. Low level of accomplishment
2. Poor attitude, lack of self-confidence
3. Lack of goals/objectives
4. Lack of enthusiasm
5. Lack of interest in the company's business
6. Inability to sell or express yourself
7. Unrealistic salary demands
8. Poor appearance
9. Lack of maturity, no leadership potential
10. Lack of extracurricular activities
11. Lack of preparation for the interview, no knowledge about company
12. Objecting to travel
13. Excessive interest in security and benefits
14. Inappropriate background

Department of Labor studies have proven that smart, "prepared" job hunters can increase their beginning salary while getting a job in *half* the time it normally takes. (4½ months is the average national length of a job search.) Here, from PREP, are some questions that can prepare you to find a job faster.

Are you in the "right" frame of mind?

It seems unfair that we have to look for a job just when we're lowest in morale. Don't worry *too* much if you're nervous before interviews. You're supposed to be a little nervous, especially if the job means a lot to you. But the best way to kill unnecessary fears about job hunting is through 1) making sure you have a great resume and 2) preparing yourself for the interview. Here are three main areas you need to think about before each interview.

Do you know what the company does?
Don't walk into an interview giving the impression that, "If this is Tuesday, this must be General Motors."

Find out before the interview what the company's main product or service is. Where is the company heading? Is it in a "growth" or declining industry? (Answers to these questions may influence whether or not you want to work there!)

Research the company before you go to interviews.

Information about what the company does is in annual reports, in newspaper and magazine articles, and on the Internet. If you're not yet skilled at Internet research, just visit your nearest library and ask the reference librarian to guide you to printed materials on the company.

Do you know what you want to do for the company?
Before the interview, try to decide how you see yourself fitting into the company. Remember, "lack of exact background" the company wants is usually the last reason people are not offered jobs.

Understand before you go to each interview that the burden will be on you to "sell" the interviewer on why you're the best person for the job and the company.

How will you answer the critical interview questions?
Put yourself in the interviewer's position and think about the questions you're most likely to be asked. Here are some of the most commonly asked interview questions:

Anticipate the questions you will be asked at the interview, and prepare your responses in advance.

Q: *"What are your greatest strengths?"*
A: Don't say you've never thought about it! Go into an interview knowing the three main impressions you want to leave about yourself, such as "I'm hard-working, loyal, and an imaginative cost-cutter."

Q: *"What are your greatest weaknesses?"*
A: Don't confess that you're lazy or have trouble meeting deadlines! Confessing that you tend to be a "workaholic" or "tend to be a perfectionist and sometimes get frustrated when others don't share my high standards" will make your prospective employer see a "weakness" that he likes. Name a weakness that your interviewer will perceive as a strength.

Q: *"What are your long-range goals?"*
A: If you're interviewing with Microsoft, don't say you want to work for IBM in five years! Say your long-range goal is to be *with* the company, contributing to its goals and success.

Q: *"What motivates you to do your best work?"*
A: Don't get dollar signs in your eyes here! "A challenge" is not a bad answer, but it's a little cliched. Saying something like "troubleshooting" or "solving a tough problem" is more interesting and specific. Give an example if you can.

Q: "What do you know about this organization?"

A: Don't say you never heard of it until they asked you to the interview! Name an interesting, positive thing you learned about the company recently from your research. Remember, company executives can sometimes feel rather "maternal" about the company they serve. Don't get onto a negative area of the company if you can think of positive facts you can bring up. Of course, if you learned in your research that the company's sales seem to be taking a nose-dive, or that the company president is being prosecuted for taking bribes, you might politely ask your interviewer to tell you something that could help you better understand what you've been reading. Those are the kinds of company facts that can help you determine whether or not you want to work there.

Go to an interview prepared to tell the company why it should hire you.

Q: "Why should I hire you?"

A: "I'm unemployed and available" is the wrong answer here! Get back to your strengths and say that you believe the organization could benefit by a loyal, hard-working cost-cutter like yourself.

In conclusion, you should decide in advance, before you go to the interview, how you will answer each of these commonly asked questions. Have some practice interviews with a friend to role-play and build your confidence.

STEP FOUR: Handling the Interview and Negotiating Salary

Now you're ready for Step Four: actually handling the interview successfully and effectively. Remember, the purpose of an interview is to get a job offer.

A smile at an interview makes the employer perceive of you as intelligent!

Eight "do's" for the interview

According to leading U.S. companies, there are eight key areas in interviewing success. You can fail at an interview if you mishandle just one area.

1. **Do wear appropriate clothes.**

You can never go wrong by wearing a suit to an interview.

2. **Do be well groomed.**

Don't overlook the obvious things like having clean hair, clothes, and fingernails for the interview.

3. **Do give a firm handshake.**

You'll have to shake hands twice in most interviews: first, before you sit down, and second, when you leave the interview. Limp handshakes turn most people off.

4. **Do smile and show a sense of humor.**

Interviewers are looking for people who would be nice to work with, so don't be so somber that you don't smile. In fact, research shows that people who smile at interviews are perceived as more intelligent. So, smile!

5. **Do be enthusiastic.**

Employers say they are "turned off" by lifeless, unenthusiastic job hunters who show no special interest in that company. The best way to show some enthusiasm for the employer's operation is to find out about the business beforehand.

6. Do show you are flexible and adaptable.

An employer is looking for someone who can contribute to his organization in a flexible, adaptable way. No matter what skills and training you have, employers know every new employee must go through initiation and training on the company's turf. Certainly show pride in your past accomplishments in a specific, factual way ("I saved my last employer $50.00 a week by a new cost-cutting measure I developed"). But don't come across as though there's nothing about the job you couldn't easily handle.

7. Do ask intelligent questions about the employer's business.

An employer is hiring someone because of certain business needs. Show interest in those needs. Asking questions to get a better idea of the employer's needs will help you "stand out" from other candidates interviewing for the job.

8. Do "take charge" when the interviewer "falls down" on the job.

Go into every interview knowing the three or four points about yourself you want the interviewer to remember. And be prepared to take an active part in leading the discussion if the interviewer's "canned approach" does not permit you to display your "strong suit." You can't always depend on the interviewer's asking you the "right" questions so you can stress your strengths and accomplishments.

Employers are seeking people with good attitudes whom they can train and coach to do things their way.

An important "don't": Don't ask questions about salary or benefits at the first interview. Employers don't take warmly to people who look at their organization as just a place to satisfy salary and benefit needs. Don't risk making a negative impression by appearing greedy or self-serving. The place to discuss salary and benefits is normally at the second interview, and the employer will bring it up. Then you can ask questions without appearing excessively interested in what the organization can do for you.

Now...negotiating your salary

Even if an ad requests that you communicate your "salary requirement" or "salary history," you should avoid providing those numbers in your initial cover letter. You can usually say something like this: "I would be delighted to discuss the private details of my salary history with you in person."

Once you're at the interview, you must avoid even appearing *interested* in salary before you are offered the job. Make sure you've "sold" yourself before talking salary. First show you're the "best fit" for the employer and then you'll be in a stronger position from which to negotiate salary. **Never** bring up the subject of salary yourself. Employers say there's no way you can avoid looking greedy if you bring up the issue of salary and benefits before the company has identified you as its "best fit."

Don't appear excessively interested in salary and benefits at the interview.

Interviewers sometimes throw out a salary figure at the first interview to see if you'll accept it. You may not want to commit yourself if you think you will be able to negotiate a better deal later on. Get back to finding out more about the job. This lets the interviewer know you're interested primarily in the job and not the salary.

When the organization brings up salary, it may say something like this: "Well, Mary, we think you'd make a good candidate for this job. What kind of salary are we talking about?" You may not want to name a number here, either. Give the ball back to the interviewer. Act as though you hadn't given the subject of salary much thought and respond something like this: "Ah, Mr. Jones, I wonder if you'd be kind enough to tell me what salary you had in mind when you advertised the job?" Or ... "What is the range you have in mind?"

Don't worry, if the interviewer names a figure that you think is too low, you can say so without turning down the job or locking yourself into a rigid position. The point here is to negotiate for yourself as well as you can. You might reply to a number named by the interviewer that you think is low by saying something like this: "Well, Mr. Lee, the job interests me very much, and I think I'd certainly enjoy working with you. But, frankly, I was thinking of something a little higher than that." That leaves the ball in your interviewer's court again, and you haven't turned down the job either, in case it turns out that the interviewer can't increase the offer and you still want the job.

Salary negotiation can be tricky.

Last, send a follow-up letter.

Mail, e-mail, or fax a letter right after the interview telling your interviewer you enjoyed the meeting and are certain (if you are) that you are the "best fit" for the job. The people interviewing you will probably have an attitude described as either "professionally loyal" to their companies, or "maternal and proprietary" if the interviewer also owns the company. In either case, they are looking for people who want to work for *that* company in particular. The follow-up letter you send might be just the deciding factor in your favor if the employer is trying to choose between you and someone else. You will see an example of a follow-up letter on page 16.

A follow-up letter can help the employer choose between you and another qualified candidate.

A cover letter is an essential part of a career change.

A cover letter is an essential part of a job hunt or career change.

Many people are aware of the importance of having a great resume, but most people in a job hunt don't realize just how important a cover letter can be. The purpose of the cover letter, sometimes called a **"letter of interest,"** is to introduce your resume to prospective employers. The cover letter is often the critical ingredient in a job hunt because the cover letter allows you to say a lot of things that just don't "fit" on the resume. For example, you can emphasize your commitment to a new field and stress your related talents. The cover letter also gives you a chance to stress outstanding character and personal values. On the next two pages you will see examples of very effective cover letters.

Please do not attempt to implement a career change without a cover letter. A cover letter is the first impression of you, and you can influence the way an employer views you by the language and style of your letter.

Special help for those in career change

We want to emphasize again that, especially in a career change, the cover letter is very important and can help you "build a bridge" to a new career. A creative and appealing cover letter can begin the process of encouraging the potential employer to imagine you in an industry other than the one in which you have worked.

As a special help to those in career change, there are resumes and cover letters included in this book which show valuable techniques and tips you should use when changing fields or industries. The resumes and cover letters of career changers are identified in the table of contents as "Career Change" and you will see the "Career Change" label on cover letters in Part Two where the individuals are changing careers.

Date

Exact Name of Person
Title or Position
Name of Company
Address (number and street)
Address (city, state, and zip)

Addressing the Cover
Letter: Get the exact
name of the person to
whom you are writing. This
makes your approach
personal.

Dear Exact Name of Person: (or Sir or Madam if answering a blind ad.)

With the enclosed resume, I would like to express my interest in exploring employment opportunities with your organization.

Second Paragraph: You
have a chance to talk
about whatever you feel is
your most distinguishing
feature.

As you will see, I offer a blend of clinical and administrative abilities gained while excelling in a versatile work history in the medical field. I have completed extensive related training including a Medical Assistant Program and a Phlebotomy course as well as courses in Secretarial Science and Business.

Third Paragraph: You
bring up your next most
distinguishing qualities and
try to
sell yourself.

Presently a Clinical Assistant for a family practice environment, I have become known for my compassionate and professional approach to dealing with patients, physicians, and other medical professionals. My duties range from preparing patients for exams, to performing medical procedures and assisting physicians, to performing diagnostic and screening tests. I also enter data into patient charts, refill prescriptions, and administer medications and vaccinations.

Fourth Paragraph: Here
you have another
opportunity to reveal
qualities or achievements
which will impress your
future employer.

Earlier as a Phlebotomist and Medical Laboratory Aide in a Veterans Administration Hospital, I became skilled in utilizing universal blood and body fluid precautions while collecting samples and then doing all required tests on each sample. Prior to this job, I was one of three Medical Assistants in a women's clinic with five doctors and one nurse practitioner. In this capacity, I handled all aspects of procedures from screening patients, to documenting medical histories, to assisting in physical examinations as well as minor surgeries.

Final Paragraph: She
asks the employer to
contact her. Make sure
your reader knows what
the "next step" is.

If you can use an adaptable and compassionate medical professional who is knowledgeable of insurance billing, inventory control, and office operations and administration, I hope you will contact me to suggest a time when we might meet to discuss your needs. I can provide outstanding references at the appropriate time.

Sincerely,

Alternate Final
Paragraph: It's more
aggressive (but not too
aggressive) to let the
employer know that you
will be calling him or her.
Don't be afraid to be
persistent. Employers are
looking for people who
know what they want to
do.

Jodie Thomas Damon

Date

Semi-blocked Letter

Date

Three blank spaces

Exact Name of Person
Title or Position
Name of Company
Address (number and street)
Address (city, state, and zip)

Address

Dear Exact Name of Person: (or Dear Sir or Madam if answering a blind ad.)

Salutation
One blank space

Can you use an articulate and knowledgeable medical professional who offers a reputation as an enthusiastic and energetic individual who excels in communicating with others whether contributing to team efforts, instructing and mentoring other medical professionals, or educating patients and family members?

You will see from my enclosed resume that I offer a solid background of experience as a nursing professional who has often been called on to instruct, educate, and teach. Currently excelling as a Case Manager in Hospice, I manage a case load of up to 21 terminally ill patients, providing supportive care, patient assessment, and education. I joined the staff of San Diego Area Medical Center as a Registered Nurse, and then worked as a Psychiatric Nurse from November of 2000 until I was promoted into my current position.

Although I am highly regarded by my present employer and can provide outstanding references at the appropriate time, I have decided to permanently relocate back to my native Canada. I am interested in exploring career options with companies in the area that can use a highly skilled, dedicated medical professional.

Body

I offer experience in the nursing field, along with knowledge of medical facility operations including case management, data entry, and records management which combine to make me a well-rounded professional. With my enthusiastic and energetic approach and reputation as a compassionate and caring individual, I am certain that I offer a blend of skills, experience, and knowledge which would make me a valuable addition to any organization searching for a versatile and adaptable mature professional.

I hope you welcome my call soon when I try to arrange a brief meeting to discuss your needs and how I might help you. Thank you in advance for your time.

Sincerely,

One blank space

Signature

Samuel Jackson

CC: Mr. Nate Lipscomb

cc: Indicates you are sending a copy of the letter to someone

Date

Exact Name of Person
Title or Position
Name of Company
Address (number and street)
Address (city, state, and zip)

Follow-up Letter

A great follow-up letter
can motivate the
employer
to make the job offer,
and the salary offer may
be influenced by the
style and tone of your
follow-up
letter, too!

Dear Exact Name:

I am writing to express my appreciation for the time you spent with me on 9 December, and I want to let you know that I am sincerely interested in the position of Controller which we discussed.

I feel confident that I could skillfully interact with your 60-person work force, and I would cheerfully travel as your needs require. I want you to know, too, that I would not consider relocating to Salt Lake City to be a hardship! It is certainly one of the most beautiful areas I have ever seen.

As you described to me what you are looking for in the person who fills this position, I had a sense of "déjà vu" because my current employer was in a similar position when I went to work for his practice. The managing physician needed someone to come in and be his "right arm" and take on an increasing amount of his management responsibilities so that he could be freed up to do other things. I have played a key role in the growth and profitability of his practice, and that business has come to depend on my sound financial advice as much as my day-to-day management skills. Since this is one of the busiest times of the year in the medical field, I feel that I could not leave during that time. I could certainly make myself available by mid-January.

It would be a pleasure to work for a successful individual such as yourself, and I feel I could contribute significantly to your hotel chain not only through my accounting and business background but also through my strong qualities of loyalty, reliability, and trustworthiness. I am confident that I could learn Quick Books rapidly, and I would welcome being trained to do things your way.

Yours sincerely,

Jacob Evangelisto

Many people are aware of the importance of having a great resume, but most people in a job hunt don't realize just how important a cover letter can be. The purpose of the cover letter, sometimes called a **"letter of interest,"** is to introduce your resume to prospective employers.

"A Picture Is Worth a Thousand Words."

As a way of illustrating how important the cover letter can be, we have chosen to show you on the next two pages the cover letter and resume of an experienced nursing professional who is seeking a new challenge. She has found herself in a situation in which she wishes to apply for a newly created position in the hospital where she is currently employed. You will see clearly from the documents on the next page that she is approaching her job hunt in an intelligent fashion. Although she has the experience and credentials for the position, she has decided to "take no chances" in aggressively presenting herself. Because she knows that (1) the job is being advertised in numerous print media and (2) she has worked for her current employer for fewer than two years, she realizes that she must apply for the position in the same way as everyone else: with a resume and cover letter which enthusiastically express her talents, experience, and skills.

The Resume and Cover Letter are "Companion Documents."

You will see on the next two pages that the cover letter gives you a chance to "get personal" with the person to whom you are writing whereas the resume is a more formal document. Even if the employer doesn't request a cover letter, we believe that it is *always* in your best interest to send a cover letter with your resume. In the case of Carmen Santiago, whose resume and cover letter you will see on the next two pages, the cover letter provides an opportunity to say how much she wants the job. The aim of this book is to show you examples of cover letters and resumes designed to blow doors open so that you can develop your own resumes and cover letters and increase the number of interviews you have.

A cover letter is an essential part of a career change.

Please do not attempt to implement a career change without a cover letter such as the ones you see in Part Two and in Part Three of this book. A cover letter is the first impression of you, and you can influence the way an employer views you by the language and style of your letter.

Your cover letter and resume are "companion" documents.

Date

Mr. Gordon Peebles
Nurse Recruiter
Waylon University Hospital
Waylon, TX

Dear Mr. Peebles:

Experienced nurse seeking to advance within the hospital where she currently works

Although this individual already works at the hospital which is attempting to fill a newly created position, she knows that her current employer is not aware of all her talents, certifications, and aptitude for the position. Here's a tip: when applying for internal openings, don't sacrifice any formality in your approach. Make sure you have a great cover letter and resume in order to compete for the job as aggressively as the "outside" candidates.

With the enclosed resume, I would like to express my interest in the position as Clinical Educator—Cardiac Service Line, which you recently advertised in the Waylon Times.

As you will see from my resume, I offer extensive training, certifications, and experience related to critical care and cardiac patients along with experience in developing and providing inservice training for other medical professionals. I began my medical career as an LPN in 1990 and then completed my Bachelor of Science in Nursing in 1992. From 1992-96 I worked in the Georgia University Medical Center in the Medical/Surgical/Trauma Intensive Care Unit. In that job I worked in a vibrant teaching and research hospital, and I gained extensive ICU experience in a 500-bed facility which contained a Level I Trauma Center.

I joined the U.S. Army in 1996 and served my country as a Captain while working in the Medical/Surgery/Coronary Care Unit of one of the Army's largest medical centers. As a Charge Nurse and Intensive Care Nurse, I was extensively involved in training and development. I worked on a team with another RN and three medical technicians in developing a training program which became an integral part of a five- week training program. I also spearheaded orientation for ICU specialists and was commended for developing and implementing training which "produced rock-solid clinicians." I was described as an "outstanding educator" in teaching the Critical Care Course, and I revised and updated three ICU orientation/education packets and produced training which was praised for "arming orientees with the latest practice standards."

You will notice from my resume that I earned and have maintained since 1994 the C.C.R.N. certification in critical care. On my own initiative, I have aggressively pursued training opportunities related to the clinical management of the cardiac surgery patient. I enjoy sharing my knowledge with other medical professionals as well as with families and patients.

I have been with the Waylon Medical Center since 2000, and I have served as Charge Nurse, Preceptor, and Resource Person. I am eager to serve Waylon Medical Center as its Clinical Educator – Cardiac Service Line, and I respectfully request an opportunity to speak with you in person about this position. Thank you for your time.

Sincerely,

Carmen Santiago

CARMEN SANTIAGO, C.C.R.N.

1110½ Hay Street, Fayetteville, NC 28305 • preppub@aol.com • (910) 483-6611

OBJECTIVE To contribute to a medical environment that can use a highly motivated individual known for resourcefulness and personal initiative who offers extensive critical care and cardiac experience along with a proven ability to develop and implement inservice and staff training activities.

EDUCATION **Certificate of Training in Critical Care;** obtained my **C.C.R.N.** in 1994, and complete 100 hours annually in order to maintain this certification.
Continuing training, 1990-present: Completed multiple training activities related to ***Critical Care and EKG Interpretation*** sponsored by MED-ED, an AACN-approved provider; received a Certificate of Training from the U.S. Army for completing specialized training in ***Clinical Management of the Cardiac Surgery Patient;*** completed training sponsored by the Georgia Nurses Association entitled ***Multiple Trauma in the 21ˢᵗ Century.*** Completed other training including these courses:

Multisystem Organ Failure: A Pathophysiologic Approach	Critical Care Crisis
Critical Care Essentials	Critical Care Challenges
What's New in Critical Care	Intra-Aortic Balloon Pumping
Current Diagnosis and Treatment of Tachyarrhythmias	

Bachelor of Science in Nursing, University of Georgia, Atlanta, GA, 1992.
Diploma in Practical Nursing, Greyson Practical Nursing Program, Greyson, GA, 1990.
Completed **Officer Training School,** U.S. Army, Ft. Benning, GA, 1996.

CERTIFICATIONS Registered Nurse **(R.N.),** currently licensed in NC and GA.; previously certified as an **L.P.N.**
Critical Care Registered Nurse **(C.C.R.N.),** certified since 1994.

EXPERIENCE **REGISTERED NURSE & CHARGE NURSE.** Waylon Medical Center, Waylon, GA (2000-present.) Became Charge Nurse after six months; schedule 12 nurses.

CHARGE NURSE & INTENSIVE CARE NURSE. U.S. Army, Womack Army Hospital, Ft. Bragg, NC (1996-2000). In the Medical/Surgical/Coronary Care Unit of one of the Army's largest medical centers, provided skilled critical care nursing in a 100-bed facility while also supervising other RNs and technicians during a 12-hour shift.
Training and development:
- Developed a training module which became an integral part of a five-week training program; worked on a team with another RN and three medical technicians in developing this training program. Spearheaded orientation for seven ICU specialists and was commended for developing and implementing training which "produced rock-solid clinicians."
- Revised/updated three ICU orientation/education packets, and produced training which was praised for "arming orientees with the latest practice standards."
- Was described as an "outstanding educator" in teaching the Critical Care Course.

Quality nursing:
- Implemented the nursing process for critically ill patients in a 12-bed intensive care/observation status unit; planned and managed patient/nursing care activities; prepared nursing reports. On a formal performance evaluation, was praised for providing "ingenious tailored care for respiratory patients" and was described as a "clinical expert."

R.N. MEDICAL/SURGICAL/TRAUMA INTENSIVE CARE UNIT. Georgia University Medical Center, Atlanta, GA (1992-96). In a vibrant teaching and research hospital associated with the Georgia Tech Medical School, gained extensive ICU experience in a 500-bed facility.

Other experience: Worked as an LPN in a nursing home and in rural Georgia hospitals.

Date

Mrs. Samantha Smith
Administrative Director, Radiology Department
Sneeds Mayo Medical Center
1102 Kenton Road
Sneedsville, LA 23001

Dear Mrs. Smith:

With the enclosed resume, I would like to make you aware of my qualifications for the position of Radiology Staff Nurse, specifically my background as a radiology nurse with more than nine years of service to Sneeds Mayo Medical Center, and the extensive list of certifications and credentials with which I have supplemented that experience.

I am currently excelling as a Staff Registered Nurse in the Emergency Department, where my primary duty is to serve as Triage Nurse. I interview presenting patients, assigning a triage category and prioritizing the placement of patients into the appropriate treatment areas based on the nature and severity of the patient's condition. I monitor the condition of patients in the waiting area, and upgrade or downgrade their assigned triage categories based on changes in patient condition.

Although I am highly regarded within the Emergency Department, and can provide excellent references at the appropriate time, it is my desire to return to Radiology, where I previously served with distinction. As you will see, I hold certifications in ACLS, BCLS, and PALS in addition to credentials which qualify me to administer a wide range of medications specific to radiology procedures, including nuclear medicines and special procedures.

My knowledge, my skills, and above all, my personal loyalty made me a strong asset to the Radiology Department in the past and would continue to do so in the future. I was proud to be a part of the growth and development of the radiology team during the nine years I served, and I would relish the opportunity to rejoin that team. I have a deep respect for the expertise and reputation of the radiology team headed by Dr. Evans, and it is my strong desire to be of service to Dr. Quixote and the other team members.

Sincerely,

Larry French

Date

Exact Name of Person
Title or Position
Name of Company
Address (number and street)
Address (city, state, and zip)

Dear Exact Name of Person: (or Sir or Madam if answering a blind ad)

With the enclosed resume, I would like to express my interest in exploring employment opportunities with your organization and make you aware of my versatile skills and abilities which could complement your goals.

As you will see from my enclosed resume, I earned my first B.S. degree from Michigan State University where I maintained a 3.5 GPA. During my senior year I worked as many as 50 hours a week as a Research Assistant and Tutor in the university's chemistry lab.

In my subsequent job as a middle school science and math teacher, I refined my communication, organizational, and time management skills. Although I was highly regarded as a teacher and was commended for strong communication skills, I decided that I wanted to become involved in hospital administration as my primary career field, and I pursued a degree in hospital administration in my spare time while excelling in my full-time teaching position. Just recently I received my second Bachelor's degree in Hospital Administration.

My teaching experience helped me refine my verbal and written communication skills. I am highly regarded for my ability to persuade, motivate, and lead, and I am certain I could utilize those skills and talents in order to impact the bottom line of a medical organization.

If you can use a proven performer with an ability to work well with others, I hope you will contact me to suggest a time when we might talk to discuss your needs. Single and available for worldwide relocation, I would cheerfully travel as frequently as your needs require. I can provide excellent references at the appropriate time.

Sincerely,

Julie M. Vogel

CC: Dr. Nathan Rogers

Date

Exact Name of Person
Title or Position
Name of Company
Address (number and street)
Address (city, state, and zip)

Changing Careers into the pharmaceutical sales field

In this letter, a store manager is seeking to transfer her strong bottom-line orientation and impressive accomplishments in boosting sales and profit into a new industry. She is primarily interested in the pharmaceutical industry, and the letter is designed to acquaint pharmaceutical companies with her knowledge of the territory she would be covering as well as with her fine personal and professional reputation. She is hoping that the company will be willing to train a highly motivated producer who has excelled in another industry.

Dear Exact Name of Person: (or Dear Sir or Madam if answering a blind ad)

I would appreciate an opportunity to talk with you soon about how I could contribute to your organization through my excellent sales, communication, and customer service skills. I am responding to your advertisement for a Pharmaceutical Sales Representative. I am very knowledgeable of the Dallas, TX, area and offer an outstanding personal and professional reputation in the community.

As you will see from my enclosed resume, I have been highly successful in sales and operations management with a major corporation. Beginning as a Customer Service Manager, I was promoted to manage stores with increasing sales volumes of $7 million, $8.5 million, and $11.5 million annually. In my current position, I have raised total sales by 20%, and profit levels by 25% through my aggressive sales orientation.

Although I am held in high regard by my employer and can provide outstanding references at the appropriate time, I have decided that I would like to apply my sales, customer service, and communication skills within the pharmaceutical sales field. I am certain that my sales ability and strong bottom-line orientation would be ideally suited to pharmaceutical sales. As a store manager, I have become very familiar with a wide range of pharmaceutical products as I have provided oversight of store merchandising, vendor relations, and product mix. I interact with pharmacists and other healthcare professionals with regard to the range of pharmaceutical products carried by the store.

With a B.S.B.A. degree, I possess an educational background which complements my sales and management experience. My highly developed communication skills, assertive personality, and time-management ability have allowed me to effectively manage as many as 100 employees. I offer a reputation as a forceful yet tactful salesperson who is able to present ideas as well as products in a powerful and convincing fashion.

I can assure you that this is a very deliberate attempt on my part to transition into the pharmaceutical sales field, and I hope you will call or write me soon to arrange a brief meeting to discuss your current and future needs and how I might serve them. Thank you in advance for your time.

Sincerely,

Gloria Pena

Date

BY FAX TO: Human Resources Department
910-483-2439
Reference Job Code XYZ 9034

Dear Sir or Madam:

With the enclosed resume, I would like to make you aware of my interest in employment as a Pharmaceutical Healthcare Representative with Johnson & Johnson. I believe you are aware that Walter Freeman, one of your Healthcare Representatives, has recommended that I talk with you because he feels that I could excel in the position as Pharmaceutical Healthcare Representative.

As you will see from my enclosed resume, I offer proven marketing and sales skills along with a reputation as a highly motivated individual with exceptional problem-solving abilities. Shortly after joining my current firm as a Mortgage Loan Specialist, I was named Outstanding Loan Officer of the month through my achievement in generating more than $20,000 in fees.

I believe much of my professional success so far has been due to my highly motivated nature and creative approach to my job. For example, when I began working for my current employer, I developed and implemented the concept of a postcard that communicated a message which the consumer found intriguing. The concept has been so successful that it has been one of the main sources of advertisements in our office, and the concept has been imitated by other offices in the company.

In addition to my track record of excelling in the highly competitive financial services field, I gained valuable sales experience in earlier jobs selling copying equipment and sleep systems. I also applied my strong leadership and sales ability in the human services field when I worked in adult probation services. I am very proud of the fact that many troubled individuals with whom I worked told me that my ability to inspire and motivate them was the key to their becoming productive citizens.

If you can use a creative and motivated self-starter who could enhance your goals for market share and profitability, I hope you will contact me to suggest a time when we could meet in person to discuss your needs and goals and how I could meet them. I can provide strong personal and professional references at the appropriate time.

Yours sincerely,

Cheri Garcia

How do I e-mail or fax my resume?

The answer is: always with a cover letter. When you fax your resume and the cover letter introducing your resume, we recommend that you put the fax number on the top of the letter. In this way you identify to the receiver how you contacted them (remember, they may be receiving dozens of other resumes and cover letters), and you also have a record of the fax number on the top of your copy of the letter. Never send any type of correspondence in business without dating it.

PART THREE:
Resumes and Cover Letters for Entering or Advancing in the Nursing Field

In this section, you will find resumes and cover letters of individuals who are trying to use a resume as their main tool for entering or advancing in the nursing field. Even when jobhunters are entering a field where jobs are plentiful, the best jobs and the best schedules are always hard to get. A great resume can help you negotiate your best working conditions and optimum salary.

By looking over the resumes and cover letters in this section, you will see examples which demonstrate how to show clinical rotations, when to reveal your grade point average (only if it's above a 3.3, usually!), and how to present your skills and knowledge in a creative fashion in order to "make up" for a lack of experience.

When you look at one resume in this section, you will notice sections which include Computer Skills, Laboratory Knowledge, and Languages in addition to the "standard" sections such as Objective, Experience, Education, and Personal. On another resume you will see a Training section which is separate from the Education section. On another resume you will find sections called Certifications & Training as well as Technical Skills. On another resume you will see how to show off affiliations to best advantage. On several resumes, you will see how to professionally present experience as a Tutor and Mentor.

And how does one show clinical rotations on a resume? You will find some answers if you examine some of the resumes in this section.

Have you ever been a waitress or intern? A few resumes in this section will give you some ideas about how to present such experience, even when that experience appears to have little relationship to the nursing field.

Some advice to students...
If senior professionals could give students a piece of advice about careers, here's what they would say: Manage your career and don't stumble from job to job in an incoherent pattern. Learn early in your working life that a great resume and cover letter can blow doors open for you and help you maximize your salary.

Entry-level nurses are often "selling" their potential to do a job they've never done before. In this section, you will see examples of how to market your clinical rotations if you have limited or no experience in the field. This book also contains a wealth of information for experienced nursing professionals.

Date

Exact Name of Person
Exact Title
Exact Name of Company
Address
City, State, Zip

A CURRICULUM VITAE

Dear Exact Name of Person (or Dear Sir or Madam if answering a blind ad):

With the enclosed curriculum vitae describing my credentials and experience, I would like to introduce myself and express my interest in exploring employment opportunities with you as a Family Nurse Practitioner.

As you will see from my CV, I am currently finishing a Master of Science in Nursing in the Family Nurse Practitioner Program at Duke University School of Nursing. I am excelling academically and maintaining a 3.5 GPA while working full-time as an Emergency Room Nurse. I previously earned a B.S.N. and A.D.N.

One of my distinctive areas of competence is my extensive background in critical care nursing. As a Registered Nurse in the Emergency Department at Womack Army Medical Center, I supervise Licensed Practical Nurses and Medics. I expertly oversee emergency nursing, clinical nursing, and triage nursing.

In previous experience as a Critical Care Nurse Specialist in Colorado, I provided post-operative care to surgical patients in these areas: general surgery; cardiovascular, vascular, and thoracic; neurology; urology; reconstructive plastic surgery; pediatric; acute trauma; acute head trauma; multisystem failure; and orthopedic. In prior positions, I worked as a Critical Care Registered Nurse in a Cardio-Thoracic Intensive Care Unit and other Intensive Care Units as well.

I am genuinely excited about the medical care I will be able to provide as a Family Nurse Practitioner, and I have a special interest in women's health. You would find me in person to be an exceptionally strong communicator who is well equipped for the challenges of teaching and educating patients about their illnesses and treatments. As you can see from the fact that I have embarked on the adventure of obtaining my master's degree, I am an extremely hard worker who is committed to refining my skills and abilities to the highest level. Quality care is always my focus, and I am seeking a position in a practice that will value an ambitious and dedicated professional who could enhance the image and patient care of the practice.

I hope we will have the opportunity to meet in person, and I would ask that you contact me to suggest a time and place for us to meet in person if my considerable skills and talents are of interest to you. Thank you in advance for your time.

Sincerely,

Margaret Smith

MARGARET SMITH, B.S.N., R.N.

1110½ Hay Street, Fayetteville, NC 28305   •   preppub@aol.com   •   (910) 483-6611

Curriculum Vitae

Professional Credentials

Licensed Registered Nurse, North Carolina (Certificate #CYZ1230)
Certified as an **Advanced Cardiac Life Support (ACLS), Neo-natal Life Support (NALS),**
Pediatric Advanced Life Support (PALS), and **Basic Cardiac Life Support (BCLS)**
Provider by the American Heart Association.
Passed AACN-approved critical care course, 1987.

Professional Organizations

Inducted into Phi Theta Kappa National Honor Society
Member of the following professional organizations:
- American Association of Nurse Practitioners, 1991-present
- American Association of Critical Care Nurses, 1992-present
- Society of Critical Care Medicine, 1993-present

Education

Finishing **Master of Science in Nursing, Family Nurse Practitioner Program**, Duke
University Medical Center, Durham, NC; will graduate May 2003.
- Currently maintaining a 3.5 GPA in this rigorous program while working full-time as an Emergency Room nurse.

Completed Pre-Med prerequisite courses, Community College of Aurora, Aurora, Colorado, May 2000.
Bachelor of Science in Nursing (B.S.N.) Degree from Thomas Jefferson University, Philadelphia, PA, 1995.
Associate of Science Degree in Nursing (A.D.N.), Harrisburg Area Community College, Harrisburg, PA, 1987.

Residency

Dr. Demitri Anjelis, MD, Family Practice, Philadelphia, PA

Clinical Rotations for Duke University
Family Nurse Practitioner Program

- **Sexual and Reproductive Health** —three-month rotation with Drs. David Schuster and Guy Peters, Charlotte Obstetrics & Gynecology, Charlotte, NC (2001).
- **Child Health in Family Care** —three-month pediatric rotation with Dr. Masoud Caxton, Pediatrics & Adolescent Medicine, Chapel Hill, NC (2001).
- **Internal Medicine** —three-month rotation in internal medicine with Dr. Rudy Alfano, Internal Medicine & Acute Care Clinic, Burlington, NC (2000).
- **Acute and Chronic Health Problems** —three-month rotation with Drs. Robert Burton and Paul Dickson, Group Family Practice, Greensboro, NC (2000).

Publications and Papers

Published a Focus on Critical Care article, *"Panic and Concerns of Our Health Care Colleagues,"* published in 1995.

Personally completed most of the research for and co-authored a research paper, *"AnimalCare as a Nursing Intervention to Decrease the Stress Response in the Critically Ill Patient."*

Teaching Experience

Prepared and presented an instructional seminar on "Concepts of Celebrex Consumption."

Experience

REGISTERED NURSE, EMERGENCY DEPARTMENT.
Womack Army Medical Center, Fort Bragg, NC (2000-present).
Supervise Licensed Practical Nurses and Medics at this major military medical center.
Performed the following types of nursing:
- Emergency nursing
- Clinical nursing
- Triage nursing

Started with Fitzsimmons Army Medical Center in Aurora, Colorado as an **INDIVIDUAL CONTRACT NURSE** *in the Surgical Intensive Care Unit* (1995-97; *when the contract ended, applied and was selected for a position as a* **NURSE SPECIALIST, GS-11.** (1997-2000).
- Provided post-operative care to surgical patients in the following areas:
    - General Surgery
    - Cardiovascular, vascular, and thoracic
    - Neurology
    - Urology
    - Reconstructive plastic surgery
    - Pediatric
    - Acute trauma
    - Acute head trauma
    - Multisystem failure
    - Orthopedic
- Utilized Marquette monitoring systems.
- Analyzed components of oxygen delivery and consumption in treating patients.
- Was nominated for the Nightingale Award in 1998.

REGISTERED NURSE, CRITICAL CARE UNITS. Swedish Medical Center, Englewood, CO (1995-1997).
- Provided pre-operative, post-operative, and operating room critical care nursing to the following classes of patients:
    - Post-operative open heart surgery
    - Post-operative general surgery
    - Acute spinal cord injury
    - Acute trauma
    - Acute head trauma
    - Acute MI
    - Multi-system failure
- Utilized Siemens monitoring systems and clini-comp computers for nursing.
- Served as a member of the open heart surgery team.

REGISTERED NURSE, INTENSIVE CARE UNITS A & B. Phily Medical Center, Philadelphia, PA (1987-1989 and 1990-1995). Provided immediate postoperative nursing care for open heart surgery patients and acute MI patients.
- Worked with both medical and surgical IABP-Therapy patients.
- Handled TPA-Therapy for acute MI patients.
- Rendered expert care to patients requiring Ventricular Assist Devices.
- Utilized state-of-the-art Hewlett-Packard monitoring and telemetry systems for patient care.

CLINICAL COORDINATOR and **REGISTERED NURSE.** Central Pennsylvania Cardiac, Thoracic, and Vascular Surgeons, Philadelphia, PA (1990). Performed preoperative and postoperative patient education for individuals recovering from cardiac, vascular, and thoracic surgical procedures.
- Provided counseling and support for patients and family members.

Volunteer Experience

With Habitat for Humanity Project in Boston, MA, investigated issues associated with and assisted the hungry and homeless population of the Harrisburg community, to include working in several area soup kitchens.

Excellent personal and professional references are available upon request.

Date

Exact Name of Person
Exact Title
Exact Name of Company
Address
City, State, Zip

ADMISSIONS CLERK   Dear Exact Name of Person (or Dear Sir or Madam if answering a blind ad):

With the enclosed resume, I would like to make you aware of my reputation as an experienced, loyal, and highly motivated management and accounting professional with excellent communication, organizational, and motivational skills as well as a background in office management and accounting.

With First Health of Kentucky, my loyalty and dedication have been rewarded by advancement into positions of increasing responsibility. I started with the company as a registration clerk in the Emergency Room and quickly advanced to Assistant Supervisor, overseeing the activities of as many as 30 clerks, providing administrative, patient registration, and accounting services. In this position, I prepared weekly schedules for three rotating shifts of 30 employees while also providing counseling for marginal performers and conducting employee evaluations. I attended seminars on ICD-9 coding, and coded emergency room charts daily, entering them into the computer for billing.

You will also notice from my resume that I am experienced in the full range of accounting activities. Prior to my employment with First Health of Kentucky, I handled the accounting function for a furniture retailer, and in that capacity I was involved in accounts payable, cost accounting, shipping and freight reports, and inventory control.

Of course all of my jobs have involved customer service, and I offer strong customer service and public relations skills. I have frequently been commended for my gracious manner of dealing with the public and for my skill in troubleshooting difficult problems so that customer satisfaction is retained while safeguarding the company's bottom line goals.

I can provide outstanding references at the appropriate time, and I would appreciate an opportunity to talk with you in person about how my versatile skills and background could make a difference to your organization. I hope you will call and suggest a time when we might meet in person to discuss your needs and how I might serve them.

Sincerely,

James Gray

JAMES GRAY

1110½ Hay Street, Fayetteville, NC 28305 • preppub@aol.com • (910) 483-6611

OBJECTIVE

To benefit an organization that can use an experienced management and accounting professional with exceptional communication, organizational, and motivational skills who offers a background in office management and accounting.

EDUCATION

Graduated with a **Bachelor's degree** in **Business Administration, Magna Cum Laude,** with a 3.85 G.P.A.; Leighton University, Leighton, KY.
- Majored in **Accounting** with a minor in **Computer Programming.**

Have nearly completed the requirements for an **Associate's degree** in **Nursing,** Sandhills Community College, Leighton, KY; am only five courses short of this degree.

Completed **Associate's degree** in **Accounting,** Sandhills Community College, Leighton, KY.

Completed two years of course work in General Studies and Accounting, Wake Technical Community College and Wilson Technical Community College, Wake and Wilson, KY.

CERTIFICATIONS

Certified Nursing Assistant I, Kentucky certificate # 189773.

Licensed Notary Public for the state of Kentucky, commission expires 4/27/2006.

AFFILIATIONS

Member, Phi Kappa Phi national honor society.

EXPERIENCE

With First Health of Kentucky at Moore Regional Hospital, have advanced in the following "track record" of increasing responsibilities:

2000-present: **ADMISSIONS CLERK.** Leighton, KY. During the evening shift, operate the admissions office completely by myself, working without supervision since 2001; oversee all aspects of the admissions process and assisted with billing and accounting.
- Coordinate with in-patient nursing supervisor and housing supervisor on matters pertaining to patient placement and availability of beds.
- Escort patients to their rooms; ordered diagnostic testing for newly admitted patients.
- Quickly master the transition from the proprietary SMS computer system to a Windows-based system.
- On my own initiative, keep the office open until midnight in order to catch change-of-shift admissions and ensure that doctors would get paid for Emergency Room work-ups on D.R.G. if the E.R. counted as the first day of admission. This saves the hospital thousands of dollars in Medicare payments that would otherwise have been lost.

1995-00: **ADMISSIONS OFFICE CLERK.** Leighton, KY. Performed administrative, accounting, and clerical duties for the admissions office of this busy regional medical center.
- Processed inpatient registrations, took financial statements and ran credit checks on self-pay patients, and interviewed patients to acquire necessary information.
- Contacted insurance companies to verify patient coverage, get benefits information, and pre-certify inpatient services.
- Administered the Hill Burton Fund, completing applications for qualified patients.

1990-94: **ASSISTANT SUPERVISOR** and **EMERGENCY ROOM REGISTRATION CLERK.** Leighton, KY. Managed as many as 30 clerks in rotating shifts, providing direct supervision, administrative support, employee counseling and evaluation, and accounting services to the Emergency Department patient registration office.
- Coordinated patient registration efforts with billing office goals, ensuring that all patient information required by the billing department was complete and accurate.
- Coded emergency room charts daily and entered them into the computer for billing; attended seminars on ICD-9/CM coding.

Date

Exact Name of Person
Exact Title
Exact Name of Company
Address
City, State, Zip

ASSISTANT DIRECTOR OF NURSING

Dear Exact Name of Person (or Dear Sir or Madam if answering a blind ad):

With the enclosed resume, I would like to acquaint you with my strong administrative, organizational, and problem-solving skills as well as my extensive background in nursing supervision and administration.

I have earned a Bachelor of Science in nursing from Kent State University, in addition to my Associate degree in Registered Nursing and Licensed Practical Nurse programs. I have been certified as an instructor in Basic Cardiac Life Support (BCLS), and have received my ANCC Gerontological Nurse Certification.

At Elderlodge of Kent, I was hired as an RN Supervisor and was quickly promoted to Assistant Director of Nursing/Staff Development. In this position, I support the Director of Nursing, supervising 75 Registered Nurses, Licensed Practical Nurses, and Certified Medical Assistants, coordinating and directing the day-to-day operations of the nursing department to insure that appropriate levels of direct care are provided to the Residents. I am responsible for assessing, selecting, and implementing training programs for the nursing staff and developing other programs to meet the needs of the facility's employees.

As you will see from my resume, I have worked at this level of responsibility for most of my nursing administration career. In previous positions at Village Green Care Center and Carrolton of Kent, my leadership and management skills were recognized, and I was either hired at the Assistant Director of Nursing level or quickly advanced to that level and beyond.

If you can use a highly educated, articulate professional with a strong background in nursing administration and long-term care environments, I hope you will contact me to suggest a time when we might meet to discuss your need. I can assure you that I have an excellent reputation and could quickly become a valuable asset to your organization.

Sincerely,

Sandra Bush

SANDRA BUSH

1110½ Hay Street, Fayetteville, NC 28305   •   preppub@aol.com   •   (910) 483-6611

OBJECTIVE
To benefit an organization that can use a motivated, experienced administrator with strong organizational and problem-solving skills who offers a strong background of nursing supervision in long-term care environments.

EDUCATION
Bachelor of Science in Nursing (BSN), Kent State University, Kent, OH.
Associate degree, Registered Nursing (RN), Kent Community College, Kent, OH.
Licensed Practical Nurse program (LPN), Kent Technical Community College, Kent, OH.
Registered Nurse License #ZXX106744 , Expires 12/31/03.
Basic Cardiac Life Support (BCLS) Instructor, Certificate #244869872, Expires 5/31/05.
ANCC Gerontological Nurse Certification, Certificate # 8900058-09, Expires 11/30/03.

AFFILIATIONS
Member, American Society of Long Term Care Nurses
Member, Ohio Nurses Association

EXPERIENCE
At Elderlodge of Kent, was hired as an RN Supervisor, and was quickly promoted to Assistant Director of Nursing/Staff Development.
2000-present: **ASSISTANT DIRECTOR OF NURSING.** Elderlodge of Kent, OH. Support the Director of Nursing, supervising a staff of 75 RNs, LPNs, and CNAs in order to coordinate and direct the day-to-day operations of the nursing department in this busy long-term care facility.
- Perform daily rounds of the Nursing Service Department.
- Develop, implement, and maintain an effective orientation program that quickly and effectively familiarizes nursing staff with the facility, its policies and procedures, and the job duties they will be expected to discharge.
- Work closely with the Director of Nursing to ensure that a sufficient number of Registered Nurses, Licensed Practical Nurses, and Certified Medical Assistants are available for each tour of duty, in order to maintain quality resident care.
- Assess, select, and implement in-service training and other programs to meet specific needs of the facility's employees.
- Assist the Director of Nursing in preparation of employee performance evaluations.
- Serve as Coordinator for resident assessment and care planning, compiling the Minimum Data Set for Nursing Home Resident Assessment and insuring the implementation of Resident Assessment Protocols and Triggers.

1996-00: **REGISTERED NURSE SUPERVISOR.** Observed and assessed the physical and emotional health of Residents, ensuring that direct nursing care was provided.
- Made rounds with physician; notified physician of changes in resident's condition.
- Reviewed nurse's notes and C.N.A. flow sheets to insure that all documentation was descriptive of the resident care being provided.
- Admitted, transferred, and discharged residents, completing all necessary paperwork.
- Monitored all operational areas; notified the Director of Nursing of any problem areas.
- Assisted charge nurse; monitored seriously ill residents and provided nursing care.

ASSISTANT DIRECTOR OF NURSING. Village Green Care Center, Kent, OH (1991-96). Performed essentially the same duties as the **Assistant Director of Nursing** position at Elderlodge; also performed some of the duties of an **RN Supervisor.**

PERSONAL
Outstanding personal and professional references are available upon request.

Date

Exact Name of Person
Exact Title
Exact Name of Company
Address
City, State, Zip

**CERTIFIED NURSE AIDE
(CNA)**

Dear Exact Name of Person (or Dear Sir or Madam if answering a blind ad):

With the enclosed resume, I would like to make you aware of my background as a dedicated Certified Nurse Aide whose exceptional organizational and patient care skills have been proven in a challenging mental health/developmentally disabled, long term care, and home health environments.

As you will see from my resume, I completed the Certified Nurse Aide program through The Beagleton of Houndville, and received my licensure from the West Virginia Board of Nursing in 2000. In positions as a Certified Nurse Aide in long-term care and home health environments, I have demonstrated my ability to work independently while interacting with nursing staff and physicians to provide the highest possible levels of patient care.

Earlier as a Health Care Technician at a group home for clients with severe/ profound mental and physical disabilities, I monitored and recorded behavioral changes to assist the physician in determining appropriate medication and course of treatment. I programmed individual and group activities designed to improve developmental skills and increase client independence, and worked closely with clients and their families to teach and refine socialization skills.

If you can used a skilled Certified Nurse Aide with experience in a variety of challenging clinical environments, I hope you will welcome my call soon when I try to arrange a brief meeting to discuss your goals and how my background might serve your needs. I can provide outstanding references at the appropriate time.

Sincerely,

Barkley M. Basset

BARKLEY M. BASSET

1110½ Hay Street, Fayetteville, NC 28305   •   preppub@aol.com   •   (910) 483-6611

OBJECTIVE   To contribute to an organization that can use a versatile, hard-working young professional who offers a track record of accomplishments both as a Certified Nurse Aide in developmental and home health environments, as well as in distribution, warehousing, and supply.

EDUCATION &   Completed the Certified Nurse Aide certification program through The Beagleton of Hieton,
TRAINING   Houndville, WV, 2000.
Excelled in numerous training courses in leadership and management, supply and inventory control, personnel administration, and computer operation sponsored by the U.S. Army.

CERTIFICATIONS   Certified Nurse Aide, West Virginia Board of Nursing, Houndville, WV, 2000-present.
Community CPR certification (adult, child, and infant), American Heart Association, expires 11/03.

EXPERIENCE   **CERTIFIED NURSE AIDE (PRIVATE DUTY).** Houndville, WV (2001-present). Provide exceptional in-home care to a bedridden patient; perform patient assessment, monitor vital signs, and ensure that the patient was responding appropriately to treatment.
- Assist with feeding and feed the patient when necessary, as well as helping the patient perform basic personal hygiene, bathing, grooming, and dressing.

CERTIFIED NURSE AIDE. Beagleton of Houndville, WV (2000). Completed recertification as a Nurse Aide at Beagleton, then accepted this position, assisting the nursing staff and physicians in providing direct patient care services to elderly and bedridden individuals in this long-term care facility.
- Measured patient's vital signs and administered oxygen by nose feeder, mask, or tent.
- Assisted with catheterizations, setup and monitored feeding pumps, and performed accuchecks to measure blood sugar levels of diabetic patients while also handling wound care, enemas, etc.
- Assisted clients with personal hygiene, dressing, bathing, grooming, and feeding; encouraged and prepared the patient to achieve greater independence in daily living.

RESIDENT HEALTH CARE TECHNICIAN. Stimplekins Associates, Houndville, WV (1999-00). In a group home for handicapped and disabled children, programmed developmental and educational activities for individual clients and for the group; provided supervision daily and during outings.
- Monitored patient behavior and reported any incidences to the appropriate staff member while providing care to patients with severe/profound mental and physical disabilities.
- Completed PIC training; developed skills in subduing violent patients.

SUPERVISOR & INVENTORY MANAGEMENT SPECIALIST. U.S. Army, Ft. Bark, WV (1994-99). Gained a varied and well-rounded base of experience in the supply field while providing support to several different types of companies; qualified to operate forklifts up to 12,000 lbs.
- Provided leadership to as many as 20 personnel involved in stock record keeping and inventory management; developed knowledge in different types of work environments.
- Controlled equipment listings and count cards for multimillion-dollar inventories.
- Provided support for high-ticket items as copiers and fax machines.

PERSONAL   Am a fast learner who strongly believes in always giving 100%. Excellent references.

Date

Exact Name of Person
Exact Title
Exact Name of Company
Address
City, State, Zip

**CERTIFIED NURSE AIDE
(CNA)**

Dear Exact Name of Person (or Dear Sir or Madam if answering a blind ad):

I would appreciate an opportunity to talk with you soon about how I could contribute through my skills and experience as a Certified Nurse Aide (CNA).

As you will see from my enclosed resume, I graduated from a 420-hour course in Anniston, AL, and was the top student in my class with a 98.1 GPA. Since earning this certification, I have also completed a Piedmont Technical Community College course and was certified in CPR.

Presently attending PTCC in the General Studies program, I offer experience as a CNA and have worked in both home health care and nursing home settings. When I worked for a home health care organization, I provided services which included taking vital signs and recording them as well as helping patients with range-of-motion exercises, bathing, dressing, feeding, and other aspects of personal care.

Earlier for two health care centers in Alabama, I learned to work on a team which joined together in providing the best possible care for residents. I received several Letters of Recommendation for my efforts in supporting the welfare of patients. I took vital signs and entered information on charts, monitored medication, and assisted patients with many aspects of personal care.

If you can use a caring and compassionate young professional with strong patient care skills, I hope you will contact me to suggest a time when we might meet to discuss your needs. I can assure you in advance that I could rapidly become an asset to your organization.

Sincerely,

Jessica Rodriguez

JESSICA RODRIGUEZ

1110½ Hay Street, Fayetteville, NC 28305 • preppub@aol.com • (910) 483-6611

OBJECTIVE To offer excellent nursing skills in an environment where superior communication and motivational abilities would be beneficial and the ability to work well independently and as a contributor to team success would be valued.

EDUCATION Pursuing an Associate's degree, Piedmont Technical Community College, LA.
Graduated from Piedmont High School, Piedmont, LA, 2000: displayed a high level of self-motivation and ability to handle my time effectively while working in a fast-food restaurant after school and on weekends and volunteering in the school library.

TRAINING Graduated from the 420-hour CNA course, Anniston Assessment Center, AL, 1997.
- Achieved the highest average in the class with a 98.1 GPA.

CERTIFICATIONS *Certified Nurse Aide (CNA),* Anniston, AL, 1997.
CPR, Piedmont, LA, 2001.

SPECIAL SKILLS *Patient care skills:* have operated a Hoyer lift and changed IV bags
- Take vital signs and keep accurate charts and patient records
- Assist patients with personal care – feeding, bathing, dressing, and moving around
- Monitor medications
Other: offer basic computer knowledge and can type

EXPERIENCE **CERTIFIED NURSE AIDE (CNA).** Southern Hospitality Home Health, Piedmont, LA (2001-present). Contribute to the care of homebound patients in such areas of support as taking vital signs as well as helping bathe, feed, and dress patients.
- Provide patients with help doing range-of-motion exercises which would in turn allow them more freedom and in many cases lead to an eventual return to independence.
- Cook and clean patients' homes and instruct them in hygiene and personal care.
- Assist patients to the bathroom and helped them move around inside the home.
- Applied my communication skills working with patients with a variety of conditions and prognoses.
- Am known for my dependability and punctuality.

CNA. Manor Pines Nursing Center, Anniston, AL (2000-01). Learned to be part of a team working together to provide patients with the best possible care.
- Provided direct patient care which included taking vital signs and charting daily activities participated in by patients under my care.
- Assisted patients with dressing, feeding, bathing, and walking and encouraged them to take responsibility for whatever they could do on their own.

CNA. Piedmont Health Care Center, Piedmont, AL (1997-99). Received several Letters of Recommendation for my efforts on behalf of the patients and my professionalism while developing excellent nursing skills and a reputation for dedication.
- Took vital signs and entered information on the individual patient's chart.
- Monitored medications and helped give enemas.
- Charted intake and output.

PERSONAL Am a team player who works well independently. Have a reputation as a creative, dedicated hard worker. Skilled in handling multiple tasks and seeing each is done correctly. Excellent references are available.

Date

Exact Name of Person
Exact Title
Exact Name of Company
Address
City, State, Zip

Dear Exact Name of Person (or Dear Sir or Madam if answering a blind ad)

With the enclosed resume, I would like to make you aware of my background as an experienced and reliable professional with exceptional customer service skills who offers experience in medical, office administration, and other environments requiring attention to detail and strong people skills.

As you will see, I have recently completed the Certified Nursing Assistant I & II program from Langston Technical Community College and received my certification from the Michigan Board of Nursing. While completing this program, I completed internships at Langston Medical Center and Highland House of Langston, a local long-term care facility. I provided patient care in support of the nursing staff, taking vital signs, monitoring catheters and IVs, and changing IV bags. I performed wound care, cleaning wounds and replacing bandages, as well as feeding, cleaning, bathing, and turning patients. At Highland House of Langston, I was additionally responsible for the care of elderly and bedridden patients, including Alzheimer's patients. I feel that my strong combination of education, practical experience, and genuine compassion for my patients would make me a valuable addition to your operation.

If you can use a motivated, hard-working professional who is dedicated to providing quality patient care and offers a track record of success in customer-focused environments requiring attention to detail, then I look forward to hearing from you soon. I assure you in advance that I have an excellent reputation, and would quickly become an asset to your organization.

Sincerely,

Lisa Niles

LISA NILES

1110½ Hay Street, Fayetteville, NC 28305   •   preppub@aol.com   •   (910) 483-6611

OBJECTIVE
To benefit an organization that can use an experienced and dependable professional with extensive experience working in medical and other environments where attention to detail and quality customer relations are emphasized.

CERTIFICATIONS
Certified Nurse Aide I & II, listing #026943, Michigan Board of Nursing, expires 2003.
Certified in Adult & Child CPR, American Heart Association, expires 2002.

EDUCATION
Completed the course of study for Certified Nursing Assistant I and II, Langston Technical Community College, Langston, MI, 2001.
- Was evaluated as a "delightful student who performs well with patients."

EXPERIENCE
CERTIFIED NURSING ASSISTANT. Langston Medical Center and Highland House of Langston, Langston, MI (2001-present). While completing a two-month internship, provide general patient care in support of the nursing staff at this large local long-term care facility.
- Take vital signs; monitor catheters and IVs; change IV bags.
- Perform wound care, cleaning wounds and replacing bandages.
- Perform colostomies and conduct blood sugar tests.
- Feed, clean, bath, and turn patients; change bedding.
- At Highland House, am additionally responsible for care of elderly and bedridden patients, including Alzheimer's patients.

SECRETARY. Stanley Steemer, Langston, MI (1999-00). Performed administrative, clerical, and receptionist function for this busy location of the nationwide carpet cleaning company.
- Answered multi-line phone systems, directing calls, taking messages, and scheduling appointments for carpet cleaning service.
- Prepared all office correspondence, typing letters, memos, reports, and other documents; prepared monthly billing statements.
- Updated and maintained files, ensuring that all customer information was current.

BEAUTICIAN. Personal Creations, Langston, MI (1998-99). Effectively managed my time while assisting customers with a variety of hair care needs at this busy salon.
- Worked closely with customers, determining their needs and advising them.

HOME HEALTH CARE PROVIDER. (1997-98). Provided in-home health care to my husband during his illness.
- Became knowledgeable of transplants, aneurysms, heart attacks, strokes, and medical terminology related to cardiac care.
- In the aftermath of his death, learned to cope with grief and bereavement.

OPTICAL SHOP SALESPERSON. Valley Eye Clinic, Langston, MI (1992-96). Performed customer service, receptionist, and office administration duties for this busy optical shop; maintained inventory and ordered supplies.
- Worked closely with patients, assisting in the selection of eyeglass frames.
- Performed liaison between patients and optometrist.

PERSONAL
Outstanding personal and professional references are available upon request.

Date

Exact Name of Person
Exact Title
Exact Name of Company
Address
City, State, Zip

**CERTIFIED NURSING
ASSISTANT (CNA)**

Dear Exact Name of Person (or Dear Sir or Madam if answering a blind ad):

With the enclosed resume, I would like to begin the process of exploring employment opportunities within your organization. I am particularly interested in opportunities at Under the Sea Hospital. As you will recall, we spoke by telephone this morning and you asked me to fax a resume to you.

As you will see from my enclosed resume, I am a Certified Nursing Assistant II and have excelled in jobs in various types of environments including nursing homes, home health services, state hospitals, and major medical centers. On numerous occasions I have been recognized for superior initiative and outstanding performance.

I can provide excellent personal and professional references, and I would appreciate an opportunity to show you in person that my outstanding nursing skills and compassionate personality could become valuable assets to your organization.

I hope you will contact me to suggest a time when we might meet to discuss your needs and how I might help you. Thank you in advance for your time.

Sincerely,

Ariel D. Mermaid

ARIEL D. MERMAID

1110½ Hay Street, Fayetteville, NC 28305   •   preppub@aol.com   •   (910) 483-6611

OBJECTIVE

To offer my experience as a Certified Nursing Assistant (CNA) to an organization that can use my background as a nursing assistant as well as my outstanding qualities including initiative and a cheerful personality.

EDUCATION

Certified Nursing Assistant II training, Oceanville Technical Community College, Oceanville, HI, 2001.
Certificate for Nursing Assistant, Oceanville Technical Community College, Oceanville, HI, 1987.

LICENSE

License for Nurse Aide II, State of Hawaii, listing # XYA123; expires 06/2004.
HI License as Nursing Assistant #193333.

EXPERIENCE

CERTIFIED NURSING ASSISTANT. Flounder Hospital, Oceanville, HI (2000-present). Handle all the responsibilities of a nurse except for dispensing medicine, and have become widely respected because of my skill in delivering quality patient care with a cheerful and outgoing personality.

- Handle tube feedings, monitor blood sugar, insert foleys and D/C foleys; set up IVs for nurses and D/C IVs; monitor vital signs as well as height and weight and record them in the computer.
- Handle tracheostomies and suctioning; change colostomy bags; have become skilled with telemetry.

NURSING ASSISTANT. Tritonton of Oceanville, Oceanville, HI (1997-00). Performed routine medical diagnostic functions for residents. Ensured living areas were clean and in order. Assisted patients with bathing, eating, grooming when required. Annotated patients' status on medical records.

NURSING ASSISTANT. Scullyville State Hospital, Scullyville, HI (1992-97). In addition to regular nursing assistant duties, escorted ambulatory patients to doctor's appointments which were away from our facility. Supervised various group activities. Reported to staff on patient changes in behavior or habits. Performed "suicide watch" monitoring on unstable patients which required close observation of patient and detailed written reports of their actions in 15-minute intervals.

NURSING ASSISTANT. St. Sebastian Nursing Center, Scullyville, HI (1991). Provided and recorded routine diagnostic analysis for geriatric patients. Documented patient records.

NURSING ASSISTANT. Ursula Center Nursing Home, Ursula, HI (1988-90). Skillfully performed duties encompassing total geriatric patient care with compassion and sensitivity.

NURSING ASSISTANT. Home Health Services of Mermenton County, Scullyville, HI (1987). Blended my nursing abilities with my domestic skills to provide exceptional care for patients in their homes.

AWARDS

Have been recognized on many occasions for my outstanding performance.

- Have been presented five **Service Awards** as a testimonial to dedication to patient care.
- Was the recipient of a **Certification of Appreciation.**

PERSONAL

Interests include community affairs, family and improving my nursing skills.

Date

Exact Name of Person
Exact Title
Exact Name of Company
Address
City, State, Zip

CERTIFIED NURSING
ASSISTANT (CNA)

Dear Exact Name of Person (or Dear Sir or Madam if answering a blind ad):

With the enclosed resume, I would like to make you aware of my interest in exploring employment opportunities with your organization and introduce you to my nursing credentials.

As you will see from my resume, I became a Certified Nursing Assistant through training from Indiana State University and Terre Haute Community College. I am currently employed simultaneously by T.H.I. Home Health Care and Medical Staffing, Inc. in which I work extensively with psychiatric and geriatric patients. I am especially proud of my accomplishments because I earned my certificate in my spare time while also excelling in my full-time job in the health care field.

In previous positions, I worked with several medical staffing agencies that assisted me in gaining most of my work experience. In my full-time job, I applied my strong assessment and problem-solving skills to resolve numerous long-standing problems at each facility that I have been assigned. I can provide outstanding personal and professional references because of my outstanding personal reputation and performance.

If we have the opportunity to meet in person, you will see that I am an articulate individual with an outgoing personality and I would be well suited for your medical facility. I would enjoy the opportunity to meet with you to discuss your needs as a highly respected C.N.A. I hope you will contact me to suggest a time when we could meet in person. Thank you.

Yours sincerely,

Denise E. Ryzner

DENISE E. RYZNER

1110½ Hay Street, Fayetteville, NC 28305　　•　　preppub@aol.com　　•　　(910) 483-6611

OBJECTIVE

To contribute to an organization that can use a dedicated medical professional known for compassion and meticulous attention to detail in all aspects of patient care.

EDUCATION & LICENSES

Diploma as a Certified Nursing Assistant (C.N.A.), Terre Haute Community College, Terre Haute, IN 2000.
Licensed Certified Nursing Assistant (C.N.A.) in IN.
Medication Aide License, IN, 2000.
Certificate of Completion in Child Day Care, Indiana State Univ., Terre Haute, IN, 1998.
Certified in First Aid and CPR.
Completed extensive training sponsored by the Department of Health and Human Services in Fire Safety, record keeping, and numerous courses related to health care issues.

EXPERIENCE

CERTIFIED NURSING ASSISTANT (C.N.A.) T.H.I. Home Health Care and Medical Staffing Inc., Terre Haute, IN, (2004-present). With T.H.I., work on temporary assignments in private homes and hospitals. With Medical Staffing, have worked on temporary assignments in assisted living environments.

C.S.S.A. Department of Health and Human Services, Terre Haute, IN (2002-04). As a C.N.A., visited patients' homes and worked with individuals with physical, mental, and/or emotional limitations that prevented them from adequately meeting their own needs.
- Performed light housekeeping; took records and reported vital signs.

C.N.A. Manicare Nursing Home, Terre Haute, IN (2000-02). Worked with mentally disturbed and Alzheimer's patients' charts on MARs. Monitored vital signs and medications; assisted with feedings and bathing. Recognized/reported symptoms of illness and changes in condition. Turned patients every two hours, if necessary.

C.N.A. Village Rehabilitation Center, Terre Haute, IN (1998-00). Worked with Alzheimer's and mentally ill patients in this busy hospital.

Child Care Attendant. Tiny Tots Daycare Center, Terre Haute, IN (1997-98). Interacted with infants to 6-month-olds, including bathing and feeding. Was a Care Leader. Planned parent letters and quarterly newsletters; prepared lesson plans.

C.N.A. Woodlands Nursing, Terre Haute, IN (1996-97). Worked with mentally depressed and Alzheimer's patients, monitoring vital signs and collecting specimens. Recognized and reported symptoms of illness and changes in health; charted on MARs.

C.N.A. Illinois State Veterans Nursing Home, Terre Haute, IN (1994-96). Visited patients who were homebound and reported back to an RN. Escorted patients to appointments; assisted with personal care and sat with patients.

Child Care Attendant. Littleton Child Care, Terre Haute, IN (1994). Worked with infants to six months. Interacted with and fed and diapered. Also worked with children 6-18 months old as well as school-age children. Assisted and guided children relating to their self-concept, sensory, language and cognitive development; went on field trips with children.

PERSONAL

Enjoy working with people. Am known as reliable and as a good organizer. Excellent references on request. Am a cheerful and adaptable professional who gets along with others.

Date

Exact Name of Person
Exact Title
Exact Name of Company
Address
City, State, Zip

**CERTIFIED NURSING
ASSISTANT (CNA)**

Dear Exact Name of Person (or Dear Sir or Madam if answering a blind ad):

With the enclosed resume, I would like to make you aware of my interest in exploring employment opportunities with your organization and introduce you to my nursing credentials.

As you will see from my resume, I became a Certified Nursing Assistant through training from Massey-Hill Medical Institute and Amarillo College in Amarillo, TX. I am currently employed simultaneously by Arizona Medical Center and Roper North Hospital in which I work extensively with psychiatric and med-surg patients. I am especially proud of my accomplishments because I earned my certificate in my spare time while also excelling in my full-time job in the health care field.

In previous positions, I worked with several medical staffing agencies that assisted me in gaining most of my work experience. In my full-time job, I applied my strong assessment and problem-solving skills to resolve numerous long-standing problems at each facility that I have been assigned. I can provide outstanding personal and professional references because of my outstanding personal reputation and performance.

If we have the opportunity to meet in person, you will see that I am an articulate individual with an outgoing personality and I would be well suited for your medical facility. I would enjoy the opportunity to meet with you to discuss your needs as a highly respected C.N.A. I hope you will contact me to suggest a time when we could meet in person. Thank you.

Yours sincerely,

Lionel P. Everson

LIONEL P. EVERSON

1110½ Hay Street, Fayetteville, NC 28305   •   preppub@aol.com   •   (910) 483-6611

OBJECTIVE   To contribute to an organization that can use a dedicated medical known for compassion and meticulous attention to detail in all aspects of patient care and record keeping.

LICENSES   Licensed Certified Nursing Assistant (C.N.A.) in AZ, NM, CO, and TX.

EXPERIENCE   **CERTIFIED NURSING ASSISTANT (C.N.A.).** Arizona Medical Center and Roper North Hospital, Phoenix, AZ (2003-present). Through Keiffer Staffing agency, am currently working at two hospitals in Phoenix.
- At Arizona Medical Center, work extensively with psychiatric patients as well as med-surg.
- At Roper North Hospital, work on the oncology floor and in ICU; also work in the Radiology Lab assisting patients that needed radiation treatment.

C.N.A. & MEDICAL ASSISTANT. Maricopa County Memorial Hospital, Phoenix, AZ (2000-03). Through the Interim Medical Staffing Agency, worked in two different hospitals in Phoenix.
- Worked in the Emergency Room and in ICU; was responsible for all blood draws and EKGs.
- Provided CPR during cardiac arrests.

C.N.A. Kelly Services, Phoenix, AZ (1999-00). Through the Kelly medical staffing agency, worked on temporary assignments.
- At Roper North Hospital, worked in oncology.
- At the Candeler Group Home, which housed adults aged 15 years and older, provided supervision to mentally challenged adults who had transitioned from a state-run facility.
- At the Buncher Rehabilitation Center, provided medical care to new quadriplegics.

C.N.A. & STAFFER. Randstaff Nursing, Amarillo, TX (1997-99). Worked as a temporary staffing specialist for hospitals, medical centers, and medical facilities.
- Began with Randstaff Nursing as a temporary C.N.A. and then was recruited to assume office responsibilities related to placing C.N.A.s in temporary positions.
- As a C.N.A., worked in ER and ICU; drew blood and was responsible for EKGs.
- On a two-year assignment as a C.N.A., worked at the Farmington Prison Medical and Psychiatric Department, a permanent prison for incarcerated individuals who required medical and psychiatric care.

C.N.A. (private duty nursing). Massey-Hill Medical Institute, Amarillo, TX, (1995-97). Provided the full range of nursing care to a patient suffering from muscular dystrophy; I provided skilled nursing care and handled a wide range of personal errands until the patient passed away.

EDUCATION   **C.N.A.** I Certification. Massey-Hill Medical Institute, Amarillo, TX, 1995.
C.N.A. Certificate, Amarillo College, Amarillo, TX, 1994.
Graduated from R.E.Fields High School, Amarillo, TX, 1993.

PERSONAL   Hobbies include shopping, gardening, cooking, computer operation, and volleyball.

Date

Exact Name of Doctor
Name of Company
Address (no., street)
Address (city, state, zip)

CHARGE NURSE　　Dear Exact Name of Person (or Dear Sir or Madam if answering a blind ad):

I would appreciate an opportunity to show you soon, in person, that my superior communication skills and nursing expertise could make a valuable contribution within your office.

As you will see from my resume, I was employed at Davidson Medical Hospital for the year immediately following my graduation from nursing school. I enjoyed the satisfaction of patient contact and the team approach to medical care practiced in the hospital. Serving on the medical-surgical ward also permitted me to become proficient with sophisticated medical   technology and a variety of post-operative procedures.

I became very interested in an innovative program aimed at stimulating increased patient and family involvement in long-term medical treatment. It was especially gratifying for me to help patients adjust to their physical condition combining dietary and therapeutic measures they could control themselves.

I feel certain that my experience could benefit your patients, too, and I am sure that you would find me a warm, dedicated professional whose standards are in keeping with the high quality of your office staff. I hope you will welcome my call next week when I try to arrange a brief meeting at your convenience to discuss your current and future needs and how I might serve them. Thank you in advance for your time.

Yours sincerely,

Juanita W. Fulton

(Alternate last paragraph: I hope you will call or write me soon to suggest a time convenient for us to meet and discuss your current and future needs and how I might serve them.)

JUANITA W. FULTON

1110½ Hay Street, Fayetteville, NC 28305   •   preppub@aol.com   •   (910) 483-6611

OBJECTIVE

I want to offer my excellent communication skills and health care expertise to a medical office in need of a professional nurse with experience in post-operative procedures, patient instruction programs, and sophisticated medical terminology.

LICENSES

Am a qualified Registered Nurse. Hold current IV and CPR certification.

EDUCATION

Bachelor of Science degree in Nursing, Vanderbilt University, Nashville, TN, 2002. Conducted into the Vanderbilt Nurses Honor Society with a 4.0 GPA.

EXPERIENCE

Excelled in a track record of promotions with Davidson Medical Center, Nashville, TN:

2003-present: CHARGE NURSE. Experience in medical-surgical therapeutic procedures through treating a variety of patients, and supervise other nurses in various units.

- Supervise a staff of 12. Maintain accurate patient progress charts.
- Assist laboratory technicians working with patients on my ward.
- Train new nurses joining the staff.
- Use a computer system linking my floor with other hospital departments.
- Through motivating my staff, improve morale and efficiency on the ward, thereby cutting down on high-cost overtime hours.
- Participate in these innovative instruction programs, counseling patients and families facing long-term illnesses.
- Develop expertise with a wide range of state-of-the-art medical technology including these:
- IVAC and IMED intravenous monitoring systems; Artificial Respiration Systems; Hyperalimentation systems
- Learn to anticipate physicians' needs and "doctor's orders."

2001-03: STAFF NURSE. Provided individual patient care administering medication and other therapeutic treatment. Accompanied physicians on ward rounds.

- Developed my ability to anticipate patients' needs, providing physical comfort and emotional support.
- Learned to cooperatively contribute my skills within a team of health care professionals.
- Assisted in these and other post-operative procedures:

  stitch and staple removal   surgical dressing changes   tracheotomy care

Other experience:

POOL OPERATOR. Percy Priest Community Center, Nashville, TN (1999-01). Managed a recreational swimming facility, organizing competitive events and private instruction. Learned to budget time and money effectively.

PERSONAL

Am a careful listener and empathetic professional committed to the philosophy that "patients are people, too." Believe that preventive medicine and patient instruction are the best approach to health care.

Date

Exact Name of Person
Title or Position
Name of Company
Address (number and street)
Address (city, state, and zip)

Dear Exact Name of Person: (or Sir or Madam if answering a blind ad.)

With the enclosed resume, I would like to express my interest in exploring employment opportunities with your organization.

As you will see, I offer nursing skills honed in medical clinic and coronary step-down unit environments. Presently working as the Charge Nurse and Clinical Coordinator for a busy local clinic, I supervise two Licensed Practical Nurses and a Phlebotomist while overseeing support activities ranging from controlling inventory, to providing triage for patients being admitted, to assisting in patient and family education efforts. My daily activities include assisting in minor procedures and administration of medications as well as in phlebotomy, PFTs, nebulizer treatments, oxygen therapy, vital signs, and EKGs. I also handle administrative functions such as scheduling, providing referrals to specialists, completing insurance authorizations, filing, and operating computer systems for record keeping.

In an earlier job as a Charge Nurse and Preceptor for a coronary step-down unit, I supervised 11 people providing total patient care in a 32-bed unit. In this capacity, I personally provided and supervised others in providing the full range of pre- and post-operative care for coronary patients. I received cross -training in open-heart and medical-surgical step down, CCU, and nephrology care while also participating in educating patients and family members on all aspects of disease management including proper aftercare, dietary issues, and medication and possible drug interactions.

My education and training include an Associate Degree in Nursing and the completion of Basic and Advanced Cardiac Life Support (BCLS and ACLS) certification training.

If you can use an articulate and enthusiastic nursing professional with excellent organizational skills, I hope you will contact me to suggest a time when we might meet to discuss your needs. I can provide outstanding references at the appropriate time.

Sincerely,

Sherry Stevens

SHERRY STEVENS

1110½ Hay Street, Fayetteville, NC 28305 • preppub@aol.com • (910) 483-6611

OBJECTIVE

To benefit an organization that can use an enthusiastic professional with exceptional communication and organizational skills who offers nursing experience honed in medical clinic and coronary step-down environments, as well as experience in sales of insurance products.

EDUCATION

Associate Degree in Nursing (ADN), Rapid City Technical Community College, Rapid City, WA, 1998.
Completed two years of college-level course work in General Studies, Rapid City Technical Community College, Rapid City, WA, 1989-1991.
Completed **Basic** and **Advanced Cardiac Life Support** certification training (**BCLS** and **ACLS**), Rapid City Valley Medical Center, Rapid City, WA, 2000 & 2001.

EXPERIENCE

CHARGE NURSE and **CLINICAL COORDINATOR.** Westside Medical Center of Rapid City Valley Health Systems, Rapid City, WA (2001-present). Supervise two Licensed Practical Nurses and a phlebotomist while overseeing operation of the nursing staff for this busy local clinic; train new personnel for the clinic.

- Entrusted with the responsibility of maintaining and monitoring inventory control and dispensing of all narcotics as well as medications from the sample closet.
- Contribute patient and family education in situations requiring tact and diplomacy.
- Perform phlebotomy, PFTs, nebulizer treatments, oxygen therapy, vital signs, and EKGs; administer medications and assist in minor procedures.
- Provide triage for all patients being admitted to the clinic, arranging the patients so that the most serious cases receive the quickest attention from the doctor.
- Schedule patients, provide referrals, complete insurance authorizations, and perform filing and basic computer operations.
- Manage the accurate and timely ordering of all supplies needed by the clinic.

CHARGE NURSE and **PRECEPTOR, CORONARY STEP-DOWN.** Rapid City Valley Medical Center, Rapid City, WA (1998-2001). Supervised as many as 11 personnel, including eight registered nurses, two Certified Nurse Aides, and a monitor technician while providing total patient care for this 32-bed facility.

- Started IVs and performed insertion of Foley catheters and NG tubes; administered medications orally, intravenously, and subcutaneously.
- Provided pre- and post-operative care for cardiac catheterization, pacemaker insertion, PTCA, cardioversion, defibrillators & CABG, and other coronary patients.
- Assisted in procedures which included stress testing, chest tube insertion, thoracentesis, lumbar punctures, and CVP lines.
- Served as Preceptor on the Coronary Care Step-Down Unit for RNs and RN candidates.
- Cross-trained in open-heart and medical-surgical step down, CCU, and nephrology.
- Performed wound care, phlebotomy, telemetry monitoring and interpretation, suture and staple removals, and 12-lead EKGs.
- Educated patient and family on proper aftercare, dietary issues, medication and possible drug interactions, and disease management.

INTERN and **STUDENT NURSE.** Various locations, Rapid City, WA (1995-1998). Performed clinical rotations in pediatrics, rehabilitation, Emergency Room, Orthopedics, Neurology, child abuse, and medical-surgical units while completing my student nurse practicum at medical facilities throughout Cumberland County.

PERSONAL

Known as an articulate communicator a with a passion for excellence.

Date

Exact Name of Person
Exact Title
Exact Name of Company
Address
City, State, Zip

CHARGE NURSE &
STAFF NURSE

Dear Exact Name of Person (or Dear Sir or Madam if answering a blind ad)

With the enclosed resume, I would like to make you aware of my background as an articulate nursing professional with exceptional communication and organizational skills who offers a background of supervision and training as well as patient care and education in critical care and nephrology environments.

In my most recent position, I excelled as a Charge Nurse and Staff Nurse on the Nephrology Unit at a major regional medical center. I specialized in peritoneal dialysis, and I have more than 13 years experience in providing care to patients suffering from renal failure. Earlier I worked as an Intermediate Care (step-down) Nurse, providing patient care for trauma, ventilator, cardiac, tracheostomy, and other patients who were transferred out of the ICU, but were not stable enough to go to a regular floor. In previous experience as a Licensed Practical Nurse, I performed phlebotomy services at a local blood bank, strictly observing all precautions related to the handling of blood products and related biohazards.

As you will see from my enclosed resume, I completed the Associate's degree in Nursing program at Gumbo Technical Community College, and have supplemented my education with courses in American Sign Language, computers, and Basic Cardiac Life Support (BCLS). Certified as a BCLS Instructor, for more than 11 years I have served as a patient educator facilitator, and my skills in this area were recognized with first-place honors at the Gumbo Area Health Education Center (GAHEC) Spring Community Fair.

If you can use an accomplished, hard-working nursing professional who is known for loyalty to her employers as well as for exceptional patient care and education skills, I hope you will call or write me soon to suggest a time when we might meet to discuss your current and future needs and how I might serve them. I can provide outstanding references and would quickly become an asset to your organization.

Sincerely,

Jenny Brook Gump

(Alternate last paragraph:
I hope you will welcome my call soon to arrange a brief meeting to discuss your current and future needs and how I might serve them.)

JENNY BROOK GUMP

1110½ Hay Street, Fayetteville, NC 28305 • preppub@aol.com • (910) 483-6611

OBJECTIVE

To benefit an organization that can use an experienced nursing professional with exceptional communication and organizational skills who offers a background in nursing supervision and training as well as patient care and education in critical care and nephrology environments.

EDUCATION

Associate of Science Degree in Nursing (ADN), Gumbo Technical Community College, Shrimp, AL, 1990.

Graduated from the **Licensed Practical Nurse** program, Gumbo Technical Community College, Shrimp, AL, 1984.

Completed a number of advanced training programs offered through Shrimp Gumbo Health Systems, including the Basic Cardiac Life Support (BCLS) Instructor course, a 16-week American Sign Language course, and more than 150 hours of ongoing education in computers.

HONORS

Selected as **Nurse of the Year** for Shrimp Gumbo Health Systems, 2000 and 1992.

LICENSES & CERTIFICATIONS

Licensed **Registered Nurse**, Alabama Board of Nursing Certificate #073573.

Certified as a Basic Cardiac Life Support (BCLS) Instructor, expires November, 2005.

AFFILIATIONS

Member, American Nurses Association, 1990-present.

EXPERIENCE

With Shrimp Gumbo Health Systems, Shrimp, AL, have advanced in the following "track record" of increasing responsibilities at this major regional medical center:

2001-present: **CHARGE NURSE** and **STAFF NURSE, NEPHROLOGY.** Supervise as many as 10 personnel on the nursing staff while serving as Charge Nurse in charge of training new employees; provide expert care to patients suffering from renal dysfunction and kidney-related disorders on this busy nephrology unit.

- Perform patient assessments in order to determine the patient's care needs and monitor treatment progress.
- Provide education on medications, diet, and other related matters to patients and their families to assist them in the transition to home care.
- Operate a variety of computerized medical equipment and computers; monitor patient's status using telemetry equipment.
- Design and create new care plans for the Nephrology Unit; formerly served on a committee planning procedures for dealing with seclusion and patient restraint issues.
- Specialize in peritoneal dialysis and care for patients with renal failure.

1991-00: **CHARGE NURSE** and **STAFF NURSE, INTERMEDIATE CARE UNIT.** Provided total patient care to medical-surgical, hospice, cardiac step-down, and other patients who were discharged from the Intensive Care Unit (ICU) but were not stable enough to receive care on the regular floors.

- Assisted physicians with procedures and performed telemetry monitoring, phlebotomy, wound care, and care and maintenance of patients with tracheostomy and NG tubes.
- Treated overflow and post-ICU patients from every specialty area in the hospital.

LICENSED PRACTICAL NURSE. John Elliott Blood Bank, Shrimp, AL (1984-1990). Performed phlebotomies, sterilizing the venipuncture site before drawing blood from the donor in order to augment the blood supply available for use by local hospitals and clinics.

PERSONAL

Excellent personal and professional references are available upon request.

Exact Name of Person
Title or Position
Name of Company
Address (number and street)
Address (city, state, and zip)

CLINICAL ASSISTANT

Dear Exact Name of Person: (or Sir or Madam if answering a blind ad.)

With the enclosed resume, I would like to express my interest in exploring employment opportunities with your organization.

As you will see, I offer a blend of clinical and administrative abilities gained while excelling in a versatile work history in the medical field. I have completed extensive related training including a Medical Assistant Program and a Phlebotomy course as well as courses in Secretarial Science and Business.

Presently a Clinical Assistant for a family practice environment, I have become known for my compassionate and professional approach to dealing with patients, physicians, and other medical professionals. My duties range from preparing patients for exams, to performing medical procedures and assisting physicians, to performing diagnostic and screening tests. I also enter data into patient charts, refill prescriptions, and administer medications and vaccinations.

Earlier as a Phlebotomist and Medical Laboratory Aide in a Veterans Administration Hospital, I became skilled in utilizing universal blood and body fluid precautions while collecting samples and then doing all required tests on each sample. Prior to this job, I was one of three Medical Assistants in a women's clinic with five doctors and one nurse practitioner. In this capacity, I handled all aspects of procedures from screening patients, to documenting medical histories, to assisting in physical examinations as well as minor surgeries.

If you can use an adaptable and compassionate medical professional who is knowledgeable of insurance billing, inventory control, and office operations and administration, I hope you will contact me to suggest a time when we might meet to discuss your needs. I can provide outstanding references at the appropriate time.

Sincerely,

Jodie Thomas Damon

JODIE THOMAS DAMON

1110½ Hay Street, Fayetteville, NC 28305   •   preppub@aol.com   •   (910) 483-6611

OBJECTIVE
To contribute to an organization that can use a skilled medical professional with excellent clinical/administrative abilities and a congenial attitude when dealing with patients and others.

EDUCATION
Graduated from the Medical Assistant Program, Mercer Career Institute, Chicago, IL.
Completed Phlebotomy course, Hunter Vocational School, Chicago, IL.
Completed Secretarial Sciences Studies, City College of Chicago, Campus in Germany.
Continuing my education in business at Clarksville Technical Community College, TN.

EXPERIENCE
CLINICAL ASSISTANT. Riverbend Family Practice, Clarkesville, TN (2000-present). Utilize phlebotomy skills in an LPN working position. Am known for my professional and compassionate attitude in my interactions with patients, physicians, and other staff members while expertly performing all aspects of the job of Clinical Assistant.
- Prepare the patient for exams; perform medical procedures, and assist physician during exams; perform diagnostic and screening tests.
- Chart pertinent data in patients' medical records while also scheduling patients for consultations and diagnostic tests, refilling prescriptions, and assisting office manager and physicians in other tasks; administer medications and vaccinations.

MEDICAL LABORATORY AIDE. Veterans Hospital, Clarkesville, TN (1998-00). Worked primarily as a Phlebotomist as well as a Lab Aide.
- Performed venipuncture on inpatients, outpatients, and employees throughout the hospital complex utilizing universal blood and body fluid precautions.
- Collected patient samples with sufficient volume and correctness to do all tests required; performed positive identification of patient and specimen through entire process of phlebotomy, accessioning, receiving, aliquoting, distributing, and storage.
- Acted as the first-line contact between the Clinical Laboratory and the patient.
- Became very knowledgeable of the VA procedures used to review patient data, answer telephones, and count or record numerical data on AMIS reports.
- Handled patient information in a confidential and professional manner.
- Skillfully applied my knowledge of inventory procedures used to classify chemical reagents, antibiotics, expendable supplies, data, and files while utilizing my ability to interpret commercial chemical nomenclature, calculate simple ratio equations, and safely mix chemical ingredients.

MEDICAL ASSISTANT. Women's Health Center of Radcliff, Radcliff, KY (1996-98). As one of three Medical Assistants for five doctors and one nurse practitioner, handled the screening of OB patients, obtaining vital signs, determining weight, and collecting urine specimens; documented medical histories; assisted doctors in physical examinations as well as minor surgeries/biopsies, colonoscopy, IUD insertions/removal, NORPLANT insertions/removals, Cone Leep biopsies; ensured OSHA regulations were followed.
- Set up procedure room; explained procedures and postoperative care to patients.
- Priced and ordered instruments needed for office operation or instrument repair.

Other experience:
RED CROSS VOLUNTEER. Radcliff, KY and Ft. Campbell, KY (1996-present). While working full-time, volunteered up to 30 hours per week at Blanchfield Army Hospital.

PERSONAL
Can provide outstanding references. Knowledgeable of insurance billing.

CAREER CHANGE

Exact Name of Person
Exact Title
Exact Name of Company
Address
City, State, Zip

GROUP HOME PROVIDER

Dear Exact Name of Person (or Dear Sir or Madam if answering a blind ad):

With the enclosed resume, I would like to make you aware of my interest in exploring employment opportunities with your organization and introduce you to my nursing credentials.

As you will see from my resume, I am working on a full-time position with Peachtree Home Care as a Group Home Provider while I am currently being trained for my Nursing Assistance certification through training from Springfield Technical Community College. I operate a fully licensed group home for young and mature adults aged 20-45, all women. All adults were disabled, either mentally or physically. I assist in all areas of life ranging from personal hygiene to personal transportation.

In previous positions, I worked with several fast food and convenient stores which allowed me to gain management experience. In my full-time job, I applied my strong assessment and problem-solving skills to resolve numerous long-standing problems at each facility that I have been assigned. I can provide outstanding personal and professional references because of my outstanding personal reputation and performance.

If we have the opportunity to meet in person, you will see that I am an articulate individual with an outgoing personality and I would be well suited for your medical facility. I would enjoy the opportunity to meet with you to discuss your needs as a highly respected caregiver. I hope you will contact me to suggest a time when we could meet in person. Thank you.

Yours sincerely,

Natalie J. Waybright

NATALIE J. WAYBRIGHT

1110½ Hay Street, Fayetteville, NC 28305   •   preppub@aol.com   •   (910) 483-6611

OBJECTIVE
To apply my background as a caregiver combined with my proven management abilities.

EXPERIENCE
GROUP HOME PROVIDER. Peachtree Home Care, Springfield, MA (2003-present). Operate a fully licensed group home for young and mature adults aged 20-45, all women. All adults were disabled, either mentally or physically, and I assist them in all areas of life ranging from personal hygiene to personal transportation.
- Maintain detailed records and medical reports.
- Work part-time as a Data Processor with the Mail Boxes, Etc., and am involved in processing up to 800,000 pieces of outgoing mail per day by inputting zip codes, addresses, and often business names.

MANAGER. Popeye's, Springfield, MA (2002-03). Supervised up to 18 employees who included food prep, cashiers, cooks, order takers, cleaning staff, and others.
- Became known for effective management, quality control, and customer service.

MANAGER. Chick-Fil-A, Springfield, MA (1999-02). Managed all administrative/operations functions for this busy fast food chain including cooking, inventory control/ordering, making bank deposits, training, and supervising.

CONVENIENCE STORE MANAGER & CREDIT CARD REPORT PROCESSOR:
Excelled in the management of the following retail store operations in Springfield, MA:
SEVEN-ELEVEN (1999)
EXXON (1996-99)
CIRCLE K (1994-1996)
- Managed the overall daily operations, including accounts receivable and payable.
- Maintained inventory records, daily sales records, and made bank deposits.
- Hired, trained, and scheduled personnel. Approved time cards and computed payroll.
- Prepared daily and weekly reports; monitored cash received for assigned vendors and reconciled cash received with appropriate sales.
- Generated a weekly report reflecting the status of financial transactions.

CUSTOMER SERVICE CLERK. Uniforms-R-Us, Springfield, MA (1994). Assisted customers with the selection and ordering of appropriate uniforms.
- Processed orders and maintained customer files. Maintained inventory control.

BANK TELLER. Bank of Springfield, Springfield, MA (1993-94). Became known for excellent customer service skills performing banking transactions using computerized banking system.
- Accurately handled large sums of money and balanced drawer at close of business.
- Frequently performed the duties of Head Teller.

EDUCATION
Currently completing courses for a Nursing Assistant Certificate at Springfield Technical Community College.
Completed extensive professional training related to operations management and customer service sponsored by employers including Popeye's, Chick-Fil-A, Mail Boxes.
Completed computer software/hardware and retail management and bookkeeping training.
Graduated from Franklin-Murray High School, Springfield, MA.

PERSONAL
Am well-organized, detail-oriented, and highly dependable. Enjoy work requiring personal initiative and responsibility. Offer an exceptionally strong customer service orientation.

Date

Exact Name of Person
Title or Position
Name of Company
Address (number and street)
Address (city, state, and zip)

HEAD NURSE   Dear Exact Name of Person: (or Dear Sir or Madam if answering a blind ad.)

With the enclosed resume, I would like to indicate my interest in your medical center and my desire to explore employment opportunities.

As you will see from my enclosed resume, I offer experience as a Head Nurse and am known for my compassionate style when dealing with patients and their families. I decided on a career in nursing after working in administrative support roles at two medical offices and discovering my strong desire to become more involved in patient care.

I hope you will welcome my call soon to arrange a brief meeting at your convenience to discuss your current and future needs and how I might serve them. Thank you in advance for your time.

Sincerely yours,

Belinda Warren

(Alternate last paragraph:
I hope you will call or write me soon to suggest a time convenient for us to meet and discuss your current and future needs and how I might serve them. Thank you in advance for your time.)

BELINDA WARREN

1110½ Hay Street, Fayetteville, NC 28305   •   preppub@aol.com   •   (910) 483-6611

OBJECTIVE

To contribute to an organization that can use a skilled nursing professional who offers effective communication skills along with a reputation as a hard-working and compassionate person.

EDUCATION

Associate's degree in Nursing, Towson Technical Community College (TTCC), MD, 2000.
Certificate in **Surgical Technology,** TTCC, 1984; completed extensive on-the-job training at Towson Medical Center.
Certified CPR Instructor.

EXPERIENCE

HEAD NURSE. Cliffdale Primary Care, Towson, MD (2000-present). In addition to supervising the clinic staff of nine LPNs, lab technicians, and phlebotomists, order supplies and equipment while overseeing and controlling the completion of numerous tests and procedures which include:

pulmonary function testing	flex sigmoidoscopy
stress testing	visual acuity testing
peak flow meter usage	immunizations/vaccinations
monitoring EKGs	sterilization of equipment

- Act as liaison between pharmaceutical company representatives and physicians; accept samples and stock pharmaceutical supplies for clinic use.
- Assist during in-office surgical procedures.
- Make insurance referrals and authorizations along with referrals to other doctors.

FULL-TIME NURSING STUDENT. Towson Technical Community College, MD (1999-00). Placed on the President's List in recognition of my academic achievements.

CLINICAL STAFF MEMBER and **ADMINISTRATIVE ASSISTANT.** Medical Drive Obstetrics and Gynecology, Towson, MD (1987-93). Handled support activities ranging from taking patients' vital signs, to answering phones and routing messages, to setting up appointments and making referrals to other medical practices.

- Called in prescriptions; also conducted telephone triage by advising patients and helping determine how urgent their situation was.
- Developed mutually beneficial relations with pharmaceutical representatives, including acting as liaison between them, the physicians, and the nursing staff.

SURGICAL ASSISTANT. Dr. Dennis Michaels, Towson, MD (1984-87). Provided chairside assistance in periodontal surgeries as well as handling office support activities including making appointments, preparing surgical instruments, taking X-rays, and working with ultrasound equipment.

Highlights of earlier experience:
Gained skills in sales, office operations, credit application processing, and letters/contract preparation.

SPECIAL SKILLS

Am proficient with various office machines including typewriters, copy machines, personal and office computers, and X-ray and ultrasound equipment.

PERSONAL

Offer exceptionally strong communication skills. Excellent references.

Date

Exact Name of Person
Exact Title
Exact Name of Company
Address
City, State, Zip

HEALTH TECHNICIAN   Dear Exact Name of Person (or Dear Sir or Madam if answering a blind ad):

With the enclosed resume, I would like to make you aware of my interest in exploring employment opportunities with your organization.

As you will see from my resume, I have worked with the public all my life and I feel good about the contributions I have made to the physical and mental health of others through my positive attitude and outgoing personality. A dedicated Christian, I believe that a positive attitude is a key to good mental and physical health, and I excel in communicating with others in a way that they find uplifting, motivating, and encouraging. I have obtained numerous certifications and credentials during my career which include being certified as an Emergency Medical Technician, becoming trained as an Alcohol and Drug Abuse Counselor, and becoming certified as a Mental Health Specialist, Massage Therapist, and Paramedic. I was motivated to earn all those certifications because I thought they would enable me to reach out to others in a positive and helpful manner. My greatest satisfaction seems to come from helping others, and I have a proven ability to work effectively with others in a team situation.

You will notice that most of my paid professional work has been in the medical field as a Health Technician. During my spare time, I have excelled as a songwriter, composer, and singer as well as an ordained Presbyterian youth minister and counselor.

I am in the process of relocating to New York where extended family lives, and I am seeking employment with an organization that can make use of a versatile individual with a true desire to contribute to an organization and to others. I can provide strong personal and professional references, and I hope you will contact me to suggest a time when we might meet to discuss your needs.

Yours sincerely,

Vincent C. Ivey

VINCENT C. IVEY

1110½ Hay Street, Fayetteville, NC 28305   •   preppub@aol.com   •   (910) 483-6611

OBJECTIVE

I want to contribute to an organization that can use a versatile and outgoing professional who offers an outstanding personal and professional reputation along with a strong desire to contribute to an organization which provides quality services and products.

EDUCATION

Bachelor of Arts degree in Religion & Sociology, Wilmington College, Wilmington, DE, 2004.

COUNSELING

Completed Alcohol & Drug Abuse Training, Paul S. Hutton Veterans Hospital, Newark, DE. Accreditation in Occupational Hearing Conservation. Certified Mental Health Specialist II.

COMMUNICATION SKILLS

Completed Customer Relations Training, Department of Health and Human Services.
Musical talents: Am a concert singer of gospel music. Songwriter, singer, composer.
- In college at University of Delaware and at Wilmington College, was a tenor soloist under the direction of Dr. Michael Hollingsworth and Dr. Andrew Merritt. In the U.S. Army, continued as a soloist with the Fifth Squadron Soldier's Chorus as the group performed throughout the U.S.
- **Publications:** Published a CD entitled *The Storm Is Over No*w and other songs. Authored publications including *Yet I'll Rise, What I Have Found,* and *What a Wonder.*
- **Public speaking:** Extensive public speaking as a Presbyterian youth minister.

MEDICAL SKILLS

Certified Emergency Medical Technician (EMT) (certificate # 654321); certified in CPR. Certified Massage Therapist (certificate # 98765432); certified Paramedic (certificate # 1234).

EXPERIENCE

HEALTH TECHNICIAN. Department of Health and Human Services, Wilmington, DE (2003-present). Supervise four junior health technicians at this in-processing station which processed up to 280 people weekly undergoing physical examinations for entrance into this government agency. Complete paperwork reviewed by other government officials.

HEALTH TECHNICIAN. Paul S. Hutton Veterans Hospital, Newark, DE (2000-03). Provided aid to the injured, sick, and shut-in. Screened and triaged patients as appropriate. Utilized proper aseptic techniques and infection control procedures.
- Performed a wide variety of tasks under the supervision of a physician's assistant or medical doctor which included minor surgical, medical, or nursing treatment; applied and removed sutures; treated burns, blisters, and insect bites.
- Obtained lab readings; rendered tine tests; reported and documented positive reactions.
- Set up and operated specialized equipment such as resuscitation equipment, EKG monitors, and other equipment.
- Earned a reputation as a caring and nurturing professional who had the ability to lift up the spirits of patients and families through my positive outlook on life.

NURSING ASSISTANT. Wilmington Health Care Systems, Newark, DE (1998-00). Performed post-operative care which included irrigating indwelling catheters, performing gastric tube irrigations, and applying simple sterile dressings.
- Operated medical equipment; collected specimens; monitored patient's vital signs.

Highlights of other experience: CHIEF, PHYSICAL EXAMINER. Worked under the supervision of a flight surgeon and performed rigorous flight physicals.

PERSONAL

Have a compassionate, empathetic personality with a strong desire to help others.

Date

Exact Name of Person
Title or Position
Name of Company
Address (number and street)
Address (city, state, and zip)

**HOME HEALTH CARE
REGIONAL DIRECTOR**

You will see a steady
progression of
advancement in the resume
of this home health care
professional. Her industry
is expanding, and she is
using this resume and
cover letter as "fishing
bait"
to catch the best job.

Dear Exact Name of Person: (or Dear Sir or Madam if answering a blind ad.)

With the enclosed resume, I would like to indicate my interest in your organization and my desire to explore employment opportunities.

As you will see from my enclosed resume, I am an experienced home health care manager currently excelling as Regional Director of 12 branch offices with 35 administrative personnel reporting to me. Although I am held in high regard by my current employer and can provide excellent references at the appropriate time, I am attracted to your company because of its #1 ranking in the home health care industry.

I hope you will welcome my call soon to arrange a brief meeting at your convenience to discuss your current and future needs and how I might serve them. Thank you in advance for your time.

Sincerely yours,

Terri Alligood

(Alternate last paragraph:
I hope you will call or write me soon to suggest a time convenient for us to meet and discuss your current and future needs and how I might serve them. Thank you in advance for your time.)

TERRI ALLIGOOD

1110½ Hay Street, Fayetteville, NC 28305 • preppub@aol.com • (910) 483-6611

OBJECTIVE

To offer my strong background in health care management to an organization that can use a mature professional known for leadership and self-motivation as well as analytical and problem-solving abilities which enhance my practical nursing and patient care skills.

EXPERIENCE

Advanced in administrative roles with Comprehensive Home Health Care, Atlanta, GA:
REGIONAL DIRECTOR. (2001-present). Oversee operational areas including patient management, regulatory affairs, corporate planning and development, and financial management of 12 branch offices and a work station; manage 35 people in 12 locations.
- Coordinate each office's accounts receivable issues and concerns while working with the accounts receivable supervisor.
- Assist in the development of and then managed Quality Assurance and Risk Management programs as well as policy and programs in all operating areas.
- Ensured compliance with applicable federal, state, and local laws, regulations, and rules.

ASSISTANT ADMINISTRATOR and **DIRECTOR OF PROFESSIONAL SERVICES (DPS).** (1995-01). Continued to function as DPS after earning a promotion to assist the administrator in overseeing activities in each branch office and ensuring that staff members received adequate training and supervision.

DIRECTOR OF PROFESSIONAL SERVICES. (1990-95). Held responsibility for managing both clinical and operational activities in the Augusta branch office.

HOME HEALTH NURSE and **HOSPITAL COORDINATOR.** (1985-90). Provided home health care to patients while keeping primary care staff informed of the disposition of their patients when they received hospital care; received updates from hospital staff on our patients and developed contacts with their physicians.

STAFF REGISTERED NURSE. Numerous locations in SC (1981-85). Ensured that general medical and surgical patients received total nursing care; assessed physical and mental health and recorded information on patient charts; implemented treatment plans.

EDUCATION

Bachelor of Science in Nursing degree, Orion State University, Orion, MT, 1983; 3.9 GPA.
Associate of Science degree in Nursing, Sandhills Community College, Carthage, NC, 1981; with honors.

LICENSES

Home Health Nurse certification from the American Nurses' Credentialing Center, 1995.
Licensed Registered Nurse in Georgia, certification number 123245
Licensed Registered Nurse in South Carolina, license number 34578

AFFILIATIONS

American Nurse's Association, 1992-present
Georgia Association for Home Care Intermediary Relations Committee, 1995-present
Georgia Association for Home Care Ethics Subcommittee, 1997-01
Georgia Association for Home Care Provider Services Committee, 1996-01

AWARDS

Award for Academic Excellence in Nursing, May 2001; Award for Academic Excellence, April 2000. Georgia "Great 100 Nurses," October 2000
Hanni Schultz Memorial Award for Academic Excellence, May 2000

PERSONAL

Am results oriented. Have an enthusiastic, caring manner which makes others comfortable.

Date

Exact Name of Person
Title or Position
Name of Company
Address (number and street)
Address (city, state, and zip)

HOSPICE CASE MANAGER

Dear Exact Name of Person: (or Dear Sir or Madam if answering a blind ad.)

Can you use an articulate and knowledgeable medical professional who offers a reputation as an enthusiastic and energetic individual who excels in communicating with others whether contributing to team efforts, instructing and mentoring other medical professionals, or educating patients and family members?

You will see from my enclosed resume that I offer a solid background of experience as a nursing professional who has often been called on to instruct, educate, and teach. Currently excelling as a Case Manager in Hospice, I manage a case load of up to 21 terminally ill patients, providing supportive care, patient assessment, and education. I joined the staff of San Diego Area Medical Center as a Registered Nurse, and then worked as a Psychiatric Nurse from November of 2000 until I was promoted into my current position.

Although I am highly regarded by my present employer and can provide outstanding references at the appropriate time, I have decided to permanently relocate back to my native Canada. I am interested in exploring career options with companies in the area that can use a highly skilled, dedicated medical professional.

I offer experience in the nursing field, along with knowledge of medical facility operations including case management, data entry, and records management which combine to make me a well-rounded professional. With my enthusiastic and energetic approach and reputation as a compassionate and caring individual, I am certain that I offer a blend of skills, experience, and knowledge which would make me a valuable addition to any organization searching for a versatile and adaptable mature professional.

I hope you welcome my call soon when I try to arrange a brief meeting to discuss your needs and how I might help you. Thank you in advance for your time.

Sincerely,

Samuel Jackson

(Alternate last paragraph:
I hope you will call or write me soon to suggest a time convenient for us to meet and discuss your current and future needs and how I might serve them. Thank you in advance for your time.)

SAMUEL JACKSON

1110½ Hay Street, Fayetteville, NC 28305   •   preppub@aol.com   •   (910) 483-6611

OBJECTIVE   To offer a combination of experience, education, and strong well-defined personal strengths to an organization that can benefit from my knowledge of the medical field as well as from my communication, teaching, and decision-making skills.

EDUCATION & TRAINING   Completed a three-year program leading to a **Diploma in Nursing,** Seneca College, Montreal, Quebec, Canada, 1995.
Began a training program in January 2002 with Comprehensive Home Health Care, San Diego, CA; earning certification to provide home health care on a case-by-case basis.

EXPERIENCE   **San Diego Area Medical Center, San Diego, CA:**
HOSPICE CASE MANAGER. (2001-present). Manage a case load of as many as 21 terminally ill patients, handling admissions processing, patient assessment, and education as well as performing home visits to care for the patient.
- Instruct patients and their family members on matters related to pain management, medications and their side effects, and disease process.
- Conduct weekly meetings (attended every two week by the physician) with the patient's care team to discuss care and treatment of the patient.
- Provide supportive care and counseling during home visits to terminally ill patients.

PSYCHIATRIC NURSE. (2000-01). Transferred from a ward with from five to 10 patients, was selected to provide nursing care for anywhere from four to 12 patients.
- Demonstrated the ability to work independently and respond to challenges and change on a demanding ward where communication and interaction were especially important.

REGISTERED NURSE. (1998-00). Supervised an L.P.N. and a Patient Care Assistant (P.C.A.) while handling nursing assessments, patient care, and case management for an average patient load of from four to eight at any time.
- Provided care support which included IV and LAB therapy as well as medication education for patients.
- Gained experience in patient administration support such as data entry and records management.
- Implemented a system of checking doctor's orders for accuracy and to prevent errors and then trained other personnel on how to apply this information.
- Contributed my knowledge and mentoring skills as a preceptor for nursing students.

REGISTERED NURSE. Sunnybrook Hospital, Toronto, Ontario, Canada (1996-98). Cited for my communication skills and ability to deal with patients and their families with compassion and concern, provided patient care including dispensing medications through I.V. therapy and oral injections.
- Was often called on to provide wellness education and predischarge education and was recognized for my ability to explain medical care procedures clearly and simply.
- Rotated charge nurse duties with other qualified members of the nursing team.
- Served as a mentor and example for student nurses rotating through the hospital's precepting program. Was a member of the skin care committee.

MEDICAL TECHNICIAN. The Hospital for Sick Children, Montreal, Quebec, Canada (1991-95). Worked in a research facility.

PERSONAL   Am an enthusiastic, energetic, and outgoing individual. Possess the ability to adapt quickly.

Date

Exact Name of Person
Exact Title
Exact Name of Company
Address
City, State, Zip

Dear Exact Name of Person (or Dear Sir or Madam if answering a blind ad):

With the enclosed resume, I would like to express my interest in a position for Licensed Practical Nurse at the Primary Care Clinic located in Orono, ME.

As you will see from my enclosed resume, I offer indepth experience in providing all types of nursing care including geriatric, substance abuse, coronary, emergency room, intensive care, surgical, and med/surg. I am currently employed by the Northeastern Medical Center in Biddeford, ME. From 1998-01, I worked at the Marion County Detention Center through a local staffing agency, and for nearly two years, I performed essentially the same job as the one for which you are advertising. As an LPN in this clinical setting, I made appointments, took vital signs, assisted doctors in examinations, performed physical assessments, drew blood, started IVs, and performed first aid when needed.

I am proficient with software including Word, and I am known for my excellent communication skills. Both at the Marion County Detention Center and at the Northeastern Medical Center, I have handled responsibilities related to patient teaching and family teaching. I offer strong interpersonal skills, and my extensive nursing experience allows me to interact confidently with patients as well as with other medical professionals.

I am certain I would be an asset to your organization, and I hope you will contact me to suggest the next step I should take in pursuing this employment opportunity.

Sincerely,

Patricia S. Hines

PATRICIA S. HINES

1110½ Hay Street, Fayetteville, NC 28305 • preppub@aol.com • (910) 483-6611

OBJECTIVE

I want to contribute to an organization that can use an experienced nursing professional who offers in-depth knowledge of medical terminology along with a clinical background which includes critical care, intensive care, emergency room, surgical, med/surg, and geriatric nursing.

EDUCATION

Completing **B.S. in Registered Nursing,** University of New England, Biddeford, ME; previously completed all except two months of the formal R.N. Program at Concord College before I had to withdraw because of a family emergency.
Completed extensive training in IV push drugs and procedures, Concord College, Athens, WV, 2002.
Earned LPN's Diploma, Nursing, Fairmont State College, Fairmont, WV, 1998.
Completed several computer classes at Fairmont State College, Fairmont, WV, 1998.

COMPUTERS

Experienced with computer software including Word, Excel.

LICENSE

Licensed LPN.

EXPERIENCE

LICENSED PRACTICAL NURSE (LPN). Northeastern Medical Center, Biddeford, ME (2003-present). Excel in my Licensed Practical Nurse duties while working with Northeastern. Provide direct patient care, take vital signs, start IVs, administer medications, work with EKGs, implement treatments, and assist doctors in various procedures.
- Handle family teaching in order to assure the best quality after-hospital care for patients.
- Assist physicians with procedures including lumbar punctures.
- Work on rotating day/evening shifts.
- Have become known for my ability to quickly identify changes in patients' condition; my extensive nursing experience allows me to react promptly to such situations. Respond to codes promptly, and am experienced in utilizing emergency equipment.
- Deal with a wide range of patients who are being treated for ailments ranging from substance abuse to coronary problems.

Excelled in simultaneous per diem jobs in Athens, West Virginia:
2002-03: NURSING HOME LPN. Sunray Nursing Home, Athens, WV. In this part-time, per diem job, supervise up to seven CNAs in nursing home environments; have worked as a Resource Nurse in the 120-bed facility in Collierville, where I have been placed in charge of the entire facility. Also have worked per diem at Englecove Rehabilitation Center.
2001-03: HOSPITAL LPN. Interim Staffing, Athens, WV. Work on a per diem basis for this agency which staffs Summers Memorial Hospital.

Other experience:
PRISON LPN. Marion County Detention Center, Fairmont, WV (1998-01). For nearly two years, I worked through the Pelligan Staffing at the Marion County Detention Center. Assisted in providing care in a timely manner and assisted the clinical staff with patients and clinical procedures.
- Received patients, took vital signs, prepared patients to see doctors.
- Excelled in all aspects of clinical nursing.

PERSONAL

Resourceful problem solver. Unlimited personal initiative. Excellent references available on request. Effective communicator.

Exact Name of Person
Exact Title
Exact Name of Company
Address
City, State, Zip

**LICENSED PRACTICAL
NURSE (LPN)**

Dear Exact Name of Person (or Dear Sir or Madam if answering a blind ad):

I would appreciate an opportunity to talk with you soon about how I could contribute to your organization through my nursing skills and outgoing personality.

As you will see from my resume, I am a highly skilled LPN with extensive experience in hospitals and nursing home environments. In my current position, I work with geriatric patients on a skilled nursing floor, where I am frequently in charge of the 155-bed facility and staff. I am known as a caring individual with strong organizational and management abilities.

If you can use a compassionate and efficient nursing professional who is willing to work flexible schedules as your needs require, I hope you will call or write soon to suggest a convenient time for us to meet and discuss your needs. I can provide outstanding personal and professional references. Thank you in advance for your time.

Yours sincerely,

Chris Chambers

CHRIS CHAMBERS

1110½ Hay Street, Fayetteville, NC 28305 • preppub@aol.com • (910) 483-6611

OBJECTIVE

Am applying for a position as a Licensed Practical Nurse. Offer a variety of indepth experience as an LPN in the past 18½ years. Am certain that, with my past experience and diversified knowledge, I would be of great assistance to both patients and doctors.

EDUCATION

Graduated from Central Washington Technical College, Seattle, WA, with a degree in Practical Nursing.

EXPERIENCE

LICENSED PRACTICAL NURSE (LPN). Highland House of Seattle, Seattle, WA (2001-present). Work with geriatric patients on a skilled nursing floor; on occasion; am frequently placed in charge of the 155-bed facility and staff.

LICENSED PRACTICAL NURSE (LPN). Carrollton Nursing Home and Cumberland County Detoxification Unit, Mental Health Center, Seattle, WA (1998-01). Worked as a Contract Nurse (PRN) for the Carrollton Nursing Home at which I was employed full-time while also working for the Cumberland County Detoxification Unit from 1998-2001.

LICENSED PRACTICAL NURSE. Village Green Care Center, Seattle, WA (1997). Cared for 30 patients on a Medicare-skilled floor and gained extensive hands-on training in the areas of medication and administration, gastrostomy feeding, taking verbal and written orders, writing nursing summaries, demonstrating skills as a charge nurse, as well as providing treatments and assessments of the patient on admission and on a daily basis.

LICENSED PRACTICAL NURSE. Cumberland Hospital, Seattle, WA (1994-96). Cared for mentally disturbed adolescents in a long-term setting. Received additional training related to teaching adolescents basic behavioral skills in a group setting, administering medication, and preparing written documentation.

LICENSED PRACTICAL NURSE. Metroplex Home Health Agency, Killeen, TX (1992-93). Cared for patients in their private homes. Received hands-on training related to teaching patients proper diet techniques, giving insulin injections, and preparing changes and other documentation pertaining to care provided. Was known for my attention to detail in carefully following verbal and written orders.

LICENSED PRACTICAL NURSE. Cape Fear Valley Medical Center, Seattle, WA (1989-91). Over a one-year period, excelled in floating assignments that included extensive experience in medical/surgery, orthopedics, urology, and OB-GYN. Gained extensive hands-on experience in team leadership, treatment administration, giving PRN medications, taking verbal and written orders, conducting charting, and writing nursing care plans.

LICENSED PRACTICAL NURSE. Durham County General Hospital, Durham, NC (1984-89). Worked in a medical and surgical intensive care unit. Received additional training related to the care of patients on respirators, and completed a basic IV insertion course.

LICENSED PRACTICAL NURSE. Chapel Hill, NC (1980-84). Gained experience in cardio-thoracic surgery and in kidney transplant operations. Completed an EKG course and received additional hands-on training in monitoring cardiac arrhythmias and patients on dialysis.

PERSONAL

Am a caring professional who understands patient needs for warmth and empathy.

Date

Exact Name of Person
Exact Title
Exact Name of Company
Address
City, State, Zip

**LICENSED PRACTICAL
NURSE (LPN)**

Dear Exact Name of Person (or Dear Sir or Madam if answering a blind ad):

With the enclosed resume, I would like to make you aware of my background as a Licensed Practical Nurse with exceptional organizational, communication, and patient relations skills who has excelled in a track record of accomplishment in obstetrics/gynecology and medical/surgical, and geriatric nursing in challenging environments worldwide.

As you will see, I have completed the Practical Nurse and Medical Specialist course from the Academy of Health Sciences at Fort Harbor, WA. I have supplemented these programs with numerous additional military training programs, including the Medical Proficiency Training Program, Algorithm-Directed Troop Medical Care Course, Deployable Medical Systems New Equipment Training, Medical Management of Chemical Casualties, and Hazard Communication Program.

Currently working as a Licensed Practical Nurse providing medical-surgical care on a 20-bed intermediate care ward at a busy 296-bed DEPMEDS-equipped Combat Support Hospital, I supervise and train 13 personnel at the Fort Harbor Medical Inprocessing Center, which handles more than 1,200 soldiers monthly. I also oversee the security and maintenance of more than $300,000 worth of medical equipment, immunization medicines, and expendable supplies. On my own initiative, I have organized and developed a Breast Health Awareness Program for females inprocessing to Fort Harbor, and I served as a phlebotomist for the Operation Life Gift Bone Marrow Drive.

My earlier nursing experience was focused in obstetrics and gynecology. In Korea, I served on a 42-bed mixed ward comprising a 17-bed newborn nursery, a six-bed labor and delivery unit, and a 19-bed obstetrics and gynecology unit. In that position, I supervised a staff of three, acted as Preceptor to newly assigned personnel, and took on additional responsibilities as Infection Control Officer for the Ward, Fire & Safety Officer, and Time Schedule Coordinator. At Fort Port, I served as a Licensed Practical Nurse in the 25-bed obstetrics and gynecology ward of a busy regional medical center.

If you can use an experienced nursing professional with a strong background in obstetrics and gynecology and exceptional patient relations skills, I hope you will contact me to suggest a time when we might meet.

Sincerely,

Irene Fisher

IRENE FISHER

1110½ Hay Street, Fayetteville, NC 28305 • preppub@aol.com • (910) 483-6611

OBJECTIVE
To benefit an organization that can use an experienced licensed practical nurse with exceptional organizational and patient relations skills who offers a background in obstetrics/gynecology and medical/surgical nursing in challenging environments worldwide.

EDUCATION
Completed the **Practical Nurse Course** and **Medical Specialist Course** at the Academy of Health Sciences, Fort Harbor, WA.
Supplemented my education with a large number of medical courses taken as part of my military training, including:
- Medical Proficiency Training Program, Fort Harbor, WA, 1998.
- Algorithm-Directed Troop Medical Care Course, Fort Harbor, WA, 1996.
- Deployable Medical Systems New Equipment Training, Fort Port, NY, 1996.
- Medical Management of Chemical Casualties, Fort Port, NY, 1996.
- Hazard Communication Program, Korea, 1994.

LICENSES
Licensed Practical Nurse for the state of Washington, certificate #054772, expires 12/31/03.
Licensed Practical Nurse for the state of New York #0024016, expires 1/31/03.

EXPERIENCE
As a Licensed Practical Nurse with the United States Army, excelled in demanding positions while advancing in a track record of accomplishment:
LICENSED PRACTICAL NURSE. U.S. Army, Fort Harbor, WA (2000-present). Serve as a Practical Nurse on this 20-bed Intermediate Care Ward which is part of a busy, 296-bed DEPMEDS-equipped Combat Support Hospital.
- Supervise and train 13 hospital personnel in proper operational procedures for the Medical Inprocessing Center, handling more than 1,200 soldiers per month.
- Oversee the security and maintenance of more than $300,000 worth of equipment, immunization medicines, and expendable supplies.
- Provide total nursing care for 20 medical-surgical patients during deployments.
- On my own initiative, organized and developed a Breast Health Awareness program for all females inprocessing to Fort Harbor.
- Served as a phlebotomist for the Operation Life Gift Bone Marrow Drive.

LICENSED PRACTICAL NURSE. U.S. Army, Korea (1996-00). Provided patient care services for a 42-bed mixed ward including a 17-bed newborn nursery unit, a six-bed labor and delivery unit, and a 19-bed obstetrics and gynecology unit.
- Supervised three personnel and served as Preceptor for newly assigned personnel.
- Assisted in the performance of Cesarean sections, administered medication both orally and intravenously, and obtained lab specimens.
- Admitted and discharged patients; provided patient education on infant care and post-circumcision care.
- Monitored high-risk laboring patients as well as patients with no complications.
- Served as Infection Control Officer for the ward, as well as Fire & Safety Officer and Time Schedule Coordinator.

LICENSED PRACTICAL NURSE. U.S. Army, Fort Port, NY (1992-1996). Performed nursing care on a 25-bed Obstetrics & Gynecology ward in a busy medical center.
- Performed patient admission orientation, and education; conducted 10 preoperative training courses for more than 150 patients. Provided patient care, including obtaining lab specimens, starting IVs, and administering medication both orally and intravenously.

CAREER CHANGE

Date

Exact Name of Person
Exact Title
Exact Name of Company
Address
City, State, Zip

MEDICAL BILLING CERTIFICATION WITH NURSING EXPERIENCE

Here is an example of a resume in which the previous work experience has nothing in common with the degree program.

Dear Exact Name of Person (or Dear Sir or Madam if answering a blind ad):

With the enclosed resume, I would like to make you aware of my background as an enthusiastic young professional with an education in Medical Billing who offers proven skills related to medical office administration, records management, and medical billing which have been tested in busy hospital environments.

Recently, I have been excelling as a Night Auditor for several different hotels while pursuing my diploma in Medical Billing. Using Microsoft Excel, I generated revenue and expense reports as well as reconciling daily receipts to ensure that all funds are accounted for. I have been recognized by these employers as an enthusiastic, reliable worker who adheres to a high work standard while providing exceptional customer service.

Earlier, I served with distinction as a Medical Corpsman in the U.S. Navy. While assisting nursing professionals and physicians in busy hospital environments, I performed a number of medical and administrative functions, including patient screening, updating and maintenance of patient medical records, phlebotomy, and patient billing. I completed inpatient registration of new clients, screening the patient and creating a file containing their medical history and major complaint. While serving as Medical Receptionist in the Medical Clinic, it was also my responsibility to obtain patient insurance information, file insurance claims, perform patient education, and provide administrative and clerical support to the office.

As you will see from my enclosed resume, I have recently completed a diploma program in Medical Billing from an accredited correspondence school, which included course work in Medical Terminology, Medical Claims Procedures, and CPT/ICD-9 coding. I have also received a diploma in Medical Science and graduated from the U.S. Navy's three-month Medical Corpsman School, completing courses in a variety of medical disciplines. I feel that my strong combination of education and practical experience would make me a valuable addition to any medical office.

Highly regarded by my previous employers, I can provide outstanding letters of recommendation at the appropriate time. I assure you in advance that I have an excellent reputation and would quickly become an asset to your organization.

Sincerely,

Gerald Faich

GERALD FAICH

1110½ Hay Street, Fayetteville, NC 28305 • preppub@aol.com • (910) 483-6611

OBJECTIVE   To benefit an organization that can use an enthusiastic, reliable young professional with strong communication and organizational skills who offers an education in medical billing and experience in medical office administration, patient screening, billing, and auditing.

EDUCATION   Completed **Certification in Medical Billing** through an accredited correspondence course, 2001. Courses included:

Medical Terminology	Anatomy and Physiology
Procedural Coding	Diagnostic Coding
Medical Claims Procedures	CPT/ICD-9 Coding

Earned diploma from a Screener's course in Medical Science, Great Lakes, IL, 1999.

Graduated from the U.S. Navy Medical Corpsman School, a three-month program which included courses in:

Venipuncture and Phlebotomy	Medical Records Management
Patient Screening and Assessment	Medical Office Administration

COMPUTERS   Familiar with popular computer systems and software including Windows, Microsoft Word, and Microsoft Excel. Have quickly mastered new software, including a variety of proprietary systems specific to the military and to the medical profession.

EXPERIENCE   **NIGHT AUDITOR.** Various locations throughout Fargo, IL (2000-present). Have served with distinction, working simultaneously as Night Auditor and "Manager on Duty" for several different hotels while completing my education in Medical Billing.
- Generate daily revenue and expense reports in Microsoft Excel and reconciled daily receipts to ensure that all funds were accounted for; handled large volumes of cash.
- Supervise the night shift hotel staff while performing customer service, bookkeeping, and guest check-in.
- Personally credited with increasing total revenue at one hotel by seven percent.
- Recognized by my employers as an enthusiastic, reliable worker who adheres to a high work standard and excels at customer service; can provide letters of recommendation.

NURSING ASSISTANT. U.S. Navy, Great Lakes, IL (1996-00). After completing extensive military training in various medical disciplines, served as a Hospital Corpsman; assisted nurses and physicians, providing patient care in busy hospital environments.
- Performed patient screening and initial assessment for more than 100 patients per week; utilized extensive knowledge of medical terminology and abbreviations.
- Completed patient registration, verifying insurance information and utilizing the DEERS military dependent eligibility system; gained valuable experience in medical billing.
- Updated and maintained medical records for more than 1,000 patients, documenting all medical visits, treatments, and changes to patients' medical history.
- Served as a Medical Receptionist at the Medical Clinic; answered phones, scheduled appointments, screened patients, and pulled, updated, maintained, and filed charts.
- Operated a computer, utilizing a variety of proprietary software specific to military medical environments to prepare reports, patient histories, and other documents.
- Conducted patient education related to subjects such as side effects of prescribed medication and proper home care procedures for patients being released.

PERSONAL   Enthusiastic individual with a results-oriented attitude. Outstanding references.

CAREER CHANGE

Date

Exact Name of Person
Exact Title
Exact Name of Company
Address
City, State, Zip

**NATURAL SCIENCES
GRAD WITH
BIOTECHNOLOGY
KNOWLEDGE**

A career in nursing is ahead of this young professional, and she is using her resume to show off her medical skills, office skills, certifications, license, honors, education, and experience. The cover letter gives her a chance to add the "warmth" and "personality" that can sometimes be lacking in a resume.

Dear Exact Name of Person (or Dear Sir or Madam if answering a blind ad):

With the enclosed resume, I would like to make you aware of my strong educational background in science and medicine, my highly developed analytical and problem-solving skills, and my extensive laboratory experience.

As you will see, I am currently completing a Bachelor of Science degree in Natural Sciences with a concentration in Biology from Wright State University. In addition to the rigorous course load of my degree program and my teaching responsibilities, I have taken on courses from the biotechnology program, which have provided me with the opportunity to develop cutting edge knowledge and learn to operate state-of-the-art laboratory equipment. While learning the fundamentals of DNA manipulation, I have used micropipettes, centrifuges, thermocyclers, and gel electrophorens apparatuses. I have studied techniques of DNA cloning, restriction digestion, transformation, plasmid isolation, bacterial culturing, and gel electrophorens. During a one-year project, I assisted on work involving the cloning of microbial resistant genes from the clinical isolation of *Klebsiella pneumoniae*.

If you can use an educated professional with highly developed analytical and technical skills who offers a strong background in laboratory testing, I look forward to hearing from you soon to suggest a time when we might meet to discuss your needs. I can assure you in advance that I have an excellent reputation and would rapidly become a valuable addition to your organization.

Sincerely,

Elka Westervelt

ELKA WESTERVELT

1110½ Hay Street, Fayetteville, NC 28305   •   preppub@aol.com   •   (910) 483-6611

OBJECTIVE

To benefit an organization that can use an articulate and intelligent young professional with exceptional technical and analytical skills who offers a strong educational background in scientific and medical testing in laboratory environments.

EDUCATION

Completing a **Bachelor of Science degree in Natural Sciences,** with a concentration in Biology, Wright State University, Dayton, OH. Will receive degree in May 2003.

Have studied a wide range of difficult courses related to science and medicine, including:

Cellular and Molecular Biology	Techniques in Microbiology	Genetics
Radiation Biology	Comparative Anatomy	Chemistry I
Integrated Zoology	Calculus w/Analytic Geometry	Chemistry II
General Physics I, II, & III	Anatomy & Physiology I & II	Botany
Ecology and Evolution	Elementary Statistics	Spanish I & II
Animal Development	Intro. To Computer Science	
Vertebrate Physiology	Special Problems (lab assignments)	

Completed 52 hours of **field experience teaching science** to local high school students.

**TECHNICAL
SKILLS**

Excelled in a number of additional courses from the biotechnology program, developing skills in the following areas:

- Fundamentals of DNA manipulation using state-of-the-art equipment such as micropipettes, centrifuges, thermocyclers, and gel electrophorens apparati.
- Techniques of DNA cloning, restriction digestion, transformation, plasmid isolation, bacterial culturing, and gel electrophorens.
- Spent a year on work involving the cloning of microbial resistant genes from clinical isolation of *Klebsiella pneumoniae.*

EXPERIENCE

TELEMARKETER. Big Starr Telemarketing, Dayton, OH (Summers 2000, 2001, 2002). During summer breaks, demonstrated my exceptional verbal communication and listening skills while excelling in this stressful telephone direct sales environment.

- Quickly developed a rapport with customers, uncovered their objections, and used product knowledge and persuasion to close the sale.
- Provided direct marketing sales and support, presenting customers with the benefits and advantages of various products offered by the company.

CUSTODIAN. North High School, Dayton, OH (1999). In a part-time job while in college, performed general maintenance, cleaning, and landscaping services in order to beautify and prepare the school's interior, exterior, and grounds for the fall enrollment.

SEWING MACHINE OPERATOR. D& D Jeans, Dayton, OH (1997-1998). Worked in this commission-based position in a busy clothing production plant.

COOK and **CASHIER.** Burger King, Dayton, OH (1995-1996). Honed my skills in teamwork and time management while cooking and providing customer service for this local branch of the large national fast food chain.

- Was frequently called upon to accept the additional responsibility of training new employees due to my patience and exceptional communication skills.
- Provided customer service, taking food orders and operating a cash register.

PERSONAL

Excellent personal and professional references are available upon request.

Date

Exact Name of Person
Exact Title
Exact Name of Company
Address
City, State, Zip

Dear Exact Name of Person (or Dear Sir or Madam if answering a blind ad):

With this letter and enclosed resume, I would like to indicate my strong interest in the job of Occupational Health and Safety Nurse for which I understand you will soon be hiring.

Although I am held in very high regard by my current employer and feel that I am making important contributions to the smooth operation of the Central Illinois Medical geriatric and extended care ward, I feel that my skills and background would be a very good fit in your organization. A native of the area who lives within two miles of the plant, I have several family members who are currently valued Lang Environmental Inc., employees or have retired from your company. I am confident that I understand the environment a nurse would be working in and would be able to quickly become a productive member of your staff.

As you will see from the resume, I was originally hired as a Staff Nurse in 2000. In 2003, I was promoted to Night Charge Nurse and am excelling in this position where I am known as a caring and compassionate professional who is highly organized, detail oriented, safety conscious, and skilled in dealing with others. My interpersonal relations skills are one of my greatest strengths and I am highly effective in building harmonious working relations as well as in educating other medical professionals, patients, and their families.

With excellent problem-solving abilities, I am becoming skilled in using our automated systems and am becoming proficient in computer operations and applications. With charting, doctors' orders, and other record keeping already automated, the medical center is currently involved in automating medication administration using bar codes. My ward is one of the first areas of the center to go through this process and is currently serving as a test site for these procedures while all the problems are worked out before the system is integrated into the operations of the entire hospital.

If you can use an RN with my skills, experience, and abilities, I hope you will consider my strong interest and call or write me soon to suggest a time when we might have a brief discussion of how I could contribute to Lang Environmental. I will provide excellent professional and personal references at the appropriate time.

Sincerely,

Carlos L. Furman

CARLOS L. FURMAN

1110½ Hay Street, Fayetteville, NC 28305   •   preppub@aol.com   •   (910) 483-6611

OBJECTIVE

To offer a reputation as a hard charger who excels in finding ways to improve the quality of patient care and administrative procedures to an organization in need of a mature nursing professional who also offers strong computer skills and awareness of safety issues.

EDUCATION & TRAINING

Associate Degree Nursing (A.D.N.), Danville Community College, Danville, IL, 1999; achieved a 3.8 GPA.
- Made the Dean's List for Fall of 1999. Earned an award from the state nursing association in recognition of scholastic achievement and nursing skills.

Studied the following computer courses: COBOL, RPG, Assembler, and Basic languages; MS Windows, MS Word, Intermediate MS Word, and many nursing courses.

CERTIFICATIONS & LICENSES

Gerontological Nursing Certificate, Central Illinois Medical Center, Danville, IL, 2000.
Registered Nurse, Illinois RN License #987654, 1999

EXPERIENCE

Excelled in a track record of promotions with Central Illinois Medical Center, Danville, IL:
2003-present: NIGHT CHARGE NURSE/RN. Am known for my emphasis on safety, positive and assertive leadership, and true concern and compassion for others displayed while supervising a staff of up to four RNs, LPNs, and NAs on the 50-bed geriatric and extended care ward.
- Have been credited with making numerous and far-reaching changes to procedures which have resulted in reducing friction among staff members.
- Have been recognized for my interpersonal skills, am adept at working with doctors, medical staff, pharmacy staff, and other personnel supporting ward activities.
- Simplify procedures including the way doctor's orders and medication renewals were handled in ways which greatly improved the work flow and reduced confusion.
- Effectively educate patients and their family members on medical and health issues and on the progress and expectations for their particular disease or medical condition.
- Cited for my awareness and ability to recognize signs of instability, have on several occasions intervened and helped ensure a patient quickly received emergency care.
- Prepare monthly, quarterly, and annual assessments, forms, charting, patient education, for my primary patients; revised forms which improved information flow between shifts.
- Was promoted to a supervisory role in 2003 after making numerous contributions to the smooth operation of this ward as a Staff Nurse.

2000-03: MEDICAL-SURGICAL STAFF NURSE. Quickly progressed from a new RN graduate to an effective, accomplished, and proficient nurse while refining skills in every area of nursing and patient care.
- Assessed patients and planned, implemented, and evaluated their care.
- Earned recognition for my communication skills while educating patients and families.

Highlights of other experience: Contributed through a wide range of skills and abilities by doing literally whatever needed to be done to keep a rest home running smoothly and saved thousands of dollars through skill in purchasing, Danville Home Care, Danville, IL.
- Created, revised, and updated detailed job descriptions for nursing and patient care personnel; prepared billing statements and maintained records; scheduled employees; completed minor equipment repairs; transported patients; oversaw patient activities.

PERSONAL

Member, INA (Illinois Nursing Association). Common sense, the ability to take action and get results, and extreme safety consciousness are among my greatest strengths.

Date

Exact Name of Person
Exact Title
Exact Name of Company
Address
City, State, Zip

NURSE ANESTHETIST

Dear Exact Name of Person (or Dear Sir or Madam if answering a blind ad):

With the enclosed resume, I would like to make you aware of my interest in exploring employment opportunities with your organization.

As you will see from my resume, I have recently completed my B.S. degree in Nursing. Although I have worked in nearly many aspects of anesthetist nursing (pediatric, cardio-thoracic surgery, emergency-trauma, and acute psychiatric), I have also excelled in administrative, teaching, and program management positions. While earning my A.D.N. from Armstrong Atlantic University, I worked at Saint Joseph's Hospital.

At Ridgeview Medical I orientated new employees and students from local colleges and the critical care school here in Savannah, GA. In my position as a Nurse Anesthetist, I reviewed capital/non-capital budgets and make recommendations on allocations and projections. Also in these positions I have developed strong and effective communication skills.

I am confident that I could become a valuable asset to an organization that can use a resourceful individual with a strong bottom-line orientation, and I hope you will contact me to suggest a time when we might meet to discuss your needs.

Yours sincerely,

Duane M. Lewis

DUANE M. LEWIS

1110½ Hay Street, Fayetteville, NC 28305 • preppub@aol.com • (910) 483-6611

OBJECTIVE   I want to benefit an organization that can use a dedicated Nurse Anesthetist who offers strong problem-solving abilities, communication skills, and management skills.

EDUCATION   **Bachelor of Science degree in Nursing,** Georgia Southern University, Statesboro, GA, 2001. Completed courses involving Anesthesia Training and Techniques, Saint Joseph's Hospital, Savannah, GA, 2000.
Received A.D.N., Armstrong Atlantic University, Savannah, GA, 1997.
Graduated from Winnbrook High School, Savannah, GA, 1994.

EXPERIENCE   **NURSE ANESTHETIST.** Memorial Health University Medical Center, Statesboro, GA (2004-present). Provide direct patient care full-time in Medical-Surgical ICU, ER-Trauma, Neurological Step Down Unit, Acute Psychiatric units, and rotate to Pediatric ICU, Cardio-Thoracic Surgical ICU. Usually perform Charge Nurse duties.

NURSE ANESTHETIST. Ridgeview Medical Hospital, Statesboro, GA (2002-04). Orientated new employees; precepted students from local colleges and from the internal critical care school. Interviewed candidates for unit manager positions and interviewed new RNs. Reviewed capital/non-capital budgets and make recommendations on allocations and projections.

Excelled in a track record of promotions with Saint Joseph's Hospital, Savannah, GA:
1999-02: NURSE ANESTHETIST. Administered medications according to physician orders. On my own initiative, made many lasting contributions to this health care facility. Identified methods of saving time and money without compromising safety. For example, developed charts as well as sign-in/sign-out sheets to help staff control inventory. Took the initiative when I discovered intake/outtake problems, and designed new procedures which eliminated the problems. Identified staff training deficiencies, and developed training sheets which permitted the documentation of all training.

1996-99: STAFF ANESTHETIST. Made significant contributions to client safety. Reduced the occurrence of medical errors and client accidents through applying my strong analytical and problem-solving skills. Taught staff members safe medication administration procedures, and provided the supervisory follow-up after training which was necessary. Was able to resolve many long-standing problems at this facility. Prepared written reports daily; maintained seizure records, vigilantly maintained notes for psychologists, and prepared shift reports.

Other experience:
STAFF ANESTHETIST/LOCUM TENENS. Palmetto Lowcountry Behavioral Health, Savannah, GA, (1993-96). Assisted physicians with procedures including behavior restraints. Worked on rotating day/evening shifts. Became known for my ability to quickly identify changes in patients' condition; my extensive nursing experience allowed me to react promptly to such situations.

PERSONAL   Excellent assessment skills. Adapt quickly to new environments. Am an outgoing individual. Can provide excellent personal and professional references.

Date

Exact Name of Person
Exact Title
Exact Name of Company
Address
City, State, Zip

Dear Exact Name of Person (or Dear Sir or Madam if answering a blind ad):

I would appreciate an opportunity to talk with you soon about how I could contribute to your organization through my formal education as a Registered Nurse as well as through my outstanding personal qualities.

As you will see from my resume, I completed several clinical rotations while earning my nursing degree; these gave me hands-on experience in medical-surgical nursing, newborn and maternal care nursing, and psychiatric nursing. In every situation, I was commended for my excellent communication skills and ability to deal professionally with doctors, nurses, patients, administrators, and other personnel.

Extremely active as a student, I was involved in the Nursing Students Association and was an elected delegate to the National Student Nurses Association Conference in New York. I have always been regarded as an outgoing individual with an ability to relate well to people on all levels.

You would find me in person to be a congenial individual who always strives to do my best in all situations. I am a mature individual who raised two children before embarking on my lifelong dream of becoming a nurse. I can provide outstanding personal and professional references.

I hope you will call or write me soon to suggest a time convenient for us to meet and discuss your current and future needs and how I might serve them. Thank you in advance for your time.

Sincerely,

Ragina Raftery

RAGINA RAFTERY

1110½ Hay Street, Fayetteville, NC 28305   •   preppub@aol.com   •   (910) 483-6611

OBJECTIVE

To contribute to an organization that can use a Registered Nurse with excellent judgment and decision-making skills who offers a strong desire to make a significant contribution to medical, surgical, and patient care activities.

EDUCATION

Associate of Applied Science degree in Nursing, Averett College, Danville, VA, 2003. Completed Rape Crisis Intervention Volunteer Training, January 2001.

RN LICENSE

Valid until February 13, 2004.

CERTIFICATIONS

Certified Nursing Assistant I and II; CPR Certified.

MEDICAL SKILLS

- Am trained in patient assessment, medication administration, catheterizations, sterile dressing changes, charting, and patient education.
- Skilled in using IV pumps, CPM (continuous passive motion) machine, and AccuChek.

OFFICE SKILLS

- Computer knowledgeable.
- Skilled in using office machines including faxes, copiers, printers, and typewriters.

EXPERIENCE

2000-2003–While earning my nursing degree, have excelled in the following clinical rotations:
Medical-Surgical Nursing Clinical Rotation: Danville Medical Center, Danville, VA. Provided total patient care while administering medications, assisting with activities of daily living including body mechanics, nutrition, and safety.
- Took vital signs; made dressing changes.
- Learned tracheotomy suctioning techniques.
- Applied sterile dressings and handled tube feedings.

Maternal and Newborn Nursing: Danville Medical Center, Danville, VA. Attended mothers through labor and delivery of infants.
- Became proficient in relaxation techniques during labor.
- Became a breast-feeding specialist.
- Completed one rotation in Neonatal ICU.
- Cared for critically ill newborns as well as healthy newborns.

Psychiatric Nursing: Danville Hospital, Danville, VA. Was commended for my compassionate attitude and my excellent communication skills while working in the adult unit.

1998-00: While earning my nursing degree, also worked part-time for LOMAC, Danville, VA: As **TREASURER,** was proudly associated with this fine organization and played a key role in the daily business operation of the day program for autistic adults; LOMAC is a nonprofit organization funded by the county which has evolved into the County Mental Health Day Program of today.
- Worked closely with the Board of Directors and was accountable to the board.
- Was responsible for more than $70,000 per year in cash and disbursements.

HONORS

- Member, Nursing Students Association, Averett College
- Delegate, National Student Nurses Association Conference in New Orleans

CAREER CHANGE

Exact Name of Person
Exact Title
Exact Name of Company
Address
City, State, Zip

NURSING GRAD WITH CLINICAL ROTATIONS

This young Registered Nurse has many clinical rotations and much leadership experience to show off on his resume.

Dear Exact Name of Person (or Dear Sir or Madam if answering a blind ad):

With the enclosed resume, I would like to make you aware of my desire to explore employment as a Registered Nurse.

As you will see, I will shortly graduate with an Associate's degree in Nursing and am seeking employment in the San Diego area, where my extended family lives. While earning my degree, I excelled in numerous clinical rotations and internships. I have worked in med-surg, ortho/neuro, labor and delivery, long-term care, psychiatric, and substance abuse environments.

I have taken the time to work actively in student organizations, and I have held numerous elected offices in student nursing associations. I can provide outstanding personal and professional references.

If you can use an educated professional with highly developed analytical and technical skills, I hope you will contact me to suggest a time when we might meet to discuss your present and future needs. I can assure you in advance that I have an excellent reputation and would rapidly become a valuable addition to your organization.

Sincerely,

Andrew Reese

ANDREW REESE

1110½ Hay Street, Fayetteville, NC 28305 • preppub@aol.com • (910) 483-6611

OBJECTIVE	I want to contribute to an organization that can use a skilled young nursing professional who offers proven management and leadership skills.
CERTIFICATIONS	Certified Nurse Aide II. CPR Certification.
LICENSES	Will take the NCLEX-RN in June 2003.
EDUCATION	**Associate Degree in Nursing (ADN) degree,** Drexel University, Philadelphia, PA; will graduate May 2003. **Current GPA 3.89.**

- Named to President's List; inducted into Phi Theta Kappa Honor Society.
- Will pursue Bachelor of Science in Nursing in my spare time after receiving RN license.
- Graduated from Chambers Senior High School, Philadelphia, PA, 1998.
- Extensive management and leadership training as a U.S. Army professional, 1998-01.

EXPERIENCE

NURSING INTERN & NURSING STUDENT. Drexel University, Philadelphia, PA (2002-present). Have excelled academically, in clinical rotations, and in leadership positions with the Pennsylvania Association of Nursing Students (PANS) and the Drexel Association of Nursing Students (ANS).

Clinical Rotations: Have received the highest-possible evaluations of my performance in these clinical rotations:

- **Med/Surg:** Renfrow Memorial Hospital, Fall 2002 and 2003. Refined skills in patient care and administered oral medications; provided advanced care in Fall 2002.
- **Ortho/Neuro:** Philadelphia Medical Center, Spring 2002. Administered parenteral and IV medications; expanded my assessment skills with adult patients.
- **Labor & Delivery/Newborn:** Philadelphia Medical Center, Summer 2002. Administered IVs; refined my assessment skills related to newborns and mothers.
- **Long-Term Care:** Carrol Nursing Home, Fall 2003. Administered medications and feedings via gastrostomy tubes; gained skills in long-term care geriatric nursing.
- **Psychiatric:** Hope Hospital, Fall 2001. Gained insights into psychiatric care.
- **Substance Abuse:** Blunt Avenue Clinic, Spring 2003. Learned about substance abuse nursing practices.

Leadership in Professional Organizations: Have been elected Breakthrough to Nursing Director in both the state (PANS) and the Drexel nursing associations.

- Awarded the PANS Nursing Scholarship at PANS Annual Convention, Oct 2002.
- For the Drexel Association of Nursing Students, supervised recruiting activities; achieved a 95% retention rate of second-year students while aggressively recruiting new first-year student members.
- For the Philadelphia Association of Nursing Students, am supervising membership recruitment and retention for all 78 nursing schools in Pennsylvania.
- Represented the state nursing association at the Pennsylvania State Legislature; have played a key role in planning the 2001 mid-year conference.

MEDEVAC OPERATIONS MANAGER. U.S. Army, Ft. Sill, OK (1998-02). For a medevac company at a large U.S. military base, was promoted to manage an average of seven people and up to 40 personnel while assuring the availability of 15 helicopters and medevac assets.

PERSONAL

Can provide outstanding references. Proven leadership and management skills.

CAREER CHANGE

Exact Name of Person
Exact Title
Exact Name of Company
Address
City, State, Zip

NURSING GRAD WITH CNA AND PHLEBOTOMY INTERNSHIPS

The Objective of the resume is a blend of all-purpose and specific. He mentions his specialized knowledge of the automotive industry as well as his sales and management skills which are transferable to any field.

Dear Exact Name of Person (or Dear Sir or Madam if answering a blind ad):

With the enclosed resume, I would like to acquaint you with my exceptional organizational and communication skills as well as my experience in Phlebotomy and as a Certified Nursing Assistant I & II.

A Certified Nursing Assistant, I have earned a certification in Phlebotomy from the American Society of Phlebotomy Technicians as well as a certification in Medical Terminology. Currently pursuing an Associate's degree in Nursing in the evenings at Carthage University, I expect to complete the requirements for the Licensed Practical Nurse program by June of 2004, and the Registered Nurse requirements in June of 2004.

In my most recent position, I worked a four-month internship in Phlebotomy at several area hospitals. Earlier in a four-month Certified Nursing Assistant Internship, I performed, cleaned, and maintained tracheostomies and catheters, inserted and cleaned feeding tubes, and assisted nurses in providing patient care.

While pursuing my nursing degree and working in the above positions, I simultaneously oversee the operation of J & D 24-hour Towing, a successful small business. I interview and hire all new employees, handle accounts payable and receivable, and process weekly payroll. In an earlier position with Quick Stop, I served as Assistant Manager in this convenience store chain. I feel that my versatile experience, supervisory skills, and education would make me a valuable addition to your organization.

If you can use a highly motivated professional with strong organizational and communication skills, I hope you will contact me to suggest a time when we might meet. I can assure you that I have an excellent reputation and would quickly become an asset to your organization.

Sincerely,

Young Sikh Sondheimer

YOUNG SIKH SONDHEIMER

1110½ Hay Street, Fayetteville, NC 28305 • preppub@aol.com • (910) 483-6611

OBJECTIVE

To contribute to an organization that can use a dedicated and hard-working medical professional with exceptional communication and organizational skills as well as certifications in Phlebotomy and as a Certified Nursing Assistant I & II.

EDUCATION

Completing **Associate of Arts degree in Nursing** program at Carthage College, Kenosha, WA.
- Will complete the Licensed Practical Nurse requirements in June, 2004, and the Registered Nurse requirements in June, 2004.

Completed the Phlebotomy, Certified Nursing Assistant I & II, and Medical Terminology courses, Carthage College, Kenosha, WA, 2002.

CERTIFICATION

Certified in Phlebotomy, American Society of Phlebotomy Technicians, certificate XYZ123, 2001.
Certified Medical Assistant I & II, certificate #0922929, 2001.
Earned a certification in Medical Terminology, certificate #0923931, 2001.

EXPERIENCE

COLLEGE STUDENT and **SMALL BUSINESS OWNER.** J & D 24-hour Towing, Kenosha, WA (2002-present). Assumed ownership of his business after the death of my father; oversee all operational aspects of this successful towing company while simultaneously pursuing my Associate's degree in Nursing.
- Interview and hire all new employees; process weekly payroll and manage accounts payable/ accounts receivable.
- Update and maintain all licenses and permits.

Completed the following internships while pursuing my Associate's degree in Nursing and simultaneously running a small business:
PHLEBOTOMY INTERNSHIP. Veterans Administration Hospital, Kenosha, WA; Good Hope Hospital, Kenosha, WA; and Harnett Manor, Lillith, WA (2001). Completed this internship program while earning my certification in phlebotomy.
- Prepared patients for phlebotomy, sterilizing the venipuncture site and tying off the vein before drawing blood for laboratory testing and diagnosis.
- Retrieved records from the computer to determine what tests are to be performed.
- Maintained strict adherence to safety regulations and guidelines related to the handling and disposal of all blood products and related biohazards.

INTERNSHIP, CERTIFIED NURSING ASSISTANT I & II. Veterans Administration Hospital, Kenosha, WA; Good Hope Hospital, Kenosha, WA; and Harnett Manor, Lillith, WA (2000). Performed the duties of a CNA while completing a four-month internship; assisted nurses in providing patient care while pursuing my nursing degree.
- Performed tracheostomies and administered catheters; cleaned and maintained catheters and tracheostomy tubes; turned stroke and heart patients every two hours.

ASSISTANT MANAGER. Quick Stop, Kenosha, WA (1996-1999). Managed this busy location of the regional convenience store chain; oversaw all facets of operation, including human resources, inventory control and purchasing, loss prevention, and accounting.
- Supervised five employees; interviewed, hired, and trained all new personnel.
- Balanced cash registers and safe, tracking all discrepancies and recording overages, shortages, and sales figures on daily transaction logs.

PERSONAL

Excellent personal and professional references are available upon request.

Date

Exact Name
Exact Title
Exact Name of Organization
Exact Address
City, State zip

**NURSING HOME
ADMINISTRATOR**

If you want to compare the
resumes and cover letters
of two nursing home
administrators, compare
this resume with the
resume of Ms. Reese on the
following page. Ms. Spears,
unlike Ms. Reese, has
worked for numerous
organizations.

Dear Exact Name of Person: (or Dear Sir or Madam if answering a blind ad)

With the enclosed resume and this cover letter, I would like to make you aware of my interest in being considered for the position of Long-Term Care State Facilitator. In addition to my expert knowledge of nursing center administration and long-term care, I offer a reputation as a highly effective communicator, creative problem solver, and skilled crisis manager.

As you will see from my resume, I am a Licensed Nursing Home Administrator (L.N.H.A.) and have excelled in administrative positions within the nursing care field. In most of my jobs, I have taken on a wide range of problems and have developed and implemented solutions that improved the census, boosted morale, improved staff skills, and resolved a wide range of problems which had resulted in deficiencies.

In my current position, I have decreased deficiencies from eight to one while increasing the census from 87% to 99%. In my previous position, I increased the census from 90% to 97% while decreasing deficiencies from 14 to five. I am skilled at planning, organizing, and directing administrative functions and monitoring conformance to regulatory guidelines. In one job, I took over the management of an organization which was experiencing a variety of staffing problems, and I restored confidence in the staff while improving public relations and profits.

I am well aware of the many significant contributions your organization makes to the long-term care industry. As an administrator, I have utilized the services you provide in inservice training as well as in mediation and problem solving. Based on my understanding of your role within the nursing home and long-term care industry, I feel I could make valuable contributions through my ability to establish and maintain outstanding relationships as well as through my highly professional approach to solving problems within our very unique industry.

I hope you will give me the opportunity to talk with you in person about my interest in this position. I can provide outstanding personal and professional references at the appropriate time, and I can assure you in advance that I am a loyal and hard-working professional who would be a valuable addition to your team. Thank you in advance for your time.

Yours sincerely,

Maureen Spears, L.N.H.A.

MAUREEN SPEARS, L.N.H.A.

1110½ Hay Street, Fayetteville, NC 28305 • preppub@aol.com • (910) 483-6611

OBJECTIVE

To offer my exceptionally strong problem-solving, public relations, marketing, and communication skills to an organization that can use a skilled administrator with expert knowledge of nursing center administration and long-term care.

EXPERIENCE

NURSING HOME ADMINISTRATOR. NC Nursing Center, Charlotte, NC (2002-present). Through my public relations, leadership, and strong administrative abilities, have accomplished numerous ambitious goals which included boosting patient and staff morale, improving staff training and effectiveness, strengthening community relations, and making facility improvements.
- Cut deficiencies from eight to one; increased census from 87% to 99%.

ADMINISTRATOR. Dunn Nursing Center, Dunn, NC (1998-02). Took over the management of this organization which experienced a suspension of admissions; was given a provisional license and four months later received a permanent license for the first time in its three-year history.
- Increased the census to 97% from 90%.

ADMINISTRATOR. Raleigh Nursing Center, Raleigh, NC (1994-98). Through my management and problem-solving skills, played a key role in "turning around" an 84-bed nursing facility experiencing numerous internal difficulties.
- Just 12 days after I was hired, the facility received its provisional license and, six months later, regained its licensure status; then I recruited, hired, and trained department heads.

ADMINISTRATOR. Primary Care of Raleigh, Raleigh, NC (1992-94). Led this 70-bed long-term care facility to show a profit for the first time in four years while also increasing the census from 90% to 95%; reduced aged receivables to 22% of total receivables.
- Planned, organized, and directed all administrative functions and monitored conformance to guidelines promulgated by regulatory agencies.
- Within one month, hired and trained four new department heads and worked with them to dramatically improve the quality of services provided.

ADMINISTRATOR. The North Carolina Diabetes Institute, Inc., Morganton, NC (1990-92). Took over the management of an organization that was experiencing a variety of staffing problems; stabilized and restored confidence in the staff while improving public relations, increasing the census, and boosting profits.
- Planned and directed administration for this 56-bed long-term facility.

EDUCATION & TRAINING

A.S. degree, Banking and Finance, Whetmore College, Reading, PA, 1989.
Completed 50-week **Administrator-in-Training and Medical Terminology Course.**
Licensed Nursing Home Administrator **(L.N.H.A.)** and **CPR** certified.
Completed courses in finance, customer service, word processing, and management.

PERSONAL

Outstanding references. Proven leader with strong human relations and communication skills.

Date

Exact Name
Exact Title
Exact Name of Organization
Exact Address
City, State zip

No matter how experienced and refined a senior manager might get, a job hunt is still an intimidating exercise filled with anxiety. This nursing home administrator is "leaving home" professionally since she is leaving the only professional home she has ever known.

Dear Exact Name of Person: (or Dear Sir or Madam if answering a blind ad)

With the enclosed resume, I would like to make you aware of my interest in utilizing my considerable experience in health care management within your organization.

As you will see from my enclosed resume, I served Elder Village of Oklahoma City as its Licensed Nursing Home Administrator for the past 19 years. In 2001, I resigned from that position in order to seek new opportunities and new challenges. Currently I am working with an in-home care organization as a consultant on a special project which involves its marketing program as well as the correction of several deficiencies recently noted by the Division of Facility Services.

I excelled in every aspect of my job at Elder Village, from public relations, to budgeting, to Medicare and Medicaid insurance billing, to human resources and personnel administration. I am an expert in dealing with matters pertaining to regulation and compliance, and I am proud of the fact that the Division of Facility Services inspected Elder Village on all state and federal compliance and gave the facility a 100% deficiency-free inspection survey result—an almost unheard-of accomplishment.

As I look back over my accomplishments at Elder Village, I am especially proud of my achievements related to human resources administration and personnel management. It was my responsibility to manage a staff of up to 170 people, who included 35 licensed nurses as well as employees involved in dietary, housekeeping, social services, physical therapy, and other activities. I created the organization's human resources policies and procedures, oversaw the development of the organization's first employee manuals, and maintained constant vigilance over personnel files to assure employee compliance with all regulations pertaining to licenses, certifications, and other matters.

If you can use a hard-working professional with vast knowledge related to health care management, I hope you will contact me to suggest a time when we could meet. I can assure you in advance that I have a strong bottom-line orientation and am known for my highly creative approach to problem solving and decision making.

Sincerely,

Myrna Joan Reese

MYRNA JOAN REESE

1110½ Hay Street, Fayetteville, NC 28305   •   preppub@aol.com   •   (910) 483-6611

OBJECTIVE   To offer my management, public relations, and customer service skills to an organization that can use a respected manager with proven versatility in business administration.

LICENSE &
CERTIFICATIONS   Licensed Nursing Home Administrator by the State of Oklahoma. All areas of health care as it relates to long-term skilled care including certified in CPR, Fire Safety, Drug Management, and other areas.

EDUCATION   **Bachelor of Science degree in Business Administration,** Oklahoma State University. Completed extensive ongoing professional education in all areas related to health care trends and management as well as business administration including budgeting and finance, human resources administration, other areas.

EXPERIENCE   *For 19 years, was the administrator of Elder Village of Oklahoma City, a nursing home and medical facility known for the highest quality standards; resigned from this position in order to pursue other opportunities. In May 2001, the Division of Facility Services inspected Elder Village on all state and federal regulations compliance; the facility was given a 100% deficiency-free inspection/survey result. With more than 600 regulations to comply with, this is considered an almost impossible task to accomplish, and my management skills were considered the key to this rare accomplishment.*

NURSING HOME DIRECTOR and MEDICAL FACILITY MANAGER. Elder Village of Oklahoma City, Oklahoma City, OK (1986-04). Took over the management of this facility and directed its growth over the next 19 years; Elder Village is a skilled nursing care and heavy rehabilitation facility which employs up to 170 people while providing nursing care and services for 159 patients.

- **State-of-the-art facility:** Provided oversight for numerous renovations and construction projects which resulted in a comfortable home for the 159 residents of this facility that provides services including round-the-clock nursing and physical therapy.
- **Human resources administration**: Developed all human resources policies and procedures; oversaw the development of the organization's first employee manuals. Take pride in the fact that many of the facility's current employees have worked at Elder Village for nearly 20 years.
- **Staff:** Hired and managed the 170-person staff which included 35 licensed nurses as well as employees in all functional areas.
- **Personnel Administration:** Maintained continuous vigilance over personnel files to assure up-to-date compliance of all personnel with regulations pertaining to their licenses, certifications, current CPR, health cards, TB testing, documentation of all time sheet discrepancies, vacation days, paid leave days, leaves of absence, family medical leave, inservice certification, drug testing, and any drug rehabilitation programs.
- **Medicare and Medicaid Insurance billing:** Provided stringent oversight for billing for this facility which was Medicare, Medicaid, and VA Certified.
- **Budgeting and Finance:** Managed budgeting related to $7 million in annual revenues; figured payroll calculations for every payroll period.
- **Quality Assurance:** Developed continuous Quality Improvement Programs for each department and was vigilant in maintaining quality assurance in all departments.
- **Outstanding Reputation in the community and with regulators:** Maintained excellent public relations with physicians, hospitals, health organizations, and patients' families and friends; was monitored by 52 licensing agencies, and handled numerous regulatory visits, announced and unannounced, from the Division of Facility Services, Department of Social Services, Department of Human Resources, Fire Marshal, others.

PERSONAL   Hardworking. Creative. Honest. Detail Person. People Person. Superior communicator. Am in excellent health and ready for a new challenge for my management abilities!

Date

Exact Name of Person
Exact Title or Position
Company Name
Company Address (number and street)
Company Address (city, state, and ZIP)

NURSE LIAISON   Dear Exact Name of Person (or Dear Sir or Madam if answering a blind ad)

With the application and enclosed resume, I would like to formally express my interest in receiving consideration for a position with your organization at the Lyster Army Community Hospital. Your company has been recommended to me by an employee, Becky Walters, who is a Discharge Planner.

As you will see from my resume I received my B.S.N. degree from the Medical College of Alabama in Huntsville in 1987. Since then I have earned a reputation as a compassionate, well-organized, and articulate professional and have built a strong background of versatile experience in private and public health environments. I believe that my background and education would allow me to contribute in any number of positions in the new medical center, and I am especially interested in pursuing jobs in discharge planning and utilization review.

Although I am highly regarded by my present employer (a TownCenter-related company), I will be leaving this organization in October to pursue other opportunities in the healthcare field where my compassionate manner of working with patients and families, my excellent presentation and communication skills, and my organizational and administrative abilities will be of value. I am certain that my track record of excellent performance in jobs which have included Nurse Liaison, Hospice Coordinator, Case Manager, Clinical Nurse, and Community Health Nurse would allow me to bring important skills to the new facility as it begins to serve this large military community.

With experience which has ranged from public health, to home health, to hospice, to long-term care, to clinical nursing I offer the maturity and adaptability to move into a new facility and quickly become an asset. If you can use an energetic and compassionate professional who is known for possessing a high level of initiative, I hope you will call me soon to arrange a brief meeting to discuss your goals and how my background might serve your needs. I can provide outstanding references at the appropriate time.

Sincerely,

Patricia T. Stewart

PATRICIA STEWART

1110½ Hay Street, Fayetteville, NC 28305 • preppub@aol.com • (910) 483-6611

OBJECTIVE

To contribute a diverse background in all phases of patient care to include assisted living, long-term care, and hospice environments where the ability to ensure that the details of planning for and providing care and discharging patients were carried out with compassion.

EDUCATION

B.S.N. degree, Medical College of Alabama, Huntsville, AL, 1987.
Have completed continuing education and training programs emphasizing pain control and chemotherapy as well as BCLS/CPR and infection control.

EXPERIENCE

NURSE LIAISON. TownCenter-related companies, Huntsville, AL (2003-present). Conduct assessments of patients based on referrals in order to determine the person's placement into long-term, assisted living, domiciliary, intermediate, or rest home-level care.

- Took over a newly created position and have been credited with increasing community awareness of the assisted living option while educating patients and their families.
- Work with discharge planners and case managers to form accurate assessments.
- Conduct outreach to local physicians and am in constant touch with 15 different offices.

Earned advancement in public health care with the Huntsville Regional Home Health Hospice, Huntsville, AL (1996-03):
2000-03: HOSPICE COORDINATOR. Was credited with "dramatically increasing referrals through networking" as coordinator of patient care services for the Hospice care portion of the hospital's programs.

- Supervised three registered nurses, three home health aides, and a chaplain.
- Made arrangements for and coordinated education and development activities for staff members and volunteer workers.
- Provided marketing support services for the program; developed a patient care guide distributed to patients and their family members; updated policy manuals.
- Participated in developing and ensuring compliance with the operating budget.

1996-00: CASE MANAGER and **CLINICAL NURSE.** Supervised nursing aides to ensure implementation of care plans while personally providing care to home health patients.

HOME IV NURSE. Missile City Home Therapeutics, Huntsville, AL (1995-96). Provided individualized, specialized IV infusion therapy in a variety of patient care situations.

COMMUNITY HEALTH NURSE. Lyster Army Community Hospital, Ft. Rucker, AL (1995). Implemented nursing care and provided educational services to individuals and families who had been exposed to or were suffering from infectious diseases or illnesses.

- Performed the hospital's HIV Hospital Admissions testing study.
- Applied knowledge and communication skills presenting a variety of formal lectures.
- Performed physical assessments and developed patient care plans for HIV and AIDS.

CASE MANAGER. Hospice Home Health Services of Montgomery County, Montgomery, AL (1990-95). Excelled in meeting the special needs of the terminally ill and their families while providing quality nursing care and assisting in the training of hospice workers.

REGISTERED NURSE. Community Health Clinic, Germany (1989). Performed a wide range of nursing duties for an outpatient clinic serving a large military community.

PERSONAL

Am highly organized and known for my ability to educate, train, and inform others.

Date

Exact Name of Person
Exact Title or Position
Company Name
Company Address (number and street)
Company Address (city, state, and ZIP)

NURSING SUPERVISOR   Dear Exact Name of Person (or Dear Sir or Madam if answering a blind ad):

With the enclosed resume, I would like to make you aware of my background as a Licensed Practical Nurse and also express my interest in exploring nursing opportunities with your organization. I am particularly interested in the Director of Resident Services position which you recently advertised.

As you will see from my resume, I am currently excelling as a Nursing Supervisor at The Rehabilitation and Health Care Center of Village Green. I supervise up to seven Licensed Practical Nurses while also supervising up to 14 CNAs.

In previous jobs as a Charge Nurse, I worked in settings which included an Alzheimer's Unit with 42 patients as well as a nursing home.

I can provide excellent references at the appropriate time, and I would enjoy an opportunity to talk with you in person about my ability to make valuable contributions to your organization.

Sincerely,

Dorothy Dix

DOROTHY DIX

1110½ Hay Street, Fayetteville, NC 28305 • preppub@aol.com • (910) 483-6611

OBJECTIVE
I want to contribute to an organization that can use an experienced Licensed Practical Nurse who offers extensive management skills and supervisory abilities.

EDUCATION
Lemuel Shattuck Hospital School of Practical Nursing, Jamaica Plain, MA, 1993-94.
Graduated from Dorchester High School, Dorchester, MA, 1980.

LICENSE
Licensed LPN, NC Certificate #045241; renewal date 12/31/03
Community CPR Certificate, AHA, 6/23/04

EXPERIENCE
NURSING SUPERVISOR. The Rehabilitation and Health Care Center of Village Green, Nashville, TN (2002-present). Supervise 4-7 Licensed Practical Nurses while also supervising 10-14 CNAs; monitor resident care rounds, monitor medication pass and treatments, and provide inservices to LPNs and CNAs.
- Assist nursing staff as needed with lab specimen collection and IV therapy.
- Notify MDs and family members as needed.
- Prepare end-of-shift supervisor's report.
- Monitor staff at Carolina Inn of Village Green, an assisted living facility.
- Assist with monthly summaries as well as with nightly and weekly chartings.

CHARGE NURSE & LICENSED PRACTICAL NURSE. Whispering Pines Nursing Home, Nashville, TN (2000-02). As Charge Nurse, was the supervisor of the 11-7 shift; supervised 3-5 nursing assistants while also administering medications and performing treatments.
- Was the Team Leader for the Eden Alternative Program.

RECEPTIONIST. H&R Block, Nashville, TN (1999-00). In this seasonal position, distributed tax return checks, filed completed tax returns, answered telephones, set up client appointments, and processed rapid refund returns.

LICENSED PRACTICAL NURSE. Village Green Care Center, Nashville, TN (1998-99). Was a Charge Nurse for skilled geriatric patients while supervising 3-5 Certified Nursing Assistants.

RESEARCH ASSISTANT. Beth Israel Hospital, Department of Pathology, Boston, MA (1997-98). Was involved in training laboratory personnel as well as in the histological preparation of research samples. Maintained laboratory equipment and supplies. Prepared Epon embedded 1 Micron samples.

LICENSED PRACTICAL NURSE. Sherril House, Inc., Boston, MA (1996-97). Was Charge Nurse of an Alzheimer's Unit with 42 patients; supervised six CNAs.

LICENSED PRACTICAL NURSE. Oak Haven Nursing Home, Roxbury, MA (1995-96). Was Charge Nurse for 34 patients; supervised three CNAs.

PERSONAL
Enjoy helping others. Have excellent people skills. Am a highly motivated self-starter and go- getter who enjoys making a difference in others' lives.

Date

Exact Name of Person
Exact Title
Exact Name of Company
Address
City, State, Zip

Dear Exact Name of Person (or Dear Sir or Madam if answering a blind ad):

With the enclosed resume, I would like to make you aware of my background as an articulate young professional with exceptional communication, organization, and patient care skills who offers an educational background and clinical rotation experience in various occupational therapy environments.

As you will see from my enclosed resume, I am currently excelling both academically and in clinical rotations while completing my Bachelor of Science degree in Occupational Therapy. Currently maintaining a 3.89 GPA, I will graduate in May and test for certification as an Occupational Therapist Registered in September of 2002. I previously earned an Associate of Applied Science degree in Accounting and completed two years college course work in Biology before entering the Occupational Therapy program.

I have excelled in clinical rotations at Charles Mental Health Center and at Northeastern Regional Rehabilitation Center, where I demonstrated my creativity, problem-solving ability, and therapeutic skills. In addition to preparing a multimedia in-service presentation for the Occupational Therapy department using Microsoft PowerPoint, I also designed and created a new adaptive tool for patients with hemiparesis. Currently, I am beginning a Pediatric Outpatient rotation.

If you can use a dedicated, accomplished young professional with a strong desire to make a contribution in the field of Occupational Therapy, I look forward to hearing from you soon. I assure you in advance that I have an excellent reputation and would quickly become an asset to your organization.

Sincerely,

Deborah Lucas

DEBORAH LUCAS

1110½ Hay Street, Fayetteville, NC 28305 • preppub@aol.com • (910) 483-6611

OBJECTIVE   To offer my education and experience in Occupational Therapy to an organization that could benefit from the services of a creative and dedicated professional with exceptional communication, problem-solving, and patient care skills which have been tested in a variety of clinical environments.

EDUCATION   **Bachelor of Science in Occupational Therapy**, Hastings College, Hastings, NE; currently maintaining a **3.89 GPA**, will graduate May 2002.
- Named to the **President's Honor List** three times, for achieving a perfect **4.0 GPA** for the semester, and the **Dean's List**, for a **3.5 GPA** or better.
- Received the prestigious Thomas Foundation scholarship, a $16,000 award in recognition of my extensive hours of volunteer work.
- Completed two years of college-level course work towards a Bachelor of Science in Biology at Hastings College before entering the Occupational Therapy program, 1997-1999.

Associate of Applied Science degree in Accounting, Hastings Community College, Hastings, NE, 1996.

CERTIFICATIONS   Will test for Occupational Therapist Registered through the National Board for Certification in Occupational Therapy, September 18, 2002.

AFFILIATIONS   Member, American Student Occupational Therapy Association, 1997-present.
Treasurer, Phi Beta Lambda, 1997-1999.

EXPERIENCE   **OCCUPATIONAL THERAPY INTERN** and **STUDENT.** Hastings College, Hastings, NE (2000-present). Have excelled academically, in clinical rotations, and in leadership positions with the American Student Occupational Therapy Association.
Clinical Rotations: Have received the highest-possible evaluations of my performance and been praised for my creativity and problem solving while completing these clinical rotations:
Pediatric Outpatient: Caring Hands, Hastings, NE (Mar 2001-present). Apply my growing knowledge and exceptional care skills while providing occupational therapy to children.
Rehabilitation: Northeastern Regional Rehabilitation Center, Hastings, NE (Jan-Mar 2001). Demonstrated resourcefulness while further honing my patient care skills during this clinical rotation at a major regional rehabilitation center; performed patient assessment and evaluation in order to establish a plan of care.
Mental Health: Charles Mental Health Center, Hastings, NE (May-Aug 00). Gained valuable experience in helping clients with schizophrenia and bipolar disorder to develop problem-solving ability as well as social and communication skills; held a money management workshop and conducted weekly money management group meetings to help patients achieve a greater sense of personal responsibility.

THERAPY ASSISTANT. Titus Rehabilitation Hospital, Hastings, NE (1996-99). Performed more than 240 hours of volunteer work, assisting with patient activities under the supervision of an Occupational Therapist.

ACCOUNTING CLERK and **DATA ENTRY CLERK.** Kearns Guidance & Navigation Corporation, Charles, NE (1994-96). Started with this major defense contractor as a Data Entry Clerk and quickly advanced to a position of increased responsibility.

PERSONAL   Excellent personal and professional references are available upon request.

Date

Exact Name of Person
Exact Title or Position
Name of Company
Address (no., street)
Address (city, state, zip)

OPERATING ROOM NURSE

Dear Exact Name of Person:

I would appreciate an opportunity to talk with you soon about obtaining a position as a staff nurse in your hospital's operating room.

During my nursing career, I have demonstrated my wide-ranging skills in various medical and surgical specialties in both military and private hospitals and medical centers.

Most recently, as an Operating Room Nurse in a 280-bed medical instruction hospital averaging 450 cases per month, I perform demanding, critical duties as O.R. Staff Nurse while simultaneously acting as charge nurse of the OB/GYN, oncology, and infertility service serving 18 physicians.

Previously, as Assistant Charge Nurse I planned, directed, and coordinated nursing care of a 25-bed multi-service surgical/orthopedic unit during acute, pre-operative, and postoperative periods. In addition to conducting orientation and training, I was chosen to serve on the air transportable hospital providing medical and surgical care under adverse conditions.

In prior jobs as a Staff Nurse and Critical Care Nurse, I refined my skills in delivering high-quality patient care. You would find me to be a dedicated, versatile professional who gains great satisfaction from helping others. I hope you will welcome my call to arrange a brief meeting during that week to discuss your current and future needs and how I might serve them. Thank you in advance for your time.

Yours sincerely,

Heidi K. Eden

(Alternate last paragraph:
I hope you will call or write me soon to suggest a time at your convenience for us to meet and discuss your current and future needs and how I might serve them. Thank you in advance for your time.)

HEIDI K. EDEN

1110½ Hay Street, Fayetteville, NC 28305   •   preppub@aol.com   •   (910) 483-6611

OBJECTIVE

I want to contribute my skills as a registered nurse to a health care facility seeking a dedicated, versatile professional well-rounded in managing and delivering general and specialized patient care.

EDUCATION

Currently enrolled in the **Bachelor of Science Degree in Nursing (B.S.N.)** program, Central Michigan University, Hill Air Force Base, UT.
Hold an **Associate of Science (A.S.) Degree in Nursing**, Georgian Court College, Lakewood, NJ, 1996.

EXPERIENCE

OPERATING ROOM NURSE. U.S. Air Force, Hill Air Force Base, UT (2003-present). In a 280-bed teaching hospital averaging 450 cases per month, perform demanding duties as O.R. staff nurse and simultaneously as charge nurse of the OB/GYN, oncology, and infertility service serving 18 physicians.
- Act as "circulating" team leader in various surgical procedures.
- Have been selected to act as a preceptor in the O.R. nurse internship program.
- Handle all types of surgical emergencies.
- Act independently as a peri-operative nurse.
- Increase efficiency by updating and reorganizing the OB/GYN service.
- Organize activities of personnel and equipment to facilitate optimal patient care.

ASSISTANT CHARGE NURSE. U.S. Air Force, Yokota Air Force Base, Japan (2001-03). Planned, directed, and coordinated nursing care of a 25-bed multi-service surgical/orthopedic unit during acute, preoperative, and postoperative periods.
- Conducted orientation and training, both in classroom settings and on-the-job.
- Gained skills in the intricacies of time management scheduling 8 personnel to maintain quality patient care.
- Was chosen to serve on the air transportable hospital and the quality assurance committee.
- Earned a Commendation Medal for rapid assessment of emergency illnesses and injuries, averting life-threatening situations.

NURSE. U.S. Air Force, McGuire Air Force Base, NJ (1998-01). Promoted health maintenance, rehabilitation, and home care practices in a 25-bed neuro/pulmonary/allergy unit by instructing patients and their families and developing individualized short- and long-range nursing care plans.
- Was recognized for significantly increasing medical awareness through educational sessions.
- Learned the importance of patient/family support.

CRITICAL CARE NURSE. Lakewood Memorial Hospital, Lakewood, NJ (1996-98). Provided care for the critically ill in an 15-bed ICU/CCU facility.

TRAINING

Completed coursework in medical treatment under adverse conditions through the use of an air transportable hospital, and in nursing service management, U.S. Air Force School of Medical Sciences, 1999-01.

PERSONAL

Am personable and work well with many different types of people. Can handle pressure and react calmly and logically to emergencies. Gain great satisfaction from helping others. Willing to relocate.

Date

Exact Name of Person
Exact Title
Exact Name of Company
Address
City, State, Zip

**OPERATING ROOM
STAFF NURSE**

Dear Exact Name of Person: (or Dear Sir or Madam if answering a blind ad)

With the enclosed resume, I would like to make you aware of my interest in exploring opportunities where my versatile nursing background and reputation as a skilled nursing professional would be valued.

As you will see from my resume, I offer a broad base of experience and knowledge with an emphasis on operating room experience. I also am familiar with heart team procedures and ambulatory care settings. Since 2000 I have been an Operating Room Nurse for the Ambulatory Surgical Center in Atlanta, GA, where I work with doctors from Village Surgical Associates on general cases such as laparoscopic gall bladders, hernias, and other LS procedures as well as other practices such as orthopedic, ENT, GYN, plastics, and endo patients.

At Valley View Medical Center in Atlanta, I was an OR Staff Nurse/Relief Head Nurse and then was handpicked as a member of the center's "Heart Team." I attended a three-month program in Open Heart Surgery at Atlanta Metropolitan University and then acted as one of the four nurses on Dr. George Smith's team of specialists.

Although I am well respected and satisfied with my present position, I am in the process of relocating to your area because my husband has started a new job with the Sheriff's Department.

I hope you will contact me soon to arrange a brief meeting to discuss my background and how I might contribute to your organization. Thank you in advance for your time and consideration of my qualifications.

Sincerely,

Maria Luisa Cardenas

MARIA LUISA CARDENAS

1110½ Hay Street, Fayetteville, NC 28305 • preppub@aol.com • (910) 483-6611

OBJECTIVE   To contribute to a medical organization that can use a Registered Nurse who has acquired expert knowledge of operating room, heart surgery, and general medical cases while earning a reputation as a skilled nursing professional with superior time management skills.

EDUCATION   **R.N.,** Waynesville Technical Community College, GA, 1996.
& TRAINING   Completed a three-month training program in Open Heart Surgery, Atlanta Metropolitan University, GA, 1997.
L.P.N., Columbus Community College, Columbus, GA, 1987.
Attended the American Medical Association 30-day Supervisory Course, 1992.
Completed Medical Corpsman (L.P.N.) training, U.S. Army, 1979.

LICENSES   **Registered Nurse,** Georgia License #229883, expires December 2005.
& CERTIFICATION Have current Advanced Cardiac Lifesaving Certification (ACLS).
Am certified in CPR and First Aid.

EXPERIENCE   **OPERATING ROOM STAFF NURSE/RELIEF HEAD NURSE.** Ambulatory Surgical Center, Atlanta, GA (2000-present). Manage 30 nurses and scrub technicians while working with physicians from Village Surgical Associates and other practices on a block schedule.
  • Specialize in general cases which included laparoscopic gall bladders, hernias, and surgical patients as well as regular general cases.
  • During surgical procedures, manage two scrub nurses while scrubbing and circulating as an assistant to doctors.
  • Was a major contributor to decisions on upgrades for laparoscopic equipment.

OR NURSE and **RELIEF HEAD NURSE.** Valley View Medical Center, Atlanta, GA (1998-00). Managed a staff of approximately 30 nurses and scrub technicians and was handpicked as part of the medical center's newly formed "Heart Team."

HEART TEAM CIRCULATING AND SCRUB NURSE. Valley View Medical Center, Atlanta, GA (1997-98). Received advanced training in open heart surgical procedures in a three-month program at Atlanta Metropolitan University; participated in nearly 1,000 heart surgeries.
  • As a member of the team of specialists handpicked for the "Heart Team" headed by Dr. George Smith, was one of four nurses selected to assist in this specialized area.

FULL-TIME STUDENT. Waynesville Technical Community College, GA, and Quincy State Junior College, IL (1993-96). Completed course work leading to licensing as an R.N.

SUPERVISORY L.P.N. Equifax, Atlanta, GA (1991-93). Coordinated schedules and supervised 30 RNs who performed insurance physicals.

OPERATING ROOM NURSE and **PRIMARY CARE NURSE.** Hendersonville Memorial Hospital, Hendersonville, GA (1989-91). Simultaneously with the job with Equifax, also worked in the neurological ward for nine months and in the operating room for one year.

Highlights of other experience:
Was an **Operating Room Nurse,** Columbia Hospital, Columbia, GA.

PERSONAL   Am a flexible and creative professional with sound decision-making skills.

Date

Exact Name of Person
Exact Title
Exact Name of Company
Address
City, State, Zip

PATIENT CARE MANAGER   Dear Exact Name of Person (or Dear Sir or Madam if answering a blind ad):

With the enclosed resume, I would like to make you aware of my interest in exploring employment opportunities with your organization and introduce you to my nursing credentials.

As you will see from my resume, I am currently employed as a Patient Care Manager for the University of Colorado's Medical Center in Boulder. I have a twenty-four hour responsibility of operational management in the Labor and Delivery Unit and Antenatal Testing Units. I also manage a regional referral center for 10 outlying counties.

I can provide outstanding personal and professional references. Because of my excellent reputation and superior academic track record at the University of Colorado and Mesa State College, I was aggressively recruited to join the Medical Center faculty. I managed 55 full-time staff members in Boulder, and I am a member in several hospital wide committees.

Although I enjoyed the challenge of providing skilled nursing care to the geriatric population, I have decided that I wish to work in a fast-paced environment which can utilize more of my clinical nursing skills and knowledge. If you can use a dedicated professional who can provide outstanding references from all previous employers, please contact me to suggest a time when we might meet to discuss your needs. Thank you in advance for your time.

Yours sincerely,

Rhonda G. Blocker

RHONDA G. BLOCKER, RN, BSN

1110½ Hay Street, Fayetteville, NC 28305   •   preppub@aol.com   •   (910) 483-6611

OBJECTIVE

To offer a reputation as a professional Patient Care Manager who excels in finding ways to improve the quality of patient care and administrative procedures to an organization in need of a mature nursing professional who offers strong computer skills and safety knowledge.

EDUCATION

Master of Science Degree in Biology and Reproductive Physiology, University of Colorado, Boulder, CO, 2000. Graduated magna cum laude.
Bachelor of Science Degree in Nursing, University of Colorado, Boulder, CO, 1999.
Bachelor of Science Degree in Agriculture, Mesa State College, Grand Junction, CO, 1992.

EXPERIENCE

PATIENT CARE MANAGER. University of Colorado Medical Center, Labor and Delivery Unit, Boulder, CO, (2002-present). Twenty four hour responsibility for operational management of 12 bed Labor Delivery Room and Antenatal Testing Units in a large county hospital with approximately 3500 deliveries per year. Manage a regional referral center for 10 outlying counties. Report to Service Line Director.

- Responsible for evaluations, schedules, performance management and payroll for 55 FTEs, to include RN, Surgical Tech, Nursing Assistant and Unit Secretary positions. Primary responsibility for management of operational and personnel budgets and development of capital budget.
- Develop supply task force to identify and implement available supply cost savings.
- Pilot and implement use of standard disposable vaginal delivery, C/S, and tubal ligation packs, with a cost savings of >$18,000 in first year. Entering trial phase for custom packs.
- Evaluate staffing patterns and change staffing levels to reflect highest census, highest activity times and days. Modify call schedule to reflect normal hours of work for RNs.
- Initiated "neonatal cart" class to familiarize Labor Delivery Room RNs and Techs with contents of neonatal emergency carts. Revamped new graduate internship program, utilized experienced RNs, Techs, and CRNAs etc. as instructors for the didactic content.
- Member of the "Patient Care" Sub-committee, Nursing Performance Recognition Committee, Neonatal Care Team, and Breastfeeding Trainer Group.

PATIENT CARE MANAGER LABOR AND DELIVERY. Gilpin Hospital, Boulder, CO (1998-02). Full responsibility on the evening shift for operational management of a 6 Operating Room Suite and a Labor Delivery Unit in a large inner city teaching, hospital, with over 1500 deliveries per year. Report to the Care Center Leader (Director).

- Joint responsibility for all schedules, annual evaluations, performance management and payroll adjustments for a staff of 45 employees.
- Served as a primary clinical resource and mentor for all staff. Instrumental in the clinical practice change from predominantly DR deliveries to primarily LDR deliveries.

ASSISTANT NURSE MANAGER (AN I) –OB. Mesa Regional Hospital, Grand Junction, CO (1995-97). Primary responsibility on AM shift for labor and delivery unit with 2500 deliveries per year, serving low to very high risk patients in an inner city teaching facility. Coordinator for the Neonatal Care Center 4-5 times per week on AM shift.

STAFF NURSE I. Delta Medical Center, Grand Junction, CO (1994-1995). Duties included: triage, charge nurse, circulating for C-sections, tubal ligations and D&C's, recovery of operative cases, transport of high risk patients by ground and caring for normal and high risk patients during the ante, intra and postpartum periods.

LICENSURES

Colorado Registered Nurse, NRP instructor, EFM certification.

Date

Exact Name of Person
Exact Title
Exact Name of Company
Address
City, State, Zip

PATIENT CARE SPECIALIST

Dear Exact Name of Person: (or Dear Sir or Madam if answering a blind ad)

I would appreciate an opportunity to talk with you soon about how I could contribute to your organization through my experience, education, and training in the medical field and knowledge of medical procedures.

As you will see from my enclosed resume, I have built a reputation as a skilled and talented young professional who is dedicated to the medical profession. While serving my country in the U.S. Army, I received extensive training as a medical specialist with an emphasis on orthopedic surgery and care. I received several medals and awards for my professionalism and for effectiveness while working in jobs as many as three skill levels above my assigned level. My adaptability and versatility have been displayed while providing patient care in a medical clinic and on frequent exercises and projects with a combat engineering unit with worldwide missions.

I am on the national registry of Emergency Medical Technicians and a Certified Nursing Assistant as well as being certified in Combat Lifesaving, First Aid, and CPR. I am also pursuing an Associate in Science degree at Tiffin Technical Community College.

If you can use an experienced medical technician who is adaptable, dedicated, and willing to work hard to achieve success, I hope you will contact me to suggest a time when we might meet to discuss your needs. I can assure you in advance that I could rapidly become an asset to your organization.

Sincerely,

Scott Cleaves

SCOTT CLEAVES

1110½ Hay Street, Fayetteville, NC 28305   •   preppub@aol.com   •   (910) 483-6611

OBJECTIVE   To contribute through my medical skills and knowledge of medical procedures to an organization that can use a self-motivated young professional who is recognized as a dedicated and exceptionally skilled individual.

EDUCATION   Pursuing an Associate in Science degree, Tiffin Technical Community College, Tiffin, OH.
Attended the U.S. Army's General Medical Orientation, Medical Specialist, Orthopedic Specialist Phase I, and Orthopedic Specialist Phase II Courses.
Completed numerous correspondence courses through the U.S. Army Academy of Health Sciences, Ft. Sam Houston, TX, including: Operating Room Specialist Sustainment, Practical Nurse Preparatory, and Practical Nurse Sustainment Courses.

TRAINING &   Attended training programs leading to certification in these areas:
CERTIFICATIONS   Emergency Medical Technician — am on the National EMT Registry
　　　Certified Nursing Assistant I
　　　Combat Lifesaving
　　　CPR and First Aid
Completed nonmedical training programs including airborne, bus driver training, hazardous materials handling and certification, and combat engineering courses as well as professional leadership development courses.

EXPERIENCE   *Have built a reputation as a talented young medical specialist, U.S. Army:*
PATIENT CARE SPECIALIST and **INSTRUCTOR.** Ft. Bragg, NC (2000-present). In a medical clinic setting, provide assistance for all phases of inpatient and outpatient care as well as simultaneously acting as an instructor in various medical subjects.
- Handle direct patient care which included conducting medical examinations, collecting and preparing specimens for lab analysis, and administering immunizations.
- Maintain accurate and up-to-date medical records on each patient.
- As an Instructor for personnel in an engineering organization, teach classes in subjects ranging from first aid and CPR; to inventory control including ordering supplies, equipment, and medications; to the proper procedures for supervising clinical and field medical facilities.
- Received the Army Commendation Medal for "meritorious achievements" while supervising supply operations during a large-scale training exercise, a job usually reserved for a professional three skill levels higher; developed sources for hard-to-find items and reduced duplications, thereby saving countless manhours and funds.
- Recognized with an Army Achievement Medal for efforts during an exercise in Georgia with an engineering unit, identified and treated two people for the early signs of heat injuries and saved them from potentially life-threatening conditions.
- Received an Achievement Medal for sustained performance during activities which included independent leadership of a cleanup crew following Hurricane Fran in North Carolina, establishment of two base camps in Haiti which are still in use, leading a construction team in Puerto Rico, and accident-free driving records in numerous projects.

ORTHOPEDIC TECHNICIAN. Lancaster, PA (1996-00). Worked in a field hospital environment where my responsibilities included assisting doctors during minor orthopedic surgical procedures and with patient care.

PERSONAL   Offer a reputation as a hard worker who can be counted on to work well with others.

CAREER CHANGE

Date

Exact Name of Person
Exact Title
Exact Name of Company
Address
City, State, Zip

Dear Exact Name of Person: (or Dear Sir or Madam if answering a blind ad)

Thank you for your recent expression of interest in my background, and I am faxing with this cover letter an updated resume which describes my current job as a Pharmaceutical Sales Representative. In my current job servicing chain drug stores and doctors' offices in 30 cities, I am consistently ranked among the company's top producers in my efforts to increase market share, develop new accounts, and boost sales of Vanceril and Proventil H.F.A. I believe my rapid success as a Pharmaceutical Sales Representative has been due in large part to my background as an R.N., and I have come to be regarded by all the doctors and pharmacists with whom I work as a trusted advisor and Marketing Consultant.

As you will see, I have lived in the San Francisco area all my life, except for a few years after high school when I worked as a model for the Legends Agency in New York. After my stint in modeling, I earned my Bachelor's degree in Business Administration in 1992 and then graduated from nursing school as an R.N. in 1998. In a job with Interim Care prior to my current position, I traveled to surrounding counties handling a patient case load and training new nurses. In a previous job, I worked for Seattle Medical Center, where I advanced to increasing responsibilities as a Staff Nurse in the Medical Intensive Care Unit, Emergency Department, and Coronary Care Unit.

With a reputation as a doer and achiever, I have worked since I was 16 years old. As a high school junior and senior, I assisted in managing a skating rink and handled sales, concessions, special events, as well as opening and closing the business. I have also excelled as a Sales Representative with a local 50-year-old business which operates all over the east coast handling mostly commercial and industrial accounts. I have negotiated contracts, prospected for customers, and resolved problems in fair and diplomatic ways.

Although I am excelling in my current job and am highly regarded by the company, I would enjoy learning how your company could make use of my considerable marketing and sales abilities. I am sure my extensive contacts and outstanding reputation within the medical community could be of value to you. You would find me in person to be a congenial individual who interacts with others with poise and professionalism. I hope you will contact me soon to suggest a time when we could meet to discuss your needs and how I might be of service to you.

Yours sincerely,

Rebecca Skenteris

REBECCA ADKINS SKENTERIS

1110½ Hay Street, Fayetteville, NC 28305   •   preppub@aol.com   •   (910) 483-6611

OBJECTIVE
To contribute to an organization that can use a persuasive communicator and proactive professional who combines outstanding sales and marketing abilities, including pharmaceutical sales experience along with professional nursing experience and a degree in Business Administration.

EDUCATION
Pursuing Master of Clinical Psychology studies, Golden Gate University, San Francisco, CA, 2001-present.

Associate of Applied Science in Nursing degree, Golden Gate Technical Community College, San Francisco, CA, 1998; excelled in extracurricular and academic activities:

- Earned **Dean's List** distinction, 1995-98.
- Was honored by selection as Marshal, Class of 1997.
- Received a faculty appointment to the Curriculum Committee and Steering Committee.
- Was named Class Historian, 1996-98.

Bachelor of Business Administration degree, cum laude, minor in Accounting and Economics, Golden Gate University, San Francisco, CA, 1992.

EXPERIENCE
PHARMACEUTICAL SALES REPRESENTATIVE. Simms-Price Pharmaceuticals, San Francisco, CA (2001-present). Manage a 30-city territory while servicing existing clients and developing new accounts.

- Because of my background as an R.N. with extensive medical knowledge and a thorough knowledge of medical terminology, quickly earned the respect of my clients; have become a respected Marketing Consultant and trusted advisor to pharmacists and doctors.
- Represent Vanceril (DS), Claritin, and Proventil H.F.A. to chain drug stores and doctors' offices.
- **Sales accomplishments**: Am ranked second in the district in total sales of Proventil H.F.A and second in percentage of growth in sales; am ranked 3rd in total sales of Vanceril Double Strength.

CASE MANAGER. Interim HealthCare, Berkeley, CA (2000-01). Traveled to surrounding counties while handling a 25-patient caseload; involved in training new nurses.

- Became skilled in time management while providing quality patient care and coordinating the efforts of physicians, ancillary medical personnel, and necessary community resources.

Excelled in the following track record of progression to increasing responsibilities, Seattle Regional Medical Center of San Francisco, CA:
2000: STAFF NURSE, CORONARY CARE UNIT. Handled patient care to include assessment, implementation of orders, treatment, and continuous monitoring of acutely ill.

1999-00: STAFF NURSE, EMERGENCY DEPARTMENT. Handled all aspects of patient care in a critical care setting while implementing triage protocol, assessing conditions and assisting with treatment, and continuously monitoring various conditions of medical, pre-surgical, and trauma-crash patients including MVAs, burns, ODs, gunshot wounds.

1998-99: STAFF NURSE, MEDICAL INTENSIVE CARE UNIT. Operated as a Float Nurse for Surgical Intensive Care Unit, Coronary Care Unit, and Cardiac Intensive Care.

MODEL. Legends Agency, New York, NY (1986-90). After graduating from high school, worked as a model in New York in commercials which emphasized my face and eyes.

COMPUTERS
Proficient with Windows, Microsoft, Quicken, and WordPerfect. Outstanding references available.

Date

Exact Name of Person
Exact Title
Exact Name of Company
Address
City, State, Zip

REGISTERED NURSE (RN)   Dear Exact Name of Person: (or Dear Sir or Madam if answering a blind ad)

With the enclosed resume, I would like to make you aware of my background as an accomplished nursing professional who offers experience in pediatrics, medical-surgical, orthopedic, and geriatric care in home health, hospital, and long-term care environments.

As you will see, I have recently completed my Associate's degree program in Nursing from Simmons Community College in Sampson, WV. I had previously completed the Licensed Practical Nurse program at Simmons Community College and have practiced as an LPN since 1996.

In my present job with Pediatric Services of America, I provide private duty pediatric home health care to critically ill children, most of whom are referred to PSA by the University of West Virginia and Kentucky Medical Centers. To enhance my abilities in this area, I attended a ventilator care seminar through PSA, as many of my patients require respirators or ventilators. I implement occupational, physical, and speech therapy programs as prescribed, and educate patients and family members on care-related issues.

While completing my Associate's degree in Nursing, I worked in a number of units at a long-term care facility. Prior to that, I served as a Licensed Practical Nurse on a 32-bed orthopedic and adolescent unit at Children's Hospital, a 175-bed pediatric teaching hospital in West Virginia. In this challenging environment, I gained valuable knowledge related to the care and treatment of orthopedic disorders resulting from birth injuries or genetic diseases.

In an earlier position at Wynhoven Nursing Center, I further developed my time management skills while supervising four nursing aides providing total patient care for 60 chronically ill patients in this long-term care facility.

If you can use a motivated, experienced nursing professional whose abilities have been tested in a wide range of challenging environments, then I look forward to hearing from you soon, to suggest a time when we might meet to discuss your needs. I can assure you in advance that I have an outstanding reputation and would rapidly become a valuable asset to your organization.

Sincerely,

Allison Hedgpeth

ALLISON HEDGPETH

1110½ Hay Street, Fayetteville, NC 28305 • preppub@aol.com • (910) 483-6611

OBJECTIVE

To benefit an organization that can use an experienced nursing professional with exceptional communication and time management skills who offers a background in pediatric, medical-surgical, orthopedic, and geriatric nursing in home health, hospital, and long-term care environments.

EDUCATION

Associate's Degree in **Nursing**, Simmons Community College, Sampson, WV, 2000. Graduated from the **Licensed Practical Nursing** program, Simmons Community College, Sampson, WV, 1996.
Have supplemented my degree programs with courses to enhance my nursing skills, including a course in ventilator care offered by Pediatric Services of America.

LICENSES

West Virginia **Registered Nurse**, certificate #158876, expires December 2003.
Licensed Practical Nurse for the state of West Virginia, expires 2003.

EXPERIENCE

REGISTERED NURSE and **LICENSED PRACTICAL NURSE.** Pediatric Services of America, Sampson, WV (2000-present). Provide private duty pediatric home health care to children who were critically ill, medically fragile, injured, or suffering from rare genetic diseases; more than 95% of my patients are referred through the University of West Virginia and Kentucky Medical Centers.
- Coordinate with doctors, nurses, families, case managers, and therapists to ensure optimum care for each patient.
- Provide ventilator and tracheostomy care and maintenance.
- Implement prescribed occupational, physical, and speech therapies; administered medication, both orally, intravenously, and by gastrointestinal tube.
- Perform family and patient education on issues related to the special care needed by critically ill or medically fragile children.
- Was recognized at a pediatric conference for my outstanding service to children with HIV and their families.

LICENSED PRACTICAL NURSE. Mary Gran Nursing Center, Sampson, WV (1998-00). Worked as an LPN, delivering quality care to elderly patients in this long-term care facility while completing my Associate's degree program in Nursing.
- Managed a work load of 33 patients, performing assessments and administering medications and treatments.
- Worked in a number of different units on alternating weekends, honing my skills in various types of nursing.

LICENSED PRACTICAL NURSE. Children's Hospital, Sampson, WV (1997-1998). Provided quality patient care for a 32-bed orthopedic and adolescent unit in a 175-bed pediatric teaching hospital associated with West Virginia State and Tulane Universities.
- Increased my knowledge related to the care and treatment of orthopedic disorders resulting from birth injuries or genetic diseases.

LICENSED PRACTICAL NURSE. Wynhoven Nursing Center, Blackridge, WV (1996-1997). Supervised and worked with four nursing aides, providing total nursing care for 60 chronically ill elderly patients on a skilled nursing unit in this long-term care facility.
- Organized and prioritized patient care; directed nursing aides under my supervision.

PERSONAL

Excellent personal and professional references are available upon request.

Date

Exact Name of Person
Exact Title
Exact Name of Company
Address
City, State, Zip

Dear Exact Name of Person: (or Dear Sir or Madam if answering a blind ad)

With the enclosed resume, I would like to make you aware of my background as a dedicated young nursing professional with strong communication and organizational skills who offers exceptional patient care skills honed in challenging environments on the Orthopedic/Neurological Surgical Unit at a major regional medical center. I am in the process of relocating to the Myrtle Beach area where my husband has accepted a new position.

As you will see, I completed my Associate Degree in Nursing (ADN) at Sandhills Community College, where I excelled in clinical rotations in ICU/CCU, Neurological/Surgical, Psychiatric, Pediatric, Obstetrics/Labor & Delivery, and Medical/Surgical nursing. I am a Licensed Registered Nurse for the state of Pennsylvania.

Since earning my RN license, I have worked on the Orthopedic/Neurological Surgical Unit at Pittsburgh Medical Center, performing skilled nursing care, patient assessment, and monitoring for pre and postoperative patients in these specialties as well as for Medical/Surgical patients. I work with a Physical Therapy team in my current position and am involved in providing a wide range of postoperative care. I am skilled in wound care and am also skilled in working with chest tubes and blood transfusions. My organizational and planning skills have served me well in my work with the peer review committee and with the organization and implementation of the hospital's United Way Fundraising campaign, which generated 18% more than the projected amount.

If you can use a nursing professional with experience in orthopedic/neurological as well as medical/surgical environments along with a genuine commitment to providing the highest possible levels of patient care, then I hope you will contact me soon to suggest a time when we might meet to discuss your needs. I can assure you in advance that I have an excellent reputation and would quickly become a valuable asset to your organization.

Sincerely,

Natalie Crudup

NATALIE CRUDUP

1110½ Hay Street, Fayetteville, NC 28305　　•　　preppub@aol.com　　•　　(910) 483-6611

OBJECTIVE　　To benefit an organization that can use a motivated young nursing professional whose exceptional communication, organizational, and patient care skills have been proven in orthopedic and neurological surgical and intensive care/critical care environments.

CERTIFICATIONS　　Licensed Registered Nurse, Pennsylvania Board of Nursing, 2002-05.
Certified in Community CPR (infant, children, and adult).

EDUCATION　　**Associate Degree in Nursing (ADN),** Sandhills Community College, Pittsburgh, PA, 2000. Received the Pennsylvania Nurse's Scholarship (2001) and Pinehurst Surgical Group Scholarship (2000) for academic excellence.
Completed a seminar, "Building People Relation Skills," 2001.
Completed a Neurosurgical Internship (16 hours).

EXPERIENCE　　**REGISTERED NURSE, ORTHO/NEURO SURGICAL UNIT.** Pittsburgh Medical Center, Pittsburgh, PA (2000-present). Provide skilled nursing care to pre- and post-operative patients in the orthopedic and neurological surgical units as well as to medical-surgical patients at this large regional medical center.
- Perform regular patient assessments and monitoring; am skilled at handling chest tubes and blood transfusions.
- Work closely with physicians as part of an interdisciplinary team to promote excellence in patient care; played a key role on the Peer Review Committee.
- Work closely with a Physical Therapy Team to provide postoperative care.
- Perform wound care on surgical patients, cleaning incision sites, checking for infection, and changing dressings.
- Develop money-saving proposals to reduce supply expenditures; organized and implemented the United Way Fundraising campaign for 2002; exceeded program objectives by 18%.

NURSING INTERN & NURSING STUDENT. Pittsburgh Community College, Pittsburgh, PA (1998-00). Excelled academically and in clinical rotations throughout the state; received several scholarships based on my academic performance, and represented the Association of Nursing Students in a number of fund-raising and volunteer activities.
Clinical Rotations: Received exceptional evaluations for my performance while completing these clinical rotations:
- **Neurological/Surgical:** Valley Medical Center, Pittsburgh, PA. Developed exceptional skills in performing patient assessment and skilled care of neurosurgical patients.
- **Medical/Surgical:** Moore Regional Hospital, Pittsburgh, PA. Refined my patient care skills and administered medication orally, intravenously, and subcutaneously.
- **Psychiatric:** Dorothea Dix and Cumberland Psychiatric Clinic, Raleigh and Pittsburgh, PA. Developed skill in the care and treatment of psychiatric patients.
- **Intensive Care Unit/Critical Care Unit (ICU/CCU):** Moore Regional Hospital, Pittsburgh, PA. Increased my abilities related to skilled nursing in challenging environments where patients required constant observation and stabilization.
- **Obstetrics/Labor & Delivery:** Valley Medical Center, Pittsburgh, PA. Served in the Newborn Nursery, NICU, Postpartem, Labor & Delivery, and Antenatal Testing units.
- **Pediatrics:** Valley Medical Center. Increased my knowledge while working with infant, juvenile, and adolescent patients.

PERSONAL　　Excellent personal and professional references are available upon request.

Date

Exact Name of Person
Exact Title
Exact Name of Company
Address
City, State, Zip

Dear Exact Name of Person: (or Dear Sir or Madam if answering a blind ad)

    I am writing to express my strong interest in exploring the possibility of becoming a Clinical Coordinator with your organization. With the enclosed resume, I would like to acquaint you with the extensive experience in emergency room, transplant center, and cardiovascular, surgical, and pediatric intensive care units which I could bring to your organization.

    Through my experience in surgical intensive care and in the transplant center, I have had the unique experience of seeing both sides of organ donation, from the courage of donors that chose to give of themselves to save the lives of others, to the miracles that transplantation can bring into the lives of the recipients. I would like to become an active part of this process, and I feel that I could make a strong contribution to your operation.

    In only four years as a Registered Nurse, I have excelled in nearly every critical and intensive care environment, and I have worked with a wide variety of patient populations. From Level I Trauma and surgical intensive care to organ transplantation in a major regional teaching hospital, where I gained experience with various "bridge to transplant" devices, I have constantly sought out formidable challenges in my career.

    If you can use a talented nursing professional with exceptional patient care skills and technical knowledge that have been proven in a variety of difficult environments, then I look forward to hearing from you soon. I assure you in advance that I would quickly become an asset to your organization, and I thank you for your time and consideration.

Yours sincerely,

Gina Sanders

GINA SANDERS

1110½ Hay Street, Fayetteville, NC 28305 • preppub@aol.com • (910) 483-6611

OBJECTIVE To benefit an organization that can use a dedicated nursing professional who thrives on challenge and offers extensive patient care experience in emergency room, transplant center, and cardiovascular, surgical, and pediatric intensive care environments.

EDUCATION **Bachelor of Science in Nursing,** State University of New York at Buffalo, Buffalo, NY, 1994; graduated **magna cum laude.**

CERTIFICATIONS Advanced Cardiac Life Support (ACLS) certification, scheduled for renewal 3/31/03. Basic Cardiac Life Support (BCLS) certification, expires 8/31/04.

AFFILIATIONS Member, **American Association of Critical Care Nurses,** 1994-present.
- **C.C.R.N.** since August, 2000.

Member, **Sigma Theta Tau International** (National Nursing Honor Society), Gamma Kappa Chapter, State University of New York at Buffalo, College of Nursing, 1999.

EXPERIENCE **REGISTERED NURSE, PEDIATRIC SPECIAL CARE UNIT.** Travel Nurse for Clinical One at Buffalo Valley Medical Center, Buffalo, NY (2002-present). Provide patient care for newborn, juvenile, and adolescent patients with a variety of serious medical illnesses that require skilled nursing in a pediatric intensive care environment.
- Contribute patient and family education in stressful situations requiring tact and diplomacy.
- Support and stabilization of pediatric population in various medical emergencies or impending crises.

REGISTERED NURSE. Northwest Texas Regional Medical Center, Amarillo, TX (1998-02). Provided patient care to post-operative cardiac, general surgery, and multi-organ trauma patients in the **Surgical Intensive Care Unit** and **Emergency Department** of this busy regional medical center which supports a Level I Trauma Unit.
- Demonstrated my versatility and adaptability while working two different departments; dealt with families and patients faced with life-changing illnesses and accidents which involved multi-organ trauma as well as severe head and spinal cord injuries.

With University Medical Center in Tucson, Arizona, advanced to positions of increasing responsibility at this major regional teaching hospital:
1996-98: **REGISTERED NURSE, CARDIOVASCULAR INTENSIVE CARE UNIT.** Excelled as a key member on a dedicated team of nurses in this challenging position with a fast-paced, aggressive University transplant center.
- Provided patient care to postoperative cardiac and vascular, heart and lung transplant, and other patients suffering from cardiac, pulmonary, and multisystem diseases.
- Gained valuable experience with "bridge to transplant" devices, including Cardio-West Artificial Heart and Ventricular Assist devices such as NOVOCOR, Thoratec, and IntraAortic Balloon Pump. Served as Clinical Preceptor for new RNs and RN candidates in the Cardiovascular Intensive Care Unit.

1994-96: **REGISTERED NURSE, CARDIAC INTERMEDIATE CARE UNIT.** Provided care for patients awaiting transplants as well as patient/family education on subjects related to lifestyle, diet, and medications after transplants; worked with a variety of patients requiring cardiac monitoring.

PERSONAL Known as a dedicated, hard-working professional with a passion for excellence.

Exact Name of Person
Exact Title
Exact Name of Company
Address
City, State, Zip

**REGISTERED NURSE &
ASSISTANT CLINICAL
COORDINATOR**

Dear Exact Name of Person (or Dear Sir or Madam if answering a blind ad):

With the enclosed resume, I would like to make you aware of my interest in exploring employment opportunities with your organization.

As you will see from my resume, I have recently completed my B.S. degree in Health Science and Psychology which adds another formal degree to my considerable experience as a Registered Nurse. Although I have worked in nearly all aspects of clinical nursing (pediatric, cardio-thoracic surgery, neurosurgical, emergency-trauma, acute psychiatric, med-surg), I have also excelled in administrative, teaching, and program management positions.

In a prior position as an Educator with Nursing Inc., a medical staffing organization, I trained other nursing professionals in medication effects and appropriate responses. In my position with Crenshaw Memorial, I have handled numerous human resource responsibilities while also reviewing budgets as well as coordinating and developing computer training for other employees. I have current knowledge in the area of reimbursable expenses for Medicare and Medicaid. Because of my strong communication skills, I have been appointed to several committees and administrative roles in which I work with physicians and medical administrators.

I am known for my unlimited personal initiative and have earned widespread respect for my ability to handle multiple simultaneous responsibilities. I offer a particular knack for excelling in sales situations, and I excelled as a Sales Associate for five years in Troy, AL while selling fine jewelry and providing outstanding customer service. I was named Top Sales Professional numerous times even though I was the youngest employee on the sales staff.

I am confident that I could become a valuable asset to an organization that can use a resourceful individual with a strong bottom-line orientation, and I hope you will contact me to suggest a time when we might meet to discuss your needs.

Yours sincerely,

Renee C. Price

RENEE C. PRICE

1110½ Hay Street, Fayetteville, NC 28305 • preppub@aol.com • (910) 483-6611

OBJECTIVE I want to contribute to an organization that can use a skilled medical professional who offers extensive nursing experience along with exceptionally strong communication and sales skills.

EDUCATION **Bachelor of Health Science & Psychology,** Troy State University, Montgomery, AL, 2002.
Associate Degree in Nursing, Troy Technical College, Troy, AL, 1999.
Completed numerous science courses and pre-nursing coursework, Troy State University, Troy, AL 1997.

LICENSES Licensed as an RN in AR (AR #123456) and TN (TN #987654321)
Received Certificates of Completion of courses related to Trauma Nurse Core Curriculum, Basic Cardiac Life Saving, Advanced Cardiac Life Saving, Pediatric Advanced Life Saving, and training related to Trauma Surgery-Neurological Patient.

EXPERIENCE **REGISTERED NURSE & ASSISTANT CLINICAL COORDINATOR.** Pike County Medical Center, Montgomery, AL (2003-present). Provide care to critically ill patients and serve as an Assistant Clinical Coordinator for one year.
- **Human resources responsibilities:** Orientate new employees; precept students from local colleges and from the internal critical care school. Interview candidates for unit manager positions and interview new RNs. Review the capital/non-capital budgets and make recommendations on allocations and projections.
- **Administrative appointments:** Am appointed to oversee Computer Program Development and computer skill training of other employees. Am in charge of staff development activities, and organize/present clinical in-services and continuing education. Am appointed to the Skin Care Committee.
- **Clinical activities:** Provide direct patient care full-time in Medical-Surgical ICU, ER-Trauma, Neurological Step Down Unit, Acute Psychiatric units, and rotate to Pediatric ICU, Cardio-Thoracic Surgical ICU. Usually perform Charge Nurse duties.

EDUCATOR. Nurses Inc., Montgomery, AL (2000-03). Refined my communication skills while instructing nursing assistants in medication side effects. Trained nursing professionals to provide the highest level of nursing care in group home settings. On my own initiative, organized quick reference data material for each group home.

REGISTERED NURSE & PROGRAM COORDINATOR. Crenshaw Memorial Hospital, Acute Care Psychiatric and Emergency Department, Troy, AL (1997-00). Co-developed a 12-step program for inpatients with alcohol/drug addictions; acted as Group Therapy Leader.
- In this job in which I worked simultaneously with the ones above, also handled extensive clinical nursing responsibilities. As Emergency Room Triage Nurse, provided care to acutely ill/emergent patients. Triaged patients and determined the severity of the illness.

Other experience:
TRAINER. Piccadilly Square Athletic Club, Troy, AL (1993-96). Instructed multiple aerobic classes weekly and assisted individuals in establishing personal training goals. Helped clients cultivate disciplined new approaches to fitness and personal training.
SALES ASSOCIATE. Gordon's Jewelers, Troy, AL (1990-93). Was Top Sales Professional numerous months; assisted clients in selecting jewelry; handled inventory control.

PERSONAL Strong references. Active in the community, was sought out as Counselor Educator for Drug Dependency Crisis of Pike County and CPR Instructor for Crenshaw County Education Center.

Date

Exact Name of Person
Exact Title
Exact Name of Company
Address
City, State, Zip

REGISTERED NURSE & CASE MANAGER

Dear Exact Name of Person (or Dear Sir or Madam if answering a blind ad):

With the enclosed resume, I would like to make you aware of my interest in exploring employment opportunities as a Registered Nurse. After living and working in South Carolina for 14 years, I have permanently relocated to Charleston in order to live near my extended family.

Currently, I am employed as a Registered Nurse and Case Manager for the Medical University of South Carolina. Before assuming responsibilities as a Case Manager, I worked in the hospital's outpatient area as well as in the Pain Management Clinic. As a Registered Nurse and Case Manager, I earned respect for my skill in helping patients and their family work through long-term placement issues. From 1998-02, I worked at the Saint Francis-Xavier Hospital in Greenville, SC where I perfected my IV skills while preparing patients and their charts for surgery. At Saint Francis, I also worked in postpartum, in post-gynecology surgery, and in the Newborn Nursery.

I have earned a reputation as a caring and compassionate individual with an ability to work effectively with patients and their families as well as with physicians and other medical professionals. If my background and skills interest you, I hope you will contact me to suggest a time when we could meet in person to discuss your needs. I can provide excellent personal and professional references. Thank you in advance for your time and courtesies.

Yours sincerely,

Lisa F. Mitchell

LISA F. MITCHELL, R.N.

1110½ Hay Street, Fayetteville, NC 28305 • preppub@aol.com • (910) 483-6611

OBJECTIVE	I want to contribute to an organization that can use a skilled Registered Nurse (R.N.) with ICU, PCU, OB, outpatient, medical, and surgical experience who offers a proven ability to communicate effectively with physicians and peers while serving the needs of patients.
EDUCATION & LICENSES	Graduated as R.N., Medical University of South Carolina School of Nursing, Charleston, SC 1990. Current RN license for SC Current BLS and ACLS (CPR) Completed Cardiology Arrhythmia course
EXPERIENCE	**At Medical University of South Carolina, Charleston, SC, worked in positions as an Outpatient R.N. and now as an R.N. & Case Manager:** **2004-present: REGISTERED NURSE (R.N.) & CASE MANAGER.** Work as an R.N. & Case Manager in the outpatient area of a busy surgical floor; also work as a Case Manager filling in on the Intensive Care and Trauma Units and the OB/Newborn Care Center. • Was commended for my skill in working through difficult long-term placement issues with patients and their families. **2002-04: REGISTERED NURSE (R.N.).** Until I assumed case management responsibilities, I worked as an Outpatient R.N., preparing patients for surgery and discharging them after providing appropriate guidance and teaching. Also worked in the Pain Management Clinic; was involved in drawing blood, performing EKGs, and other functions. Administered blood transfusions and IV antibiotics. **At Saint Francis-Xavier Hospital, Greenville, SC, worked for four years in varying capacities:** **1999-02: R.N., OUTPATIENT DEPARTMENT.** Perfected my IV skills in this position which involved working in the pre-operative area; prepared patients for surgery and prepared their charts for surgery. **1998-99: R.N.** Worked as an R.N. in postpartum, post-gynecology surgery, and in the Newborn Nursery. • Became skilled in managing the postoperative patient as I refined my OB skills. **R.N., STAFF RELIEF.** Olsten Staffing, Greenville, SC (1996-98). Worked as an R.N. in the Skilled Nursing Care Unit and the Postpartum Unit while employed as a staff relief nurse through a local medical staffing agency. **REGISTERED NURSE, OB DEPARTMENT.** Medical University of South Carolina, Charleston, SC (1993-96). Worked as an R.N. in a busy postpartum area, a newborn nursery, as well as the labor and delivery areas. Demonstrated my flexibility and adaptability while rotating to areas of primary need. **REGISTERED NURSE.** Pleasant Living Retirement Home, Charleston, SC (1990-93). Gained insight into the geriatric population while working as an R.N. in a long-term care facility.
PERSONAL	Can provide excellent personal and professional references. Am a compassionate and empathetic individual who easily establishes rapport with patients, families, and medical professionals. Relocated to Charleston, SC where my extended family lives.

Date

Exact Name of Person
Exact Title
Exact Name of Company
Address
City, State, Zip

**REGISTERED NURSE &
HEAD NURSE**

Dear Exact Name of Person (or Dear Sir or Madam if answering a blind ad):

With the enclosed resume, I would like to make you aware of my interest in exploring employment opportunities with your organization and introduce you to my knowledge of pharmaceuticals and pharmacology as well as my experience in clinical nursing and medical sales/consultation. It is my desire to work as a Registered Nurse/ Head Nurse for your medical facility.

As you will see from my resume, I am currently working in simultaneous positions as a full-time Registered Nurse/Head Nurse and as a part-time college instructor of anatomy and physiology courses for pre-med and pre-nursing students. In addition to handling clinical and supervisory responsibilities as a Head Nurse, I assumed significant bottom-line responsibilities as I marketed the benefits of non-invasive procedures. During clinical rotations as I pursued my two nursing degrees, I became knowledgeable of a wide range of pharmaceuticals used with most types of patients: renal/diabetic, ortho/ neuro, Parkinson's, Alzheimer's, dementia, med/surg, psychiatric, and labor/delivery. It was during those clinical rotations that I became aware that I wished to pursue a career in pharmaceutical sales after gaining experience in clinical nursing.

I can provide outstanding personal and professional references. Because of my outstanding personal reputation and superior academic track record, Penn Valley Community College aggressively recruited me to join its faculty on a part-time basis, and I developed and taught curricula for anatomy and physiology courses.

While obtaining my degree in nursing, I had an opportunity to undertake clinical rotations in a variety of areas. Those clinical rotations included med/surg, home health, obstetrics and pediatrics, psychiatry, public health and community health, and other observations. I am seeking employment in an environment able to use my clinical nursing skills and up-to-date knowledge. I can provide outstanding references from all previous employers.

If you can use a highly respected R.N. to represent your medical facility, I would enjoy the opportunity to meet with you to discuss your needs. I hope you will contact me to suggest a time when we could meet in person. Thank you.

Yours sincerely,

Christine M. Gautier

CHRISTINE M. GAUTIER

1110½ Hay Street, Fayetteville, NC 28305 • preppub@aol.com • (910) 483-6611

OBJECTIVE

To contribute to an organization that can use a vibrant and enthusiastic Registered Nurse with extensive knowledge of pharmaceuticals and pharmacology along with strong sales and communication skills refined through medical consulting and college teaching experience.

EDUCATION

Bachelor of Science in Nursing (BSN) degree, University of Missouri at Kansas City, MO, 2002. Excelled academically with a 3.6 GPA.
Associate of Science Degree in Nursing (ADN), Penn Valley Community College, Kansas City, MO, 1999. 3.4 GPA. Merit Scholarship recipient and President's Honor Roll member.

EXPERIENCE

Excelled in simultaneous full-time and part-time position while residing in Kansas City, KS:
2004-present: REGISTERED NURSE & HEAD NURSE. A.C. Tuttle Health Clinic, Kansas City, MO. Manage, direct, and train a nursing staff of four nurses while providing medical consulting to potential customers of non-invasive cosmetic and reconstructive procedures which included laser therapy, chemical peels, and endermology.
• Advise potential new patients on medical procedures and pharmaceutical aids.

2001-04: ANATOMY & PHYSIOLOGY INSTRUCTOR. Penn Valley Community College, Kansas City, MO. Was aggressively recruited because of my outstanding academic record and personal reputation to teach courses for pre-med, pre-nursing, pre-dental, pre-PA, and pre-physical therapy students. Developed curricula for and taught classroom and lab courses in anatomy and physiology for the Department of Mathematics, Sciences, and Health Sciences.

2001: REGISTERED NURSE. Wyanotte County Correctional Medical Services (WCCMS), Kansas City, MO. On a per diem basis, provided health services including health assessments.

Clinical rotations and other nursing employment: Kansas City, MO. Gained vast insights into pharmacology and pharmaceuticals while working in the following clinical rotations in the process of earning my two nursing degrees.
1999-01: Renal-diabetic patients: At Mid-America Nazarene Medical University, in a full-time job with renal/diabetic patients, observed insulin preparations and oral hypoglycemic agents.
1999: Ortho/neuro patients: At Pain Management Therapy Center, provided medical and surgical nursing care for orthotics, neurological, and rehab patients; observed the effects of anti-inflammatory drugs, nonsteroidal anti-inflammatory agents, basic narcotics, patient controlled analgesia pumps, and a variety of antibiotics.
1998-99: Mental health and psychiatric patients: At Central Missouri Hospital, observed patients being treated with anxiolytics, antipsychotics, sedatives/hypnotics, anticonvulsants, antimanics, antidepressants, bipolar medications, and other psychotherapeutic agents.
1998: Diabetic patients: At Penn Valley Dialysis, observed renal/diabetic treatment/dialysis.
1996-98: Med/surg and trauma patients: At Harper Hospital, performed mini-rotations in OB-GYN, gastrointestinal, OR, and ER; became knowledgeable of med/surg drugs.
1996: Parkinson's, Alzheimer's, and dementia patients: At Northwestern Nursing Home, worked with geriatric patients and observed pharmacological treatments using antihypertensive agents, antidepressants, vasodilators, and corticosteroids.

Sales experience: Kansas City, MO (1993-96). Was a Sales Consultant for four years for a bookstore while earning my college degree. Became skilled in sales/customer service.

PERSONAL

Highly motivated and intelligent individual. Fluent in conversational French.

Date

Exact Name of Person
Exact Title
Exact Name of Company
Address
City, State, Zip

REGISTERED NURSE
STUDENT

Dear Exact Name of Person (or Dear Sir or Madam if answering a blind ad):

With the enclosed resume, I would like to make you aware of my interest in exploring employment opportunities with your organization and introduce you to my nursing credentials.

As you will see from my resume, I am pursing a Bachelor of Science degree in Nursing at California State University. I have already earned an associate degree in nursing, and I was named to the President's List because of my excellent academic performance. I am especially proud of this accomplishment because I earned my degree in my spare time while also excelling in my full-time job in the health care field.

In my full-time job at an intermediate care facility for developmentally disabled adults, I advanced into a supervisory role in which I managed up to four staff members per shift. While gaining insight into the needs of mentally retarded and developmentally disabled clients, I applied my strong assessment and problem-solving skills to resolve numerous long-standing problems at the facility. For example, I reduced the occurrence of medical errors and clients accidents through the steps I took to retrain staff, educate clients, and provide clear procedures which prevented accidents. I also took strong initiative when I discovered intake/outtake issues, and I designed procedures which eliminated the problems. After discovering problems with inventory control, I took steps which ensured the proper receipt and disposition of medications and controlled substances. While in that supervisory role, I found that training and retraining is the key to successful staff performance.

While I'm obtaining my second degree in nursing, I have had an opportunity to undertake clinical rotations in a variety of areas. Those clinical rotations included med/surg, home health, obstetrics and pediatrics, psychiatry, public health and community health, and other observations. I am seeking employment in an environment which can use my clinical nursing skills and up-to-date knowledge. I can provide outstanding references from all previous employers.

Yours sincerely,

Francis G. Powell

FRANCIS G. POWELL

1110½ Hay Street, Fayetteville, NC 28305   •   preppub@aol.com   •   (910) 483-6611

OBJECTIVE   I want to benefit an organization that can use a dedicated Registered Nurse who offers strong problem-solving abilities, communication skills, and management skills.

EDUCATION   Pursing a **Bachelor of Arts degree** in **Nursing,** California State University, Fresno, CA. Received **Associate of Applied Science degree** and the **Associate Degree** in **Nursing,** Fresno City College, Fresno, CA, 2001.
- Was named to the President's List; excelled academically.

LICENSES   Licensed Registered Nurse in CA.

EXPERIENCE   **REGISTERED NURSE STUDENT.** Phillip-Handler Specialty Care, Fresno, CA (2003-present). Completing my Bachelor's Degree in Nursing in my spare time while working full-time in a residential care facility, Phillip-Handler Specialty Care.
Clinical rotations: Currently refining my nursing skills through performing clinical rotations in these areas:

Med-surg   Obstetrics and pediatrics   Psychiatry
Home health   Public health/community health   Other observations

HEALTH CARE TECHNICIAN & SHIFT SUPERVISOR. Pearlmann, Richards, and Associates, Fresno, CA (2000-03). Began working as a Health Care Technician at this intermediate care facility for developmentally disabled adults, and advanced into a supervisory role providing oversight for the care provided to six senior adults.
- Supervised up to four staff members per shift; trained new staff members.
- Supervised the receipt and storage of medications and controlled substances; inspected medications upon receipt and assured their proper
- Gained insight into the needs of mentally retarded and developmentally disabled clients.
- Implemented recreational/social development programs while assisting clients with self-help skills related to feeding and personal hygiene.
- Administered medications according to physician orders.
- On my own initiative, made many lasting contributions to this health care facility. Identified methods of saving time and money without compromising safety. For example, developed charts as well as sign-in/sign-out sheets to help staff control inventory. Took the initiative when I discovered intake/outtake problems, and designed new procedures which eliminated the problems. Identified staff training deficiencies, and developed training sheets which permitted the documentation of all training.
- Made significant contributions to client safety. Reduced the occurrence of medical errors and client accidents through applying my strong analytical and problem-solving skills. Taught staff members safe medication administration procedures, and provided the supervisory follow-up after training which was necessary. Was able to resolve many long-standing problems at this facility.
- Prepared written reports daily; maintained seizure records, vigilantly maintained notes for psychologists, and prepared shift reports.
- Extensively communicated with staff, physicians, family members, and others.

PERSONAL   Excellent assessment skills. Adapt quickly to new environments. Am an outgoing individual. Can provide excellent personal and professional references.

Date

Exact Name of Person
Exact Title
Exact Name of Company
Address
City, State, Zip

Dear Exact Name of Person (or Dear Sir or Madam if answering a blind ad):

With the enclosed resume, I would like to make you aware of my interest in exploring employment opportunities with your organization and introduce you to my nursing credentials.

As you will see from my resume, I recently resigned from my position as a Registered Nurse Supervisor in a 125-bed long-term care facility in order to seek a position which will involve me in more complex clinical nursing responsibilities. I previously worked at that same facility as an LPN Charge Nurse, and I can provide outstanding references.

Prior to entering the nursing field, I served my country with distinction in the U.S. Army and rose to the highest enlisted rank—Sergeant Major. I began my military career in the telecommunications and was subsequently selected for vital management positions in aviation and combat organizations, and I received more than 15 medals, awards, and other honors in recognition of my contributions. On numerous written performance evaluations, I was commended for "dynamic leadership ability." While managing hundreds of individuals and controlling budgets of various sizes, I took the initiative to improve safety, quality control, and human resources programs in all organizations in which I worked.

After leaving the military, I became a full-time student working toward completion of my credentials as a Registered Nurse. My clinical rotations included med-surg, home health, obstetrics and pediatrics, public health and community health, psychiatry, and other observations.

Although I enjoyed the challenge of providing skilled nursing care to the geriatric population, I have decided that I wish to work in a fast-paced environment which can utilize more of my clinical nursing skills and knowledge. If you can use a dedicated professional who can provide outstanding references from all previous employers, please contact me to suggest a time when we might meet to discuss your needs. Thank you in advance for your time.

Yours sincerely,

Carol V. Underwood

CAROL V. UNDERWOOD

1110½ Hay Street, Fayetteville, NC 28305   •   preppub@aol.com   •   (910) 483-6611

OBJECTIVE	To contribute to an organization that can use a dedicated Registered Nurse who offers extensive supervisory skills acquired in critical managerial positions.
EDUCATION	**Associate of Science Degree in Nursing,** Northcentral Technical College, Wausau, WI, 2002.

Associate in General Education, Northcentral Technical College, Wausau, WI, 2001.
- Named to the President's List with a 3.7 GPA.

Diploma in Practical Nursing, Northcentral Technical College, Wausau, WI, 2001.

Completed extensive management training sponsored by the U.S. Army including the Sergeant Major Academy, Leadership Development courses, and Instructor Training courses.

LICENSES   **Licensed Registered Nurse** in WI, #1234578; licensed LPN; hold CNA I and II.

COMPUTERS   Proficient with software including Word, Excel, PowerPoint, and numerous graphics programs.

EXPERIENCE   **REGISTERED NURSE SUPERVISOR (promoted from LPN Charge Nurse).** Wisconsin Veterans Nursing Home, Wausau, WI (2004-present). At this 125-bed long-term care facility, handle the responsibilities of an LPN Charge Nurse. After receiving my Associate Degree in Nursing in 2002 and passing the state boards, assumed the position of RN Supervisor.
- Recently resigned my position at this geriatric facility in order to seek a job which will involve me in a wider range of clinical nursing responsibilities including med-surg.

Clinical rotations: While working full-time, earned my A.S. degree in Nursing in my spare time; refined my nursing skills performing clinical rotations in these areas:

Med-surg	Obstetrics and pediatrics	Psychiatry
Home health	Public health/community health	Other observations

FULL-TIME NURSING STUDENT. Northcentral Technical College, Wausau, WI (2002-04). After serving with distinction in the U.S. Army, I decided to pursue nursing studies.

Previous experience: Served in the U.S. Army, and was promoted to the highest enlisted rank—Sergeant Major. Following are highlights of my military career:
OPERATIONS MANAGER. Fort Eustis, VA (1999-02). As the highest ranking noncommissioned officer at the rank of Sergeant Major, provided oversight for planning services supporting the 377th Med Company. Supervised more than 28 employees who included mid-level managers, clerks, drivers, communications technicians, and others.

OPERATIONS SUPERVISOR. Fort Jackson, SC (1996-99). Managed 15 individuals for combat aviation group; on my own initiative, made numerous contributions to efficiency.

PERSONNEL MANAGER & QUALITY CONTROL MANAGER. Germany (1993-96). Managed 18 office professionals while handling responsibility for quality control of personnel records for more than 800 people.

OPERATIONS CHIEF. Fort Eustis, VA (1991-93). Supervised ten people; managed training programs.

TRAINING CHIEF. Fort Carson, CO (1989-91). Supervised training activities for 120 people.

PERSONAL   Proficient with software including Word, Excel, PowerPoint, and numerous graphics programs. Can provide excellent personal and professional references.

Date

Exact Name of Person
Exact Title
Exact Name of Company
Address
City, State, Zip

RESPIRATORY CARE NURSE

Dear Exact Name of Person (or Dear Sir or Madam if answering a blind ad):

With the enclosed resume, I would like to make you aware of an experienced licensed practical nurse with exceptional time management and communication skills and a background in obstetrics and gynecology, respiratory care of ventilator patients, and general patient care.

In my most recent position with the Veteran's Administration Medical Center, I specialized in providing nursing care to respiratory patients, many of whom were totally dependent on ventilators and other life support equipment. I closely monitored the operation of this equipment to ensure that it was functioning properly. I also provided care to a number of physically challenged patients in addition to those that I cared for in my area of specialty.

At Servantes Medical Center, I served as an Obstetrics and Gynecology Nurse, where my primary responsibilities were caring for new and expectant mothers, transporting patients in labor to the delivery room, and providing nursing care in the obstetrics recovery room and newborn nursery.

I earned a certificate from the Licensed Practical Nursing Program at Sanderson Technical Community College and am licensed in the state of Oklahoma. I have supplemented my degree program with numerous continuing education courses designed to keep my medical skills up to date. My education and experience could be a valuable addition to your organization.

If you can use a motivated, caring Licensed Practical Nurse, I hope you will contact me to suggest a time when we might meet to discuss your needs. I can assure you in advance that I have an excellent reputation and would quickly become a valuable asset to your company.

Sincerely,

Megan Long

MEGAN LONG

1110½ Hay Street, Fayetteville, NC 28305 • preppub@aol.com • (910) 483-6611

OBJECTIVE

To benefit an organization that can use an experienced licensed practical nurse with exceptional organizational skills and a background in respiratory care of ventilator patients, obstetrics and gynecology, and general patient care.

EDUCATION

Graduated from the **Licensed Practical Nursing program**, Sanderson Technical Community College, Sanderson, OK, 1990.

Completed two years of additional nursing studies at the Medical Center School of Nursing in Columbus, GA.

Have attended numerous courses to supplement and update my medical knowledge, including the following:

- Communicable diseases, 60 hours, 2001.
- Orthopedics and AIDS – new methods of treatment, 60 hours, 2001.
- Ventilator care, 60 hours, 2001.
- Respiratory care, 8 hours, 2000.

LICENSES

Oklahoma Licensed Practical Nurse #009190, expires 12/31/05.

AFFILIATIONS

Secretary, Oklahoma Licensed Practical Nurses Association, 2001.

EXPERIENCE

With the Veteran's Administration Medical Center, advanced in the following "track record" of increasing responsibilities:

RESPIRATORY CARE NURSE. Sanderson, OK (2000-03). Served as a Licensed Practical Nurse, specializing in medical-surgical patients who were dependent on ventilators.

- Closely monitored the operation of respirators and other life support equipment to ensure that it was functioning properly.
- Administered medications to patients as directed by physicians.
- Performed emergency respiratory treatments, such as oxygen administration and IPPB treatments.
- Checked patient's vital signs and changed IV bags.
- Provided nursing care to other physically challenged patients in addition to my patients in the respirator ward.

LICENSED PRACTICAL NURSE. Sanderson, OK (1995-00). Provided continuous patient care in this busy medical center.

- Monitored, measured and recorded patient's vital signs; updated charts.
- Administered medication as directed by physicians.
- Transported patients between departments.
- Bathed patients and changed dressings.
- Assisted in other procedures under the supervision of registered nurses and doctors.
- Mastered time management while providing nursing care to a large number of patients within a limited amount of time.

Other experience: **OBSTETRICS and GYNECOLOGY NURSE.** Servantes Medical Center, Sanderson, OK (1990-94). Provided care as a Licensed Practical Nurse to obstetrics, gynecology, maternal, and newborn patients in this large medical center.

- Transported patients to labor room.
- Provided nursing care in obstetrics recovery room and newborn nursery.

PERSONAL

Excellent personal and professional references are available upon request.

Exact Name of Person
Exact Title
Exact Name of Company
Address
City, State, Zip

**SENIOR PROFESSIONAL
REPRESENTATIVE**

Dear Exact Name of Person (or Dear Sir or Madam if answering a blind ad):

With the enclosed resume, I would like to make you aware of my interest in exploring employment opportunities with your organization and introduce you to my knowledge of pharmaceuticals and pharmacology as well as my experience in clinical nursing and medical sales/consultation. It is my desire to work as a Sales Professional Representative with your firm.

As you will see from my resume, I excelled in simultaneous positions as a full-time Head Nurse/Staff Nurse. In addition to handling clinical and supervisory responsibilities as a Head Nurse, I assumed significant bottom-line responsibilities as I marketed the benefits of non-invasive procedures. During my employment with Broward Medical Hospital, I became knowledgeable of a wide range of pharmaceuticals used with most types of patients. It was during those clinical rotations that I became aware that I wished to pursue a career in pharmaceutical sales after gaining experience while working for a large medical center.

I can provide outstanding personal and professional references. Because of my outstanding personal reputation and superior academic track record at Nova Southeastern University aggressively recruited me to join its faculty, and I managed staff members in both Fort Lauderdale and the metro Miami medical territories.

If we have the opportunity to meet in person, you will see that I am an articulate individual with an outgoing personality which would be well suited to pharmaceutical sales. If you can use a highly respected R.N. to represent your fine product line, I would enjoy the opportunity to meet with you to discuss your needs. I hope you will contact me to suggest a time when we could meet in person. Thank you.

Yours sincerely,

Edna D. Schultz

EDNA D SCHULTZ

1110½ Hay Street, Fayetteville, NC 28305 • preppub@aol.com • (910) 483-6611

OBJECTIVE To secure a position as a pharmaceutical sales representative with a leading, growth-oriented company that can use an exceptionally qualified nursing professional with outstanding sales and communication skills.

EDUCATION **Bachelor of Science in Nursing,** cum laude, Nova Southeastern University, Fort Lauderdale, FL, 2000.
Developed a self-help support group for diabetic patients which later became the Broward County Diabetic Chapter of the National Association for Diabetes.
Completed graduate course in **Management Theory and Practice** at Florida Atlantic University, Boca Raton, FL.
Associate of Applied Science in Nursing, Broward Community College, Fort Lauderdale, FL.

EXPERIENCE **SENIOR PROFESSIONAL REPRESENTATIVE.** Cauldwell Pharmaceuticals, Fort Lauderdale, FL (2002-present). Successfully manage both Metro Miami territory (2001-03), including both community and hospital experience as well as a territory headquartered in Fort Lauderdale, FL (2002-present), including other large surrounding medical centers in the rural area.
- Develop and implement business plan for military market which resulted in formulary additions of Cauldwell products as well as reversing negative sales trends for existing Cauldwell products.
- Achieve 95% sales objective throughout pharmaceutical sales career (6.8 million dollar territory in 2002).
- Serve as class counselor for national sales training program and a mentor for new representatives.

HEAD NURSE. Broward Medical Hospital, Fort Lauderdale, FL (1998-02). Managed nursing staff at this 520-bed teaching hospital including hiring staff, scheduling, nurse education, resident supervision, and new employee orientation.
- Responsible for staff and patient education programs.

STAFF NURSE. Kindred Care Medical, Fort Lauderdale, FL (1996-98). Successfully conducted cardiac education program as well as directed patient care for the Cardio-Pulmonary Unit.

STAFF NURSE. St. Joseph's Children's Hospital, Fort Lauderdale, FL (1994-96). Provided direct patient care with emphasis upon child patient care and education at an affiliated Catholic Hospital.

HONORS Promoted to Senior Professional Representative, Cauldwell Pharmaceuticals, 2003.
Nominated as Top District Representative in the nation, 2002.
Member of the International Association of Nursing.
Member of Nova Southeastern University's Honor Society.

PERSONAL References Available Upon Request

Date

Exact Name of Person
Exact Title
Exact Name of Company
Address
City, State, Zip

STAFF NURSE   Dear Exact Name of Person: (or Dear Sir or Madam if answering a blind ad)

With the enclosed resume, I would like to make you aware of my interest in a pharmaceutical sales position with your company.

Although I am excelling in my current position as a Trauma/Surgical Intensive Care Unit Nurse at Columbus University Medical Center, I have decided that I wish to embark on a career in medical marketing and sales. My naturally outgoing personality and ability to establish strong relationships would be well-suited to pharmaceutical sales. For example, I was recently honored by being nominated by patients' families for a prestigious award given by Columbus for "outstanding care of family members." Respected for my gracious and personable style of interacting with others, I am intimately familiar with the organizational culture of hospitals and clinics and have a nurse's understanding of a wide range of pharmaceutical treatments.

Prior to graduating with a B.S. in Nursing from the University of Georgia at Atlanta in 1998, I gained clinical experience in orthopedic, pediatric, OB/GYN, community health, and surgical/ICU environments. One summer I worked with a pharmaceutical company aiding a pediatric hematologist/oncologist in research related to neutropenia.

With a reputation as an articulate and persuasive communicator, I gained valuable sales skills in summer jobs as a bank teller, a sales representative in the UGA Alumni Annual Fund office, and in Columbus University's athletic office.

I assure you that my decision to leave the clinical medical environment for pharmaceutical sales is a well-thought-out decision. I have been very deliberate about my career. Although I entered college as a Political Science major at Columbus University and excelled academically for two years, I decided to embark on a nursing career and transferred to the University of Atlanta where I maintained a 3.7 GPA in my major while earning my B.S. in Nursing. Now I wish to transfer my clinical experience and knowledge into pharmaceutical sales, and I am confident that I will be successful in contributing to a company's bottom line.

I hope you will welcome my call soon when I try to arrange a brief meeting to discuss your goals and how my background might serve your needs. I can provide outstanding references at the appropriate time.

Sincerely,

Anita Michelle Carlton

ANITA MICHELLE CARLTON

1110½ Hay Street, Fayetteville, NC 28305 • preppub@aol.com • (910) 483-6611

OBJECTIVE   To contribute my skills as an articulate and outgoing young medical professional to an organization that can use a Pharmaceutical Sales Representative who offers a track record of excellence as a nurse, outstanding communication skills, and previous sales experience.

HONOR   Have been nominated by patients' families to receive a respected award for outstanding care of their family members.

CERTIFICATIONS   Licensed **Registered Nurse,** Georgia Board of Nursing.
Certified as an Advanced Cardiac Life Support (ACLS), 1999, and Basic Cardiac Life Support (BCLS) provider, 1997, by the American Heart Association.

EDUCATION   **Bachelor of Science** in **Nursing**, University of Georgia at Atlanta, GA, May 1998.
- UNC Nursing GPA 3.5; maintained 3.7 GPA for both semesters in 1997.

B.A. in **Political Science**, University of Georgia at Atlanta, GA, 1996; **3.2 GPA**.
Completed two years of studies in Political Science, Columbus University, Columbus, GA, 1992-94. Columbus GPA 3.2; transferred to UGA in 1994 in order to pursue nursing career.
- Awarded **First Union Merit Scholarship,** 1993-94, for leadership and scholarship.

Completed training programs and workshops in CPR, BCLS, and ACLS.

EXPERIENCE   **STAFF NURSE (Trauma/Surgical ICU).** Columbus University Medical Center, Columbus, GA (2002-present). Provide total nursing care to postoperative and trauma patients at this prestigious regional medical center and teaching hospital.
- Perform patient assessment and telemetry monitoring, communicating information on the patient's response to treatment to the surgical resident or attending physician.
- Administer medications, fluids, and blood products; set up and monitor IVs.
- Provide education and support to patients and their families, performing liaison between the patient's families and doctors.

NURSE AIDE II (Surgical ICU). Columbus University Medical Center, Columbus, GA (1997-02). Was offered a job on Surgical ICU after excelling in my summer externship.
- Assisted nurses in providing care to SICU patients. Administered enteral feedings, performed dressing changes, baths, linen changes, and equipment quality control checks.

NURSE EXTERN (Surgical ICU). Columbus University Medical Center, Columbus, GA (1997). Was specially selected for this externship from a large pool of applicants, and excelled in every aspect of my first clinical care experience in one of the nation's top medical centers.
- At the end of this 10-week program in which I worked 36 hours per week providing care to critically ill surgical patients, performed RN responsibility under preceptor's supervision.

Other clinical experience: Completed three seven-week clinical rotations at UG Hospitals: one at Chris Johnson Hospital, one at Brookstone Clinic, and one at Columbus Medical Center.

Research experience: For two semesters at UGA in 1995, worked with a pediatric hematologist/oncologist in setting up a database of patients with neutropenia for Amgen, Inc.
- Once the registry was set up, the patients received a very expensive treatment, G-CSF, at no cost while the pharmaceutical company Amgen, Inc., gathered data on neutropenia.

PERSONAL   Have a thorough knowledge of the organizational culture of hospitals and clinics.

Date

Exact Name of Person
Exact Title
Exact Name of Company
Address
City, State, Zip

**STAFF REGISTERED
NURSE**

for an emergency
department

Dear Exact Name of Person: (or Dear Sir or Madam if answering a blind ad)

With the enclosed resume, I would like to make you aware of my qualifications for the position of Radiology Staff Nurse, specifically my background as a radiology nurse with more than nine years of service to Anderson Medical Center, and the extensive list of certifications and credentials with which I have supplemented that experience.

I am currently excelling as a Staff Registered Nurse in the Emergency Department, where my primary duty is to serve as Triage Nurse. I interview presenting patients, assigning a triage category and prioritizing the placement of patients into the appropriate treatment areas based on the nature and severity of the patient's condition. I monitor the condition of patients in the waiting area, and upgrade or downgrade their assigned triage categories based on changes in patient condition.

Although I am highly regarded within the Emergency Department, and can provide excellent references at the appropriate time, it is my desire to return to Radiology, where I previously served with distinction. As you will see, I hold certifications in ACLS, BCLS, and PALS, in addition to credentials which qualify me to administer a wide range of medications specific to radiology procedures, including nuclear medicines and special procedures.

My knowledge, my skills, and above all, my personal loyalty made me a strong asset to the Radiology Department in the past, and would continue to do so in the future. I was proud to be a part of the growth and development of the radiology team during the nine years I served, and I would relish the opportunity to rejoin that team. I have a deep respect for the expertise and reputation of the radiology team headed by Dr. Quantas, and it is my strong desire to be of service to him and the team.

Sincerely,

Larry French

LARRY FRENCH

1110½ Hay Street, Fayetteville, NC 28305   •   preppub@aol.com   •   (910) 483-6611

OBJECTIVE

To benefit an organization that can use an educated and experienced radiology nurse with exceptional communication and organizational skills in addition to extensive certifications and credentials specific to radiological medicine.

EDUCATION

Advanced Trauma Life Support Program, Pitt Memorial Medical Center, Greenville, SC, 1990.
Critical Care Core Curriculum, North Carolina Memorial Hospital, Chapel Hill, NC, 1988.
Associate's degree in Nursing, Sandhills Community College, Southern Pines, NC, 1986.
Completed one year of college course work at Campbell University, Buies Creek, NC, 1983.

CERTIFICATIONS

Licensed **Registered Nurse** certificate #079912, North Carolina Board of Nursing, expires December 2005.
Pediatric Advanced Life Support (PALS) Certified, expires September 2004.
Advanced Cardiac Life Support (ACLS) Certified, expires November 2002.
Basic Cardiac Life Support (BCLS) Certified, expires March 2004.

EXPERIENCE

STAFF REGISTERED NURSE. Emergency Department, Anderson Medical Center, Chapel Hill, NC (2002-present). Provide patient triage and nursing care in the Emergency Department of this busy regional medical center.
- Conduct patient assessment and initiate diagnostic procedures for appropriate presenting patients.
- Assign each patient to the appropriate triage category based on the nature and severity of the patient's condition.
- Place patients into the appropriate treatment area according to triage category and prioritize order of treatment.
- Observe and monitor all patients in the waiting room of the Emergency Department, upgrading or downgrading assigned triage categories according to patient condition.
- Demonstrate communication skills while conducting triage interviews and communicating patient needs related to condition to the supervisor or charge nurse.

STAFF REGISTERED NURSE. Radiology Department, Anderson Medical Center, Chapel Hill, NC (1993-2002). Performed patient assessment, patient and staff education, and implemented treatment plans and crisis intervention for radiology patients.
- Administered medication both orally and intravenously, to include conscious sedation, pain management, anti-coagulants, and coronary-specific medications.
- Observed cardiopulmonary measuring devices, monitoring the patient's condition and providing crisis intervention. Assisted in the development and implementation of policies and procedures for nursing practice standards in the Radiology Department.
- Conducted contrast injection I.V.P. studies to aid in patient diagnosis.
- Earned radiology-specific credentials in the following procedures: nitroglycerin I.A. infusion, urokinase infusion, contrast injection I.V.P. studies, persantine infusion study, adenosine infusion study, and dobutamine infusion study.

STAFF REGISTERED NURSE. Emergency Room, Anderson Medical Center, Greensboro, NC (1989-1993). Performed patient assessment and assignment of triage categories, trauma nursing, crisis intervention, and acute care of adults and children (infants through adolescents).

PERSONAL

Excellent personal and professional references are available upon request.

Many nursing professionals will want to seek a career in the federal government. Applications for federal employment are usually different from applications for civilian employment, and the purpose of this section is to briefly show examples of paperwork you may encounter when you apply for federal positions.

What is a "job vacancy announcement?"

When there is a job opening in the federal government, usually there is a job vacancy announcement which describes the duties and qualifications pertaining to the job. A job vacancy announcement, sometimes called a "bulletin," will also provide guidance on exactly what you must submit in order to apply for the position. Look carefully at the description of duties provided on the job vacancy announcement, and make sure you tailor your federal resume appropriately to that announcement. The announcement may suggest that you could apply for the position by submitting a form 612, a form 171, or a federal resume (or Resumix). Often that announcement will provide specifics about what should be contained in the federal resume. Some job vacancy announcements even specify how long the federal resume should be.

Is a cover letter used in applying for federal government positions?

Although a cover letter is an extremely important document when applying for civilian positions, federal positions do not usually require a cover letter. Indeed, the job vacancy announcement described above is very detailed about what you should submit, and you will probably be wasting your time if you send a cover letter when the job vacancy announcement does not ask for one.

What is a Resumix or federal resume?

The best way to describe a Resumix or federal resume is to show examples. You will find examples of federal resumes in the first few pages of this Part Four. In general, you are asked to provide more detailed information in a federal resume than in a civilian resume about matters such as your salary history and your supervisors' names and phone numbers.

What are KSAs?

Sometimes written statements, often called "narratives," are required when you apply for federal government positions, and those "elements," as they also are frequently called, relate to areas of knowledge, skills, and abilities which are required in the job advertised. These "KSAs" are extremely important in the process of determining who is the best candidate for the position.

"Civilian" resume and cover letter of Cecilia Steinberg

Date

Exact Name of Person
Exact Title
Exact Name of Company
Address
City, State, Zip

A LICENSED PRACTICAL NURSE

On the next four pages you will see the "civilian resume" and cover letter as well as the "federal resume" used by this individual to find job opportunities in both the civilian job market and the federal government. On the first two pages you will see the resume and cover letter used to compete for civilian jobs.

Dear Exact Name of Person (or Dear Sir or Madam if answering a blind ad):

With the enclosed resume, I would like to make you aware of my interest in exploring employment opportunities with your organization as a Licensed Practical Nurse.

As you will see from my resume, I received my Associate's degree and my Diploma in Practical Nursing from Oakland Community College. I began as a Medical Assistant in 2002 for a private OB-GYN practice, and I continued working at the practice as an LPN after graduating with my nursing diploma.

Prior to completing my nursing education, I worked in both retail and banking environments, and I earned advancement to supervisory roles ahead of my peers because of my excellent problem-solving and customer service skills. At Bank of America, I advanced to the position of Back-up Head Teller, and I was held in the highest regard. Prior to that at Added Dimensions at Hickory Ridge Mall, I was promoted to Sales Supervisor and was in charge of training and supervising five employees.

In addition to my nursing experience in a private clinic, I offer some experience related to med-surg patients, geriatric patients, infants, and dialysis patients through the clinical rotations I completed while earning my nursing degree.

I am known for my cheerful disposition and outgoing nature, and I am confident I will be a credit to any hospital or medical environment that can use a dedicated and hard-working nurse. I offer a reputation as a go-getter who is known for unlimited personal initiative.

Yours sincerely,

Cecilia Steinberg

CECILIA N. STEINBERG, L.P.N.

1110½ Hay Street, Fayetteville, NC 28305 • preppub@aol.com • (910) 483-6611

EXPERIENCE

LICENSED PRACTICAL NURSE. Craig-Hutton OB/GYN Medical Clinic, Bloomfield, MI (2002-present). Currently employed with this private practice as a **Medical Assistant** in 2002, and was asked to continue my employment even after I became a Licensed Practical Nurse in 2003.

- Have gained vast knowledge of obstetrical and gynecological issues and procedures. Provide assistance to physicians during examinations while providing patient care, counseling, and support.
- Carry out a therapeutic plan of care in cooperation with general supervision of a Registered Nurse based on the national Nursing Standards of Care to include evaluation, monitoring, and intervention (physical, emotional, and social aspects).
- Am involved in patient education activities which included collection of data. Oversee patient safety while maintaining, supporting, and preserving a safe environment.
- Provide for patient comfort and mental well-being. Am knowledgeable of patient rights and assure that patients' rights are preserved and protected. Promote effective customer service and customer relations and adhere to advanced medical directives per hospital protocols.
- Document nursing process, patient status, care, and services. Assist with invasive and non-invasive procedures. Clean work areas, instruments, and equipment after use. Perform/assist with the collection of laboratory specimens and other samples as required. Label specimens appropriately and dispatch specimens to lab. Obtain blood specimens by venipuncture. Test specimens and urine for sugar and acetone; test blood for glucose monitoring; and test specimens for occult blood.
- Start IVs; monitor maintenance intravenous infusion. Initiate cardiopulmonary resuscitation in emergency situations. Administer prescribed medications based upon a practical knowledge of the effects upon the physiological process of the patient's condition.
- Triage patients. Take vital signs. Supervise chart completion. Phone in prescriptions. Maintain sterile conditions, and drape and position patients. Set up/maintain special medical equipment and apparatus.

CLINICAL ROTATIONS

2001-02 (six months): **NURSING HOME NURSE.** Addison Nursing Home, Bloomfield, MI. Completed two clinical rotations which immersed me in geriatric nursing.
2001: (three months): **HOSPITAL NURSE.** Bloomfield Medical Hospital, Bloomfield, MI. Three-month clinical rotation in Med-Surg, Obstetrics, and the Infant Nursery.
2000: (six weeks): **HOSPITAL NURSE.** Xavier Hospital, Bloomfield, MI. Completed a six-week clinical rotation in this hospital, and gained experience related to Med-Surg.
1999: (two weeks): **DIALYSIS NURSE.** Northeastern Dialysis Center, Bloomfield, MI. In a two-week observation, gained insight into nursing practices in a dialysis center.

OTHER EXPERIENCE

TELLER II AND BACK-UP HEAD TELLER. Bank of America, Bloomfield, MI (1996-99). Received an award for customer service skills. Named Employee of the Month.
SALES SUPERVISOR. Added Dimensions, Hickory Ridge Mall, Bloomfield, MI (1995-96). Hired, trained, and managed five employees while scheduling employees for work. Played a key role in conducting store meetings.

EDUCATION

Received Diploma in Practical Nursing, Oakland Community College, Bloomfield, MI, 2003. Elected Class President.
Earned Associate Degree in Education, Oakland Community College, Bloomfield, MI, 2000.

LICENSE

Licensed as a Practical Nurse in Michigan, Certificate No. 1234567; Expires June 30, 2005.

Federal resume of Cecilia Steinberg

CECILIA N. STEINBERG
9546 Nathatch Road
Bloomfield, MI 53524
(999) 999-9999
E-mail: cnsteinberg@msn.com

SSN: 000-00-0000
Date of birth: March 28, 1969
Country of Citizenship: United States
Highest Federal Civilian grade held, job series, and dates of employment in grade:
Dates:

Vacancy Announcement Number: BC-000-00-0000
Position Title and Grade: Nurse, GS 09-13

A LICENSED PRACTICAL NURSE

On the previous two pages you saw the "civilian resume" and cover letter used to compete for civilian jobs. On these two pages are the "federal resume" used by this nurse to apply for federal government vacancies.

Experience: 2002-present. **LICENSED PRACTICAL NURSE.** Craig-Hutton OB/GYN Medical Clinic, 8744 Arabello Road, Bloomfield, MI 53525. Salary: $12.50 per hour. Supervisor: Carla Mitchell, 888-888-8888. Currently employed with this private practice as a **Medical Assistant** in 2002, and was asked to continue my employment even after I became a Licensed Practical Nurse in 2003.

Provide assistance to physicians during examinations while providing patient care, counseling, and support. Carry out a therapeutic plan of care in cooperation with general supervision of a Registered Nurse based on the national Nursing Standards of Care to include evaluation, monitoring, and intervention (physical, emotional, and social aspects). Am continuously involved in patient education activities which included collection of data. Oversee patient safety while maintaining, supporting, and preserving a safe environment.

Provide for patient comfort and mental well-being. Am knowledgeable of patient rights and assure that patients' rights were preserved and protected. Promote effective customer service and customer relations and adhere to advanced medical directives per hospital protocols.

Document nursing process, patient status, care, and services. Assist with invasive and non-invasive procedures. Clean work areas, instruments, and equipment after use. Perform/assist with the collection of laboratory specimens and other samples as required. Label specimens appropriately and dispatch specimens to lab. Obtain blood specimens by venipuncture. Test specimens and urine for sugar and acetone; test blood for glucose monitoring; and test specimens for occult blood.

Start IVs; monitor maintenance intravenous infusion. Initiate cardiopulmonary resuscitation in emergency situations. Administer prescribed medications based upon a practical knowledge of the effects upon the physiological process of the patient's condition. Triage patients. Take vital signs. Supervise chart completion. Phone in prescriptions. Maintain sterile conditions, and drape and position patients. Set up and maintain special medical equipment and apparatus.

Accomplishments:
- Became respected for my medical knowledge as well as my strong communication skills, and answered a large volume of calls relating to patient problems.
- Applied textbook knowledge in clinical environments.

- Gained vast knowledge of obstetrical and gynecological issues and procedures.

Clinical rotations: 2001-02 (six months): **NURSING HOME NURSE.** Addison Nursing Home, 5436 Meadowview Lane, Bloomfield, MI 53526. Salary: N/A. Supervisor/Instructor: Angela Lambert, Phone (777) 777-7777. While completing my nursing degree, completed two clinical rotations which immersed me in geriatric nursing.

2001: (three months): **HOSPITAL NURSE.** Bloomfield Medical Hospital, 1747 Kenniston Road, Bloomfield, MI 53527. Salary: N/A. Supervisor/Instructor: Dana Medford, Phone: (666) 666-6666. Completed a three-month clinical rotation in this hospital, and gained experience related to Med-Surg, Obstetrics, and the Infant Nursery.

2000: (six weeks): **HOSPITAL NURSE.** Xavier Hospital, 3625 Fargo Road, Bloomfield, MI 53528. Salary: N/A. Supervisor/Instructor: Brian Patten, Phone: (555) 555-5555. Completed a six-week clinical rotation in this hospital, and gained experience related to Med-Surg.

1999: (two week): **DIALYSIS NURSE.** Northeastern Dialysis, 2632 Wedge View Avenue, Bloomfield, MI 53529. Salary: N/A. Supervisor/Instructor: William Gordon, Phone: (444) 444-4444. Completed a two week observation and gained insight into the specific nursing practices and procedures required in a dialysis center.

1996-1999: **TELLER II AND BACK-UP HEAD TELLER.** Bank of America, 4890 Hagen Boulevard, Bloomfield, MI 53530. Salary: $9.00 per hour. Supervisor: Heather Miller, (333) 333-3333. Received an award for my exceptional customer service skills, and was frequently commended for my nurturing attitude and cheerful disposition as I processed monetary transactions and expertly performed a variety of functions within the bank.

Accomplishments:
- Advanced from Teller I to Teller II after excelling supervisory training.
- Became skilled in handling large amounts of cash with no errors, and earned a reputation as a hard worker known for attention to detail at all times.

1995-1996: **SALES SUPERVISOR.** Added Dimensions, Hickory Ridge Mall, 3837 Drury Lane, Bloomfield, MI 53531. Salary: $8.00 per hour. Supervisor: Alfreda Davidson, (222) 222-2222. Hired, trained, and managed five employees while scheduling employees for work.

Accomplishments:
- Became skilled in working on a team in order to promote quality sales results.

1993 and 1995: **CLERK.** Department of Housing and Urban Development, 3928 Leaflet Drive, Bloomfield, MI 53532. Salary: $6.00 per hour. Supervisor: David Taylor, (111) 111-1111. As a GS-03 Clerk, answered a heavy volume of phone calls while filing and handling confidential documents and making appointments for clients to reserve housing.

Accomplishments:
- Refined telephone and other communication skills as I handled customer enquiries and liaison with a variety of officials involved in providing housing for qualified families.

EDUCATION

Received Diploma in Practical Nursing, Oakland Community College, 7847 Anderson Street, Bloomfield, MI 53524; 2003.

Earned Associate Degree in Education, Oakland Community College, 7847 Anderson Street, Bloomfield, MI 53524; 2000.

Graduate of E.V. Thompson High School, 717 Coachway Road, Bloomfield, MI 53530, 1992.

LICENSE

Licensed as a Practical Nurse in Michigan, Certificate No. 1234567; Expires June 30, 2005.

HONORS & AWARDS

Elected Class President, Licensed Practical Nurse Program, Oakland Community College, 2002-03.

Employee of the Month Award, Bank of America, Bloomfield, MI, 1998.

"Civilian" resume and cover letter of Mary Saurman

Date

Exact Name of Person
Exact Title
Exact Name of Company
Address
City, State, Zip

**A PSYCHIATRIC
REGISTERED NURSE**

These are examples
of a person applying for
a civilian and federal
nursing position

Dear Exact Name of Person (or Dear Sir or Madam if answering a blind ad):

With the enclosed resume, I would like to make you aware of my interest in exploring employment opportunities with your organization. I am currently employed with Dearwood Mental Health Center as a Psychiatric Registered Nurse in Huntsville, Alabama. I also worked as a Psychiatric Registered Nurse and Charge Nurse at Sneider Memorial Hospital on a part-time basis, and I can provide excellent references from my employer as well as from all previous employers.

Nursing expertise related to med/surg, oncology, and mental health

Since obtaining my nursing degree *magna cum laude,* I have worked in various areas including med/surg, oncology, and the mental health field. Skilled at managing other LPNs, RNs, and MHTs, I offer experience as a Charge Nurse. I have coordinated day-to-day nursing activities in a psychiatric nursing unit while ensuring quality patient care through close observation of all unit activities.

Strong communication skills

In numerous letters of appreciation and commendation which I have received, I have been praised for my caring style of nursing as well as my ability to individualize my style to fit different situations. I have become respected for my ability to work well with medical professionals at all levels as well as with patients and families. I have frequently been praised for my cheerful disposition and my ability to diffuse job tensions with my sense of humor. I have become adept at counseling patients and their families in grief.

Licenses and certifications

I am licensed as a Registered Nurse in Alabama, Mississippi, and Tennessee. I am also certified in Psychiatric Nursing by the National Nurses Credentialing Center.

I am confident that I have much to offer an organization in need of a skilled and versatile nursing professional, and I hope you will contact me soon to suggest a time when we might meet to discuss your needs.

Yours sincerely,

Mary D. Saurman

MARY D. SAURMAN

1110½ Hay Street, Fayetteville, NC 28305   •   preppub@aol.com   •   (910) 483-6611

OBJECTIVE

To offer my nursing experience to an organization that can benefit from my enthusiastic, compassionate, and friendly personality as well as from my nursing skills, reputation as an open-minded individual and good listener, and talent for getting along with others.

EDUCATION & TRAINING

Bachelor of Science in Nursing degree, University of Alabama, Huntsville, AL, 2000. Graduated *magna cum laude* and was recognized as one of the class's top four students. Through training and experience while working in medical/surgical, oncology, and the mental health field, have gained and refined versatile skills.

LICENSES

Licensed as a Registered Nurse in Alabama, Mississippi and Tennessee.
Certified in Psychiatric Nursing by National Nurses Credentialing Center.

EXPERIENCE

PSYCHIATRIC REGISTERED NURSE. Dearwood Mental Health Center, Huntsville, AL (2002-present). As a Charge Nurse, coordinate and supervise day-to-day nursing activities in a psychiatric nursing unit while ensuring quality patient care through close observation of all unit activities.
- Assisted emergency room staff in evaluating patients to determine whether they meet admission criteria and provide a complete nurse assessment upon admission.
- Provided outstanding case management for adult and geriatric patients while ensuring that all standards of care were met and proper procedures followed.
- Remained alert to potential emergency or high-risk situations so that appropriate actions could be taken including transfers to other units, seclusion, or involuntary commitment.
- Participated in quality improvement activities, regular staff meetings, and hospital procedure reviews to keep up-to-date in areas including equipment familiarity as well as safety and procedural issues.

STAFF REGISTERED NURSE. Wadley County Hospital, Wadley, AL (1999-02) and Jennings Medical Center, Wadley, AL (1998-99). Supervised three LPNs while handling administrative matters and direct patient care in medical/surgical and oncology wards.
- Interviewed new patients to obtain their complete medical history; reviewed information and made initial assessments; entered information into a data base.
- Set up individual nursing plans which were regularly reviewed and altered as needed.
- Alerted physicians to problems discovered while observing and assessing patients.
- Counseled patients and family members while providing easy to understand instructions for follow up and home care as well as support through various stages of grief.
- Provided LPNs and nursing assistants with leadership and assistance with tasks beyond their qualifications along with evaluating performance and preparing work schedules.

DRUG AND ALCOHOL ABUSE COUNSELOR. Meridian Regional Hospital, Jackson, MS (1996-98). Researched information, developed a plan of instruction, and taught classes on effects of drug and alcohol, their capacity for physiological and psychological dependence, and the potential for devastating family and career; worked with volunteers and professionals while searching for solutions to legal, family, and career problems.

MENTAL HEALTH TECHNICIAN/NURSE. Mid-South Medical Center, Chattanooga, TN (1993-96). For emotionally and mentally disturbed patients, handled patient interviews, evaluated psychological and health history, monitored and recorded inappropriate behavior.

PERSONAL

Earn the trust and confidence of others through my true concern. Excellent references.

Federal resume of Mary Saurman

MARY D. SAURMAN

4025 Stirling Road, Huntsville, AL 40181

888-888-8888

E-mail: MDSaurman@compuserve.com

SSN: 000-00-0000

Country of Citizenship: United States

Geographic Preference: Alabama

Lowest Grade: GS-09

Vacancy Announcement Number: MD-00-00-0000

Position Title: Psychiatric Registered Nurse

EDUCATION

Bachelor of Science in Nursing degree, University of Alabama, Huntsville, AL, 2000. Graduated *magna cum laude* and was recognized as one of the class's top four students. Worked in medical/surgical, oncology, and the mental health field.

LICENSES

Licensed as a Registered Nurse in Alabama, Mississippi, and Tennessee.

Certified in Psychiatric Nursing by the National Nurses Credentialing Center

EXPERIENCE

PSYCHIATRIC REGISTERED NURSE II. 02/2002-present. Dearwood Mental Health Center, 1600 Plainview Avenue, Huntsville, AL 40165-0064. Supervisor: Geneve Harrelson; Phone: 777-777-7777. Salary: $40,000, Hours per week: 40. Visited clients in their homes to give injections and instructed clients on health care including diet, exercise, and hygiene. Prepared a variety of reports including a report containing a yearly health screen as well as quarterly assessments of involuntary movements. Reviewed incoming labs and reported abnormal findings to MDs. Coordinated medical appointments with the clients' primary care physicians (PCPs), and frequently escorted clients to PCPs. Called insurance companies for pre-approval on nonconforming medication. Assisted case managers with tracking some homeless clients; monitored clients for psychosis and implemented proper treatments. Assisted team and patients with treatment plans.

PSYCHIATRIC REGISTERED NURSE & CHARGE NURSE. 11/2000-02/2002. Sneider Memorial Hospital, 374 Bailey Avenue, Huntsville, AL 40158. Supervisor: Phyllis Dryer, Director; Phone: 666-666-6666. Salary: $14.00 per hour. As a Charge Nurse, coordinated and supervised day-to-day nursing activities in a psychiatric nursing unit while ensuring quality patient care through close observation of all unit activities. Made daily assignments to RNs, LPNs, and MHTs. Assisted emergency room staff in evaluating patients to determine whether they meet admission criteria and provide a complete nurse assessment upon admission. Provided outstanding case management for adult and geriatric patients. Remained alert to potential emergency or high-risk situations so that appropriate actions could be taken including transfers to other units, seclusion, or involuntary commitment. Participated in quality improvement activities, regular staff meetings, and hospital procedure reviews. Communicated with patients and their families about their diagnosis, potential problems, and the importance of complying with treatment regimens.

STAFF REGISTERED NURSE. 03/1999-11/2000. Wadley County Hospital, P.O. Box 5874, Wadley, AL 44738. Supervisor: Elizabeth Bell; Phone: 555-555-5555. and 02/1998-03/1999. Jennings Medical Center, P.O. Box 8450, 6600 Collier Street, Wadley, AL 42412. Supervisor:

Barbara Ryan; Phone: 444-444-4444. Supervised three LPNs while handling administrative matters and direct patient care in med/surg and oncology wards. Interviewed new patients to obtain their complete medical history; reviewed information and made initial assessments; entered information into a data base. Set up individual nursing plans which were regularly reviewed and altered. Alerted physicians to problems discovered while observing and assessing patients. Monitored vital signs; collected specimens; performed routine tests; dispensed medications, provided IV therapy and pre/post operative surgical care; monitored drug effectiveness while remaining alert for adverse reactions. Counseled patients and family members; provided instructions for follow up and home care. Provided LPNs and nursing assistants with leadership and assistance.

DRUG AND ALCOHOL ABUSE COUNSELOR. 12/1996-02/1998. Meridian Regional Hospital, 2039 Kensington Drive, Jackson, MS 51287. Supervisor: Frederick Harding; Phone: 333-333-3333. Researched information, developed a plan of instruction, and taught classes on effects of drug and alcohol, their capacity for physiological and psychological dependence, and the potential for devastating family and career; worked with volunteers and professionals.

MENTAL HEALTH TECHNICIAN/NURSE. 06/1993-12/1996. Mid-South Medical Center, 10700 Piedmont Avenue, Chattanooga, TN 31406. Supervisor: Paul Sheppard; 222-222-2222. For emotionally and mentally disturbed patients, handled patient interviews, evaluated psychological and health history, monitored behavior, and recorded inappropriate behavior. Successfully interacted with patients and discussed ways to alleviate problems, fears, and anxieties as well as consulting with doctors to determine therapies and medications.

PSYCHIATRIC EXPERTISE
Am highly experienced in performing duties which include the following:
Coordinating activities in a psychiatric nursing unit
Analyzing patient diagnoses, history and initial assessment
Identifying inappropriate behavior, especially threats of suicide or harm to others
Taking actions including transfers to appropriate units, seclusion, or involuntary commitment
Administering outstanding case management for adult and geriatric patients
Ensuring all standards of care are met and proper procedures followed
Helping patients to develop physical and mental diversions such as physical exercise
Interacting and counseling patient and family members on treatments
Monitoring patient behavior at all times
Establishing therapeutic relationships that facilitate treatments and the ability to console in grief

SKILLS AND KNOWLEDGE
Am experienced in these and other areas:

Physical Assessment	Intravenous Therapy and Management
Observing Signs/Symptoms of Illness	Mental-Spiritual Assessment
Blood Transfusion	Water-Seal Drainage System
Medication Administration	Observation of Reaction/Response
Tracheostomy Care	Suctioning
Bladder Irrigation	Colostomy Care
Wound Care	Crisis Intervention
Supervising and Coordinating Health Teams	Blood Glucose Testing
Hemocults	Reviewing Lab Tests
Preparing Patients for Surgery, X-Ray, and other tests	Catheter Insertion, Male and Female
Obtaining Cultures: Throat, Wound, IV Cannula	Suprapubic Catheter
Catheter Care	Volume Spirometer
Hickman and Groshong Catheters	CPR

Three-page resumix of Ruby Darlington

RUBY U. DARLINGTON, BSN

8515 Windsor Avenue

Fairfield, CT 04455

888-888-8888 H

SSN: 000-00-0000

Source: EXT

Highest Grade Held: N/A

Vacancy Announcement Number: 00000000

Position Title: Nurse (Various Specialties) (GS-0000)

NURSE LIAISON (RESUMIX)

Here is an example of a federal government resume, often called a Resumix, which shows one format used to apply for federal government positions. The job vacancy announcement which describes the position you are applying for will usually provide some guidance about what information the federal resume should contain.

EXPERIENCE

NURSE LIAISON.

Start and End Dates: March 2003-present

Hours worked per week: 40+

Current Salary: $42,000 per year

Employer's Name and Address: Sacred Heart Medical, 2494 Walden Street, Fairfield, CT 04455

Supervisor's Name and Phone Number: Kevin Hopper, 888-888-8888. Manage a project which included completing clinical assessments of patents based on referrals in order to determine their placement into long-term, assisted living, domiciliary, intermediate, or rest home-level care. Make determinations of financial feasibility. Determine the level of care needed and coordinate all phases of services required by each patient.

- Am credited for increasing community awareness of the assisted living option while educating patients and families.
- Work with discharge planners and case managers to form accurate assessments.
- Conduct outreach to local physicians and am in constant contact with 12 different offices.

HOSPICE COORDINATOR.

Start and End Dates: April 2001- March 2003

Hours worked per week: 40+

Salary: $36,500 per year

Employer's Name and Address: St. Joseph Hospice Care, 12900 Bullard Ave, Fairfield, CT

Supervisor's Name and Phone Number: Ryan Cullen, 777-777-7777.

Coordinated patient care services for the Hospice care portion of the hospital's programs. Supervised three registered nurses, three home health aides, and a chaplain. Made arrangements for and coordinated education and development activities for staff members and volunteer workers.

- Was credited with increasing referrals through networking.
- Provided marketing support services for the program.
- Developed a patient care guide distributed to patients and their family members; updated policy manuals.
- Participated in developing and ensuring compliance with the operating budget.

CASE MANAGER and **CLINICAL NURSE.**

Start and End Dates: September 1999-April 2001

Hours worked per week: 40+

Salary: $32,500 per year

Employer's Name and Address: Kindred Care-Connecticut, 8423 Cunningham Road, Fairfield, CT

Supervisor's Name and Phone Number: Sharon Blackwell, 666-666-6666. Supervised nursing aides to ensure implementation of care plans while personally providing care to home health patients.

- Assisted in community health and education efforts including such activities as preschool physicals, Community Health Fair, and Kindred Clinic staffing.
- Was certified as a Home Health Nurse by the Connecticut Medical Administration (December 1999).

HOME IV NURSE.

Start and End Dates: October 1996-September 1999

Hours worked per week: 40+

Salary: $31,250 per year

Employer's Name and Address: Hartford Therapy, 302 Lake Avenue, Hartford, CT 01644

Supervisor's Name and Phone Number: Craig Wallace, 555-555-5555. Provided individualized, specialized IV infusion therapy while working in a variety of difficult patient care situations.

- Instructed and supervised nurse's aides and family members in therapy procedures.

COMMUNITY HEALTH NURSE.

Start and End Dates: July 1994- October 1996

Hours worked per week: 40+

Salary: $27,600 per year

Employer's Name and Address: Trident Regional Hospital, 37290 Ashley Avenue, Hartford, CT 01651

Supervisor's Name and Phone Number: Laura Hartwell, 444-444-4444. Implemented nursing care and provided educational services to individual and families who had been exposed to or were suffering from infectious diseases or illnesses.

- Applied communication and instructional skills while presenting a variety of formal lectures.
- Performed physical assessments and developed patient care plans for Hepatitis and Cancer patients.
- Performed the hospital's Hepatitis Hospital Admissions testing study.

CASE MANAGER.

Start and End Dates: September 1992- July 1994

Hours worked per week: 40+

Salary: $24,225 per year

Employer's Name and Address: Extended Care Services, 39095 Price Street, Columbia, SC 22846

Supervisor's Name and Phone Number: Michelle Wheeler, 333-333-3333. Excelled in meeting the special needs of the terminally ill and their families while providing quality nursing care and assisting in the training of hospice workers.

REGISTERED NURSE.

Start and End Dates: September 1990- September 1992

Hours worked per week: 40+

Salary: $22,300 per year

Employer's Name and Address: Kindred Care of South Carolina, 4903 Cedar Creek Drive, Columbia, SC 22865

**REGISTERED NURSE
(RESUMIX)**

On the facing page you will
find another example of a
Resumix used to apply for
federal government
positions.

Supervisor's Name and Phone Number: Jacqueline Greenwood, 222-222-2222. Performed a wide range of nursing duties for an outpatient clinic in Columbia, SC. Supervised training of department personnel and evaluated their medical skills.

- Implemented a grief support group.
- Taught health education classes.
- Acted as a community liaison.

HOSPICE NURSE.
Start and End Dates: January 1989- September 1990
Hours worked per week: 40+
Salary: $8.00 per hour
Employer's Name and Address: Roper Hospital, 2348 Rutledge Avenue, Charleston, SC 29401
Supervisor's Name and Phone Number: Shirley Thompson, 111-111-1111. Provided outpatient care for terminally ill patients.

- Helped train nursing students in patient care.
- Temporality filled the role of coordinator.

STAFF NURSE.
Start and End Dates: April 1988- January 1989
Hours worked per week: 40+
Salary: NA
Employer's Name and Address: Medical University of South Carolina (MUSC), 37290 Ashley Avenue, Charleston, SC 29401
Supervisor's Name and Phone Number: Belinda Carter, 999-999-9999. Provided total care for 22 patients on the internal medicine floor in a busy hospital; was recommended for promotion to Assistant Head Registered Nurse.

STUDENT/STAFF NURSE.
Start and End Dates: May 1986-April 1988
Hours worked per week: 40+
Salary: NA
Employer's Name and Address: Medical University of South Carolina (MUSC), 37290 Ashley Avenue, Charleston, SC 29401
Supervisor's Name and Phone Number: Patricia Triplett, RN, MSN; 888-888-8888. As a student nurse, was selected to fill roles of increasing responsibility in a busy high-risk labor and delivery center. Instructed medical students in delivery procedures. Managed staffing for 15 people.

EDUCATION

Bachelor of Science in Nursing (B.S.N.) degree, Medical University of South Carolina Charleston, SC 1988.

SPECIALIZED TRAINING

Have completed continuing education courses and training programs emphasizing pain control and chemotherapy as well as BCLS/CPR and infection control.

CERTIFICATIONS & LICENSES

- Was certified as a Home Health Nurse by the Connecticut Medical Administration (December 1999).

Three-page resumix of Rhonda Greer

RHONDA GENENE GREER
9837 Dean Forest Road
Providence, RI 02894
Home phone: (111) 111-1111
Work phone: (222) 222-2222

LICENSES & CERTIFICATIONS

Registered Nurse: license number 888-888-888, issued by the State of Massachusetts, valid until 10/31/05.
BCLS Certificate: renewed 10/1/04

SKILLS

Nursing specialties: pediatric wards and clinics, medical and surgical wards.
Member of the Professional Nurses Association of America Program: received training in medical assessment and administration skills.
Computers: knowledge of ICHCS, Windows NT, and PowerPoint.
Languages: a native of Mexico, am totally bilingual in French, Spanish and German.

WORK EXPERIENCE

Registered Nurse, Xavier Regional Hospital, 2123 Harden Street, Providence, RI 02894. Supervisor: Mellisa Nevins (333) 333-3333. Salary: $49,289 (RN). Hours per week: 40. From March 1999 to present. Provide professional nursing support for Xavier with primary emphasis on screening for potential surgical procedures and secondary emphasis on screening for enrollment in special needs treatment and counseling programs.

- Apply professional nursing and related medical knowledge while evaluating the medical, psychological, and social needs of the patient and their family members and assessing their ability to cope with caring for handicapping conditions.
- Act as a consultant for medical staff, community-based support and service groups, state and federal agencies, and other concerned individuals and groups: explain program goals and objectives and educate personnel in identifying potential candidates and needs.
- Establish and maintain files, records, and logs.
- Administer and interpret first-stage and second-stage development tests.
- Inform patients and their families of findings, the consequences of enrolling in the program, and of available resources for care and support in the nearby Providence community.
- Provide screening through local clinics including the Pediatric, Geriatric, and Family Practice Clinics, as well as outlying clinics, schools, etc.

Clinical Nurse, Wentworth Medical Institute, 3278 Canebrake Road, Boston, MA 04535. $45,000. Supervisor Dillon Hancock (444) 444-4444. Salary: GS-9. Hours per week: 40. From March 1996 to March 1999. Supervised and trained as many as five people (LPNs, CNAs, and Student Nurses) while performing professional nursing duties caring for newborn and/or pediatric patients.

- Provided comprehensive care based on a combination of the needs of the patient, nursing care plan, and physician's medical plan.

- Used the nursing process and performed initial history and assessment; developed nursing care plans; determined and implemented nursing orders.
- Evaluated nursing care based on patient response and revised the nursing plan when needed.
- Administered oxygen as well as prescribed medications by oral, rectal, topical inhalation, intravenous, subcutaneous, and intramuscular routes; initiated intravenous infusions; administered blood and blood products; regulated rates and monitored infusions.
- Performed nasal-pharyngeal and gastric suction and managed a variety of other tubes as well as foley catheters.
- Set up, monitored, and operated a variety of equipment which included infant monitors, respiratory equipment, incubators, auto-infusion pumps, and traction.

Clinical Nurse, Boston Medical Center, 343 53rd Street, Boston, MA 04577, $37,000. Supervisor: Rick Hammill (555) 555-5555. Salary: GS-10. Hours per week: 40. From June 1993 to March 1996. Supervised and trained as many as five employees including LPNs, CNAs, and Student Nurses while performing Charge Nurse duties which included administrative functions duties in support of the Head Nurse with an emphasis on providing comprehensive nursing care to pediatric and adult medical and surgical patients.

- Made nursing care assignments for professional and paraprofessional staff members with various skill levels according to patient needs and staff expertise.
- Ensured staff members provided appropriate patient education, made nursing entries which were legible and correct, and dealt with emergencies appropriately.
- Verified and annotated physician's orders and advised the attending physician of significant changes in a patient's condition.
- Monitored and provided oversight during orientation and preceptorship periods in order to verify personnel were receiving appropriate and thorough training.
- Provided care for pediatric and adult medical and surgical patients ranging from those who were ambulatory to those receiving complex new or non-standard treatments.
- Cared for patients requiring intensive care such as post-operative and burn patients, accident victims, etc.
- Initiated emergency resuscitative measures and assisted physicians with further emergency responses.
- Operated specialized medical equipment such as cardiac monitoring devices. Controlled inventories of supplies and equipment in sufficient quantities.

Clinical Nurse, Dorchester Heights Medical Hospital, 5124 Habersham Road, Boston, MA 04513. Supervisor: Matthew Brushwood. (444) 444-4444. Salary: $32,800. Hours per week: 40. From February 1990 to June 1993. Provided comprehensive nursing care to patients on pediatric, general, medical, or surgical wards as well as patients in the post-anesthesia recovery unit while handling responsibilities for preparing and documenting patient health records.

- Taught patients, family members, and care providers the disease process and therapy.
- Provided on-the-job and in-service training for staff personnel and assisted with new-employee orientations.
- Prepared patients for surgical or diagnostics procedures; observed post-operative patients and those receiving medical therapy for adverse reactions; took immediate action in response to medical emergencies.
- Categorized patients according to acuity standards and entered data into an automated system.
- Administered medications by oral, subcutaneous, intramuscular, intradermal, intravenous, or inhalation routes to patients of all ages.
- Performed specialized procedures such as oxygen administration, inhalation therapy, nasal-pharyngeal and gastric suction, blood gases, gastric lavage, and others.
- Operated and monitored specialized equipment which included: cardiac monitor and defibrillator, oxygen analyzer, mist tent, IPPb, glucometer, and insulin pump.
- From April 1992 until June 1993, was given additional responsibilities as the Admission Coordinator Nurse in charge of the patient pre-admission process:

  education, pre-admission, and assessment of surgical and non-surgical patients

  prepared admissions forms, standardized care plans, teaching materials and other documentation

  coordination of services with laboratory, x-ray, EKG, anesthesia, the emergency room for unscheduled emergency response, and the Disabilities Act Program

EDUCATION   Diploma awarded upon completion of a three-year program from the School of Nursing, Tufts University, Boston, Massachusetts, February 1990.

Complete an additional 45 hours of additional training every two years, in order to update and maintain my nursing skills and certifications.

OTHER INFORMATION   Social Security number: 000-00-000

Nursing professionals who want to seek a career in the federal government may find that they must submit narrative statements called "Knowledge, Skills & Abilities" or KSAs for some positions. It is the purpose of this section to illustrate what KSAs look like when they are written effectively. Quite often you are asked to submit up to four KSAs which reveal your suitability for the job.

How do you know if you need to submit KSAs?

The job vacancy announcement which describes the duties and qualifications pertaining to the job will tell you if KSAs are required. A KSA is usually one page or two pages in length. If there is a word limit or page limit on what you are required to submit, the job vacancy announcement will specify this limit.

What is a 612?

At the end of this section, you will see an example of a form called the Optional Form 612 (OF 612) which is sometimes used to apply for federal jobs. Please note that you will submit either a resumix or a 612, but not both. Candidates for employment in the U.S. Postal Service and in other government agencies may be asked to submit a form 171 when they apply for federal employment; this book does not show samples of the 171, which is very similar to the 612.

Four KSAs of Lisa Romano

LISA K. ROMANO
SSN: 000-00-0000
CHARGE NURSE, GS-09 ANNOUNCEMENT #XYZ123

KSA #1: Ability to Assign the Work of Other Nursing Personnel

In my current position as the day **Charge Nurse** for the Adult Geriatric Unit, it my job to address the needs of the unit and make daily assignments to RNs, LPNs, and MHTs. The duties are assigned orally first thing in the morning; they are also written on an assignment board to avoid any confusion. Throughout the day, it is not only my job to take care of patients and their records but also to oversee all staff to make sure all assigned tasks are completed in a timely manner.

As a **Psychiatric Nurse and Charge Nurse**, I direct other nursing professionals in providing patient and family care using the nursing process and work in close cooperation with other members of the total treatment team in the formulation, implementation, and evaluation of the total care plans for patients. I direct other nursing professions in establishing cooperative interpersonal relationships with hospital and medical staff members in order to coordinate patient care, and I have responsibility for the milieu and contact with patients at all stages of daily life. I oversee other nursing professionals as they inform patients and families about available mental health facilities, the nature of psychiatric illness and substance abuse, treatment approaches, and the prevention and reduction of stress as well as teaching anger management techniques and discharge planning procedures.

As a Charge Nurse I am responsible for coordinating and supervising day-to-day nursing activities in the psychiatric nursing unit while ensuring the quality of patient care through close observation of all unit activities. I routinely assist emergency room staff in evaluating patients to determine whether they meet Psychiatric admission criteria and provide a complete nurse assessment upon admission. I provide outstanding case management for adult and geriatric patients while ensuring that all standards of care were met and proper procedures followed. I have earned the respect of physicians and other nursing staff for my skills, attitude, concern for patients, willingness to work long hours, and respect for confidentiality.

I must inform not only my immediate staff of patient needs, but also I must contact various hospital staffs to arrange for tests, consults, and other needs that the patient might have. Throughout the day I am constantly communicating with the patient while simultaneously collecting data on their mental status. It is my responsibility as a nurse to make sure the doctor has not overlooked or disregarded a problem, and this area of my oral communications responsibilities requires that I utilize the utmost tact, diplomacy, and delicacy.

Education and Training related to this KSA:
Hold an Associate of Science in Nursing degree from Michigan State University, Grand Rapids, MI, 1998.
Graduated **magna cum laude** and was recognized as one of the class's top four students.
Have completed professional development training related to providing nursing care in medical/surgical, oncology, and the mental health field.
Am **Certified in Psychiatric Nursing** by National Association of Nurses.
Am a licensed Registered Nurse in MI and OH.

KSA #2: Ability to communicate orally.

As a Psychiatric Nurse and Charge Nurse, I provide direct patient and family care using the nursing process and work in close cooperation with other members of the total treatment team in the formulation, implementation, and evaluation of the total care plans for patients. I establish cooperative interpersonal relationships with hospital and medical staff members in order to coordinate patient care, and I have responsibility for the milieu and contact with patients at all stages of daily life. I teach self care — medications, health care, and hygiene, and I also teach residents how to relate to others, solve problems, communicate clearly, and try out new ways of coping while helping clients progress toward less restricted living situations and less restrictive environments. I am responsible for informing patients and families about available mental health facilities, the nature of psychiatric illness and substance abuse, treatment approaches, and the prevention and reduction of stress as well as teaching anger management techniques and discharge planning procedures.

As a Charge Nurse, it is my responsibility to communicate to the staff what their duties, assignments, and responsibilities are. Assignments are made each day, and they must be orally communicated as well. I must inform not only my immediate staff of patient needs, but also I must contact various hospital staffs to arrange for tests, consults, and other needs that the patient might have. Throughout the day I am constantly communicating with the patient while simultaneously collecting data on their mental status. This is sometimes a difficult task due to the fact that some of my patients may be psychotic and sometimes quite paranoid. I must inform the doctor by telephone or in person of any changes in the patient's status that might suggest the need for immediate attention or intervention. It is my responsibility as a nurse to make sure the doctor has not overlooked or disregarded a problem, and this area of my oral communications responsibilities requires that I utilize the utmost tact, diplomacy, and delicacy so that the information I relay orally will be received in a positive and professional manner and so that all medical professionals remain firmly focused on quality patient care above all else.

As a Charge Nurse in my current position as a Psychiatric Nurse, my duties include ER admission assessments/screening. This requires me to collect data from and about the patient. I speak with not only the patient but quite often also with the family, staff, and other facilities such as nursing homes. After gathering the information, I must call the doctor and communicate a clear synopsis of the patient's problem so that the doctor can decide whether to admit the patient or not.

Education and Training related to this KSA:
Hold an Associate of Science in Nursing degree from Michigan State University, Grand Rapids, MI, 1998.
Graduated **magna cum laude** and was recognized as one of the class's top four students.
Have completed professional development training related to providing nursing care in medical/surgical, oncology, and the mental health field.
Am **Certified in Psychiatric Nursing** by the National Association of Nurses.
Am a licensed Registered Nurse in MI and OH.

KSA #3: Knowledge of pharmaceuticals and their desired effects.

My experience with pharmaceuticals is vast, considering that I have experience in oncology medical/surgical and the psychiatric fields. In each setting, no class of pharmaceuticals is used exclusively, but certain medications are used more frequently and require a more indepth knowledge of their effects, side effects, and possible allergic reactions. The most common drugs dispensed in the medical/surgical and oncology settings were antibiotic, antimicrobial, analgesic, anticoagulant and insulin.

With antibiotics and antimicrobials, I would monitor their effects, observing the prevention of infection or relief from an existing infection. Possible side effects could range from a mild rash to a fatal anaphylaxis. Working daily with these medications, I became very skilled at monitoring the patient for kidney and liver damage...another side effect of these medications. Some examples are penicillin, amoxicillan, gentamicin, timentin, and rocephin.

While serving the oncology and surgical units, I gained expertise with analgesic medications. Due to the intense suffering of our patients in the oncology unit, exorbitant amounts of analgesics are administered. I, with a doctor's order, would sometimes administer the maximum amount of these drugs to a suffering patient. Whenever an extremely high dosage is administered, I immediately became alert for possible respiratory depression or respiratory arrest. Other possible side effects might include nausea/vomiting, rashes, and decreased blood pressure. Some examples are morphine, demero, percodan, and dilaudid.

Anticoagulants are often given after surgery. These agents keep the blood from clotting, preventing embolism and thrombosis. Because they thin the blood, I would monitor for possible bruising and bleeding. Some examples are heparin and coumadin.

When administering insulin, I would watch for the reduction of blood sugar. By performing Accuchecks, I could determine blood sugar levels and the presence of hyperglycemia. Additionally, I would monitor the patient for hypoglycemia, a common side effect from insulin. Reaction time of this medication varies depending on types of insulin used, whether regular, intermediate or long-acting. Some examples include regular insulin, semilente, NPH, and lente.

While on the job in the Psychiatric setting, the most common medications that I dispense are antipsychotics, antiparkinsonion, antidepressants, antimanic, anticonvulsants, and antianxiety. When I dispense antipsychotics, I watch for reduction of hallucinations, dementia, and psychotic behaviors. The drug works by blocking dopamine receptors in the brain. Unfortunately, blocking these receptors can produce bizarre side effects resembling Parkinson's disease. Extrapyramidal symptoms include tremors, shuffling gait, and abnormal tensing and twisting of the upper torso.

Whenever a patient experiences these various symptoms, I dispense antiparksonsian medication which helps restore a natural balance of dopamine in the brain. Another side effect resulting from prolonged use of antipsychotics is Tardive Dyskinesia, which includes the following symptoms:

- bizarre facial and tongue movements
- stiff neck

Neuroleptic Malianant Syndrome (another serious side effect): high fever, rigidity, coma, possible death. Other common side effects include nausea, vomiting, sedation, and photosensitivity or blurred vision. Examples of antipsychotics are haldol, risperidone, mellaril, a prolixin.

Antidepressants are frequently used on the unit. Antidepressants are used for treatment of depression, dysthymia, and obsessive-compulsive disorder. These medications help prevent the re-uptake of dopomine, norepinephrine, and seratonin. Antidepressants relieve symptoms including sadness, tearfulness, loss of appetite, and hopelessness. Response time for these medications usually involve 2-3 weeks. Unfortunately, side effects include nausea, vomiting, sedation, blurred vision, and constipation. Antidepressants acting as monoamine oxidase inhibitors can result in hypertensive crisis if the patient fails to adhere to a monitored diet restricting foods containing tyramine. Examples include:prozac, paxil, elavil, effexor, and MAO's...parnate, nardil.

Anticonvulsive are used in the treatment of grand mal, petite mal, status epileptious, and in some instances, BiPolar. These medications depress abnormal neuronal discharge in the Central Nervous System. Possible side effects include rashes, nausea, vomiting, diarrhea, and hypotension. Some examples are tegretol, valproic acid, and gabapetin.

Antimanic medications are used to stabilize the extreme mood swings associated with BiPolar Disorder. They essentially work by altering the sodium metabolism within the nerve cells; furthermore, they enhance the re-uptake of biogenic amines in the brain, lowering levels in the body, resulting in decreased hyperactivity. Possible side effects may result in weight gain, hand tremors, headaches, and hair loss. Patients must be continuously monitored to assure proper medication dosage. Symptoms of toxicity caused from inappropriate medication dosage may result in vomiting, diarrhea, lethargy, fever, coma, and even death. Two examples follow: lithium and eskalith.

Another medication used frequently in the treatment of anxiety and Panic Disorder includes antianxiety. This drug is also used to minimize the withdrawal effects of alcoholism and prevent DT. Antianxiety medications depress the Central Nervous System and can produce a physical dependence. Nausea, constipation, dry mouth, sedation, depression, and respiratory problems are some possible side effects. Some examples include:valium, xanax, ativan, and klonipine.

Education and Training related to this KSA:
Hold an Associate of Science in Nursing degree from Michigan State University, Grand Rapids, MI, 1998.
Graduated **magna cum laude** and was recognized as one of the class's top four students. While in nursing school, studied many classes of pharmaceuticals and was tested in all of them. Have passed the state board exam, and about half the questions on that exam are related to medications and pharmaceuticals and their side effects. Have completed professional development training related to providing nursing care in medical/surgical, oncology, and the mental health field.
Am **Certified in Psychiatric Nursing** by the National Association of Nurses.
Am a licensed Registered Nurse in MI and OH.

KSA #4: Knowledge of Professional Nursing Care Principles, Practice, and Procedures.

In my current position as a Psychiatric Charge Nurse, I am expected to be a patient advocate and to provide care for the patient with mental and emotional disorders, sometimes in conjunction with physical disorders. I contribute to the effectiveness of patient care for emotionally and mentally disturbed patients by handling patient assessment interviews, collecting and evaluating psychological and health histories, monitoring behaviors, and documenting instances of ill health and inappropriate behaviors while supervising other RNs, LPNs, and MHT. As a Staff Nurse in medical/surgical and oncology, I provided the same type of assessment and care; only the disorders and ailments were mostly of a physical nature and required more technical skill with IV pumps, chest tubes, wound care, etc.

My positions which have helped me acquire expert knowledge of professional nursing care principles, practice, and procedures are these:
- **Psychiatric Charge Nurse**, Youngstown Medical Hospital, Youngstown, OH (2003-present)
- **Staff Registered Nurse**, Grand Rapids Hospital, Grand Rapids, MI (2001) and Davenport Medical Center, Dearborn, MI (1999-01)
- **Psychiatric Staff Nurse/Mental Health Technician**, Aquinas Regional Hospital, Grand Rapids, MI (1998-99)

In all of the above positions, I used my initiative and independent judgment to plan and implement professional nursing care for patients in accordance with hospital policies. I established cooperative interpersonal relationships with other hospital staff and medical staff members. Among my responsibilities, I used the nursing process and performed the initial nursing history and assessment, developed a nursing care plan, and also developed and implemented nursing orders. I evaluated patient care depending on the patient's response to that care and revised the nursing care plan accordingly. I recognized and informed appropriate personnel of changes in a patient's condition. For psychiatric patients, I followed established protocols, and I worked closely with other members of the total treatment team in the formulation of the total care plan for patients. I focused on motivating and redirecting the behavior of psychiatric patients, and I participated in group therapy sessions while also providing one-to-one counseling sessions with patients. I administered prescribed medications by oral, intramuscular, subcutaneous and topical routes, and I also prepared patients for diagnostic examinations. I identified and performed patient teaching specific to each patient's needs and initiated and completed patient discharge plan. I followed infection control procedures and practiced proper aseptic techniques at all times while also maintaining appropriate records and documents.

In my most recent position as a Psychiatric Registered Nurse, I have functioned as a Charge Nurse and am responsible for coordinating and supervising day-to-day nursing activities in the psychiatric nursing unit while ensuring the quality of patient care through close observation of all unit activities. I routinely assist emergency room staff in evaluating patients to determine whether they meet Psychiatric admission criteria and provide a complete nurse assessment upon admission. I have provided outstanding case management for adult and geriatric patients while ensuring that all standards of care were met and proper procedures followed. I continuously remain alert to potential emergency or high-risk situations so that appropriate actions can be taken to keep up-to-date in areas including equipment familiarity as well as safety and procedural issues. I have earned the respect of physicians and other nursing staff for my skills, attitude, concern for patients, willingness to work long hours, and respect for confidentiality.

Overview of skills and knowledge:

Through education, training, and experience, have acquired expert skills related to the following areas:

physical assessment	mental-spiritual assessment
observing signs/symptoms of illness	water-seal drainage system
intravenous therapy and management	blood transfusion
tracheostomy care	suctioning
bladder irrigation	colostomy care
wound care	crisis intervention
patient instruction	documentation of nursing care
Hemocults	reviewing lab tests
catheter care	suprapubic catheter
oxygen therapies	volume spirometer
Hickman and Groshong catheters	CPR
subcutaneous infusion port	cast care
Medications	

supervising and coordinating health teams blood glucose testing
medication administration observing reaction/response
preparing patients for surgery, X-ray, and various tests
obtaining cultures: throat, wound, IV cannula catheter insertion, male and female

Education and Training related to this KSA:

Hold an Associate of Science in Nursing degree from Michigan State University, Grand Rapids, MI, 1998.

Graduated **magna cum laude** and was recognized as one of the class's top four students.

Have completed professional development training related to providing nursing care in medical/surgical, oncology, and the mental health field.

Am **Certified in Psychiatric Nursing** by the National Association of Nurses.

Am a licensed Registered Nurse in MI and OH.

KSAs of Willette Gilbert

WILLETTE C GILBERT

SSN: 000-00-0000

CHARGE NURSE, GS-11 ANNOUNCEMENT #XYZ123

Charge Nurse, GS-11 Announcement #XYZ123 KSA #1

On these following page you will see examples of written KSAs (stands for Knowledge, Skills, and Abilities) which were used along with a federal resume in applying for a federal government position.

KSA #1: Ability to plan, assign, and direct the work of other nursing personnel.

Perform Charge Nurse duties on a regular basis while supervising two or three Residential Care Specialists on the evening shift at the Manor Care Rehabilitation Center. Use my initiative and independent judgment to plan and implement professional nursing care for patients in accordance with hospital policies. Am familiar with hospital policies regarding patient care. Also am responsible for knowing and following the chain of command. Am familiar with the resources available to me so that I can fill the role of Charge Nurse. Have established cooperative interpersonal relationships with other hospital staff and medical staff members. Among my responsibilities is knowing the position descriptions of nursing personnel supervised. In order to effectively delegate tasks I determine what needs to be done and what can be delegated to others. Evaluate the job performance of team members in order to determine who can best take care of each delegated task. Describe the tasks and assignments to the team members and make sure each member understands the tasks and assignments given to them and to test their listening skills. Provide the guidelines for them to report back and on how and when the assignments will be evaluated. Ensure that follow up and evaluation is as previously stated to each team member. Provide the authority, responsibility, and support needed to complete the assignment. I recognize and appreciate a job well done by giving praise that is specific, honest, sincere, and succinct. Acknowledge improvement in performance of a task and promote team synergy and cooperation. Am familiar with disruptive behaviors that may prevent co-workers from functioning well and effective in redirecting those behaviors. Endeavor to build and maintain morale to help co-workers work together smoothly. Attended and participated in the Taking Charge Workshop presented by the Education Department of St. Joseph's Medical Hospital.

Performed as a Charge Nurse as assigned at Candelier Hospital, supervising three or four Registered Nurses, one LPN or occasion, two Nursing Assistants, and a Unit Secretary. Became familiar with hospital policies governing patient care, the chain of command, available hospital resources, and position descriptions of nursing staff members supervised. Planned, assigned, and implemented nursing care for patients on the acute psychiatric unit, which treated adult patients and with substance and mental illness. Accompanied physicians on rounds, assisting them with planning, evaluating, and implementing patient care, based on the physician's medical care plans.

WILLETTE C GILBERT

SSN: 000-00-0000

CHARGE NURSE, GS-11 ANNOUNCEMENT #XYZ123

KSA #2: Ability to communicate orally.

As a Psychiatric Nurse, provide direct patient and family care using the nursing process. Work in close cooperation with other members of the total treatment team in the formulation, implementation, and evaluation of the total care plans for patients. Establish cooperative interpersonal relationships with hospital and medical staff members in order to coordinate patient care. As a Psychiatric Nurse, have responsibility for the milieu and contact with patients at all stages of daily life. Teach self care — medications, health care, and hygiene. Also teach residents how to relate to others, solve problems, communicate clearly, and try out new ways of being. Help clients progress toward less restricted living situations and less restrictive environments. Am also responsible for informing patients and families about available mental health facilities, the nature of psychiatric illness and substance abuse, treatment approaches, and the prevention and reduction of stress as well as teaching anger management techniques and discharge planning procedures.

Perform one-on-one counseling sessions with patients to facilitate a useful change in their life. Focus on motivating and redirecting the behavior of psychiatric patients. Initiate trust building and establish rapport with the patient. Using the nursing process, perform initial nursing history and assessment. Address the client's resistance if it becomes apparent due to care initiated at someone else's request or insistence, fears and misconceptions about therapy, or an unsatisfactory past therapeutic experience. Involve the patient as a full partner in the therapeutic process. Identify and perform patient teaching specific to each patient's needs. Teach patients about and prepare them for diagnostic procedures. Participate in group therapy sessions and teach patient groups on anger management, discharge planning, medications, the nature of psychiatric illness and substance abuse, and social skills.

Also serve as a patient advocate, liaison, and communicator for the delivery of individualized, safe, quality care.

Communicate on a regular basis with the unit manager to keep informed and up to date on information concerning the condition of patients, their problems, and any other issues which come up that directly affect a patient's care.

KSA #3: Knowledge of pharmaceuticals and their desired effects.

Am responsible for daily administration of prescribed medications by oral, intramuscular, subcutaneous, and topical routes. Use the "five rights" as a guide while preparing and administering medications: the right drug, right dose, right route, right patient, and the right time.

Anti-anxiety and sedative-hypnotic drugs are divided into the two categories of benzodiazepines and nonbenzodiazepines. The former exert anti-anxiety effects through potentiation of inhibitory neurotransmitter gamma-aminobutyric acid (GABA). They are prescribed for the management of anxiety, insomnia, and stress-related conditions. Other indications for their use are sleep disorders, anxiety associated with phobic disorders, post-traumatic stress disorder, alcohol and drug withdrawal, seizure disorders, and postoperative anxiety. Side effects to watch for are sedation, ataxia, irritability, and memory problems.

Transcribed medical orders and treatments to the MAR (Medication Administration Record) with responsibility for ensuring that the medication order is complete, correct, and appropriate. Read labels, check and compare them with the MAR. Am familiar with the basic action and use of each drug given as well as with the possible side effects of each drug given. Know the usual route of administration for each drug given. Ensure that medications are swallowed if given orally. Record each medication given accurately on the MAR. Must be aware of any allergies. Provide supportive nursing care to enhance the therapeutic effect and prevent complications from certain types of drugs. Take apical pulse as appropriate for certain prescribed medications and take blood pressure readings as appropriate. Ensure that patients know the name and the action of the drug they are taking, the dosages, and the times to be taken. Evaluate the effectiveness of a medication given a suitable time after its administration. Also evaluate the duration of effectiveness.

Nonbenzodiazepines are barbiturates, Chloral Hydrate, Benadryl, Atarax, Inderal, and Buspar. Tolerances can develop to the anti-anxiety effects of barbiturates. These medications are more addictive and can cause serious withdrawal reactions. Benzodiazepines are generally not strongly addictive if their discontinuation is accomplished by gradual tapering, if they have been used for appropriate purposes, and if their use has not been complicated by the use of other substances.
Some examples of benzodiazepines include the following anti-anxiety drugs:

Xanax	Librium	Serax	Tranxene	Valium
Klonopin	Ativan	Centrax		

Sedative hypnotic drugs include:

Dalmane	Restoril	Halcion

Antidepressant drugs are tricyclic antidepressants, selective serotonin reuptake inhibitors, and monoamine oxidase inhibitors (MAOIs). They are prescribed for major depressive illnesses and are also used in the treatment of panic disorders and enuresis in children. Tricyclic antidepressants appear to regulate the brain's reaction to neurotransmitters norepinephrines and serotonin. With an acceptable cardiac history and ECG within normal limits, particularly if over age 40, are safe and effective for acute and long-term depressive illness. These drugs cause sedation and anticholinergic side effects such as dry mouth, blurred vision, constipation, urinary retention, orthostatic hypertension, tachycardia, and photosensitivity. Most of these are common, short-term side effects which can be minimized with a decrease in dose. Toxic side effects are confusion, poor concentration, hallucinations, delirium, seizures, respiratory depression, tachycardia, brachycardia, and coma. Tricyclics have a 3-4 week delay before therapeutic response.

Selective Serotonin reuptake inhibitors inhibit the reuptake of serotonin at the presynaptic membrane, promoting the neurotransmission of serotonin in the brain. They are without significant anticholinergic, cardiovascular, and sedative side effects. Common side effects are nausea, diarrhea, insomnia, dry mouth, nervousness, headache, drowsiness, dizziness, and male sexual dysfunction.

Monoamine Oxidase Inhibitors block monamine oxidase in the brain and body, less norepinephrine is metabolized, increasing its availability in the synapse. Because of the potential for hypertensive crisis when tyramine-containing foods and certain medicines are taken concomitantly with these drugs, careful patient teaching is important. MAOIs are effective antidepressant and antipanic drugs.

Acute episodes of mania and hypomania and recurrent bipolar illness are treated with lithium, a naturally occurring salt. Side effects include fine hand tremors, fatigue, headache, lethargy, polyuria, polydipsia, gastric irritation, nausea and vomiting, ECG changes and weight gain. Signs of lithium toxicity are related to lithium levels and include anorexia, nausea and vomiting, diarrhea, coarse hand tremors, twitching, lethargy, fever, irregular vital signs, seizures, and coma. Blood levels must be monitored frequently. Antipsychotic drugs are dopamine antagonists and block dopamine receptors in the brain. They are prescribed to manage schizophrenias. Organic brain syndrome with psychosis, the manic phase of manic-depressive illness, and severe depression with psychosis. The nurse pays particular attention to extrapyramidal side effects. The most common drugs to treat short-term EPS are Cogentin, Artane, and Benadryl.

**Charge Nurse, GS-11
Announcement
#XYZ123
KSA #4**

KSA #4: Knowledge of professional nursing care principles, practices, and procedures.

Currently licensed to practice registered nursing in Georgia. Received an Associate of Applied Science Degree in Nursing from Armstrong Atlantic University on May 12, 2004.

Am responsible for self-growth and self-education needed to maintain competence in nursing. Keep abreast of knowledge of techniques, skills, current practices, and regulations appropriate to the age of patients served. Attend all mandatory in-service classes and staff meetings.

Attended the Better Mental Health seminar in March 2002.

Attended the Taking Charge Workshop sponsored by the Education Department of St. Joseph's Medical Hospital on March 15 and 16, 2002 and was approved for 16.2 contact hours.

Renew CPR certification annually with my last certification in August 2002.

Attended Protective Intervention Course (PIC) training at St. Luke Medical Hospital and TIP (Therapeutic Intervention Course) training at Candelier Hospital in August 2002.

Attended the Pediatric Asthma Update Workshop sponsored by St. Joseph's Hospital on April 27, 2001. This course consisted of five hours of instruction for .5 CEU and six contact hours.

Attended the Child Abuse Workshop sponsored by the St. Joseph's Hospital on April 27, 2001. This course consisted of two hours of instruction for .2 CEU and 2,4 contact hours.

Subscribe to Nursing and R.N magazines to increase my knowledge in nursing skills and procedures. Subscribe to the Duke University Medical monthly newsletter in order to stay informed of current trends in mental health.

KSAs of Heather Phillips

HEATHER PHILLIPS

SSN: 000-00-0000

NURSE/PATIENT ADVOCATE, GS-09 ANNOUNCEMENT #XYZ123

KSA #1: Ability to assign the work of other nursing personnel

In my current position as the day **Charge Nurse** for the Adult Geriatric Unit, it my job to address the needs of the unit and make daily assignments to RNs, LPNs, and MHTs. The assignments are determined by acuity of unit, the needs of each patient, and the staff scope of practice. The duties are assigned orally first thing in the morning; they are also written on an assignment board to avoid any confusion. Throughout the day, it is not only my job to take care of patients and their records but also to oversee all staff to make sure all assigned tasks are completed in a timely manner.

As a **Psychiatric Nurse** and **Charge Nurse**, I direct other nursing professionals in providing patient and family care using the nursing process and work in close cooperation with other members of the total treatment team in the formulation, implementation, and evaluation of the total care plans for patients. I direct other nursing professions in establishing cooperative interpersonal relationships with hospital and medical staff members in order to coordinate patient care, and I have responsibility for the milieu and contact with patients at all stages of daily life. I train, supervise, and monitor other nursing professionals in teaching self care — medications, health care, and hygiene, and I also teach residents how to relate to others, solve problems, communicate clearly, and try out new ways of coping while helping clients progress toward less restricted living situations and less restrictive environments. I oversee other nursing professionals as they inform patients and families about available mental health facilities, the nature of psychiatric illness and substance abuse, treatment approaches, and the prevention and reduction of stress as well as teaching anger management techniques and discharge planning procedures.

As a **Charge Nurse** I am responsible for coordinating and supervising day-to-day nursing activities in the psychiatric nursing unit while ensuring the quality of patient care through close observation of all unit activities. I routinely assist emergency room staff in evaluating patients to determine whether they meet Psychiatric admission criteria and provide a complete nurse assessment upon admission. I provide outstanding case management for adult and geriatric patients while ensuring that all standards of care were met and proper procedures followed. I continuously remain alert to potential emergency or high-risk situations so that appropriate actions can be taken. I must inform not only my immediate staff of patient needs, but also I must contact various hospital staffs to arrange for tests, consults, and other needs that the patient might have. Throughout the day I am constantly communicating with nursing personnel.

Education and Training related to this KSA:
- Hold an Associate of Science in Nursing degree from Davidson State College, Austin, TX, 1992.
- Graduated **magna cum laude** and was recognized as one of the class's top four students.
- Have completed professional development training related to providing nursing care in medical/surgical, oncology, and the mental health field.
- Am **Certified in Psychiatric Nursing** by American Nurse Association.
- Am a licensed Registered Nurse in FL and TX.

Nurse/Patient Advocate, GS-09 Announcement #XYZ123 KSA #1
On this page you see the first of three KSAs used by a nurse applying for a GS-9 position as a Nurse/Patient Advocate.

Nurse/Patient
Advocate, GS-09
Announcement #XYZ123
KSA #2

KSA #2: Knowledge of Professional Nursing Care principles, practice, and procedures

In my current position as a Psychiatric Charge Nurse, I am expected to be a patient advocate and to provide care for the patient with mental and emotional disorders, sometimes in conjunction with physical disorders. I contribute to the effectiveness of patient care for emotionally and mentally disturbed patients by handling patient assessment interviews, collecting and evaluating psychological and health histories, monitoring behaviors, and documenting instances of ill health and inappropriate behaviors while supervising other RNs, LPNs, and MHT. As a Staff Nurse in medical/surgical and oncology, I provided the same type of assessment and care; only the disorders and ailments were mostly of a physical nature and required more technical skill with IV pumps, chest tubes, wound care, etc.

Would you like to see the 612 that accompanied these KSAs? You will find it later in this section.

My positions which have helped me acquire expert knowledge of professional nursing care principles, practice, and procedures are these:

- **Psychiatric Charge Nurse**, Grandview Hospital, Tampa, FL (1997-present)
- **Staff Registered Nurse**, Mercy Regional Medical Center, Tempe, AZ (1996) and Wisteria General Hospital, Austin, TX (1993-94)
- **Psychiatric Staff Nurse/Mental Health Technician**, Memorial Medical Center, Austin, TX (1992-93)

A Psychiatric Nurse was applying for this job.

In all of the above positions, I used my initiative and independent judgment to plan and implement professional nursing care for patients in accordance with hospital policies and NANDA. I established cooperative interpersonal relationships with other hospital staff and medical staff members. Among my responsibilities, I used the nursing process and performed the initial nursing history and assessment, developed a nursing care plan, and also developed and implemented nursing orders. I evaluated patient care depending on the patient's response to that care and revised the nursing care plan accordingly. I recognized and informed appropriate personnel of changes in a patient's condition. For psychiatric patients, I followed established protocols, and I worked closely with other members of the total treatment team in the formulation of the total care plan for patients. I focused on motivating and redirecting the behavior of psychiatric patients, and I participated in group therapy sessions while also providing one-to-one counseling sessions with patients. I administered prescribed medications by oral, intramuscular, subcutaneous and topical routes, and I also prepared patients for diagnostic examinations. I identified and performed patient teaching specific to each patient's needs and initiated and completed patient discharge plan. I followed infection control procedures and practiced proper aseptic techniques at all times while also maintaining appropriate records and documents.

In my most recent position as a Psychiatric Registered Nurse, I have functioned as a Charge Nurse and am responsible for coordinating and supervising day-to-day nursing activities in the psychiatric nursing unit while ensuring the quality of patient care through close observation of all unit activities. I routinely assist emergency room staff in evaluating patients to determine whether they meet Psychiatric admission criteria and provide a complete nurse assessment upon admission.

Overview of skills and knowledge:

Through education, training, and experience, have acquired expert skills related to the following areas:

physical assessment	mental-spiritual assessment
observing signs/symptoms of illness	intravenous therapy
blood transfusion	water-seal drainage system
tracheostomy care	suctioning
bladder irrigation	colostomy care
wound care	crisis intervention
patient instruction	documentation of nursing care
supervising and coordinating health teams	blood glucose testing
Hemocults	reviewing lab tests
catheter insertion	Medications
catheter care	suprapubic catheter
oxygen therapies	volume spirometer
CPR	Hickman and Groshong catheters
subcutaneous infusion port	cast care

obtaining cultures: throat, wound, IV cannula

medication administration observing reaction/response

preparing patients for surgery, X-ray, and various tests

Education and Training related to this KSA:

- Hold an Associate of Science in Nursing degree from Davidson State College, Austin, TX 1992.
- Graduated **magna cum laude** and was recognized as one of the class's top four students.
- Have completed professional development training related to providing nursing care in medical/surgical, oncology, and the mental health field.
- Am **Certified in Psychiatric Nursing** by American Nurse Association.
- Am a licensed Registered Nurse in FL and TX.

KSA #3: Ability to communicate orally

As a **Psychiatric Nurse** and **Charge Nurse**, I provide direct patient and family care using the nursing process and work in close cooperation with other members of the total treatment team in the formulation, implementation, and evaluation of the total care plans for patients. I establish cooperative interpersonal relationships with hospital and medical staff members in order to coordinate patient care, and I have responsibility for the milieu and contact with patients at all stages of daily life. I teach self care — medications, health care, and hygiene, and I also teach residents how to relate to others, solve problems, communicate clearly, and try out new ways of coping while helping clients progress toward less restricted living situations and less restrictive environments. I am responsible for informing patients and families about available mental health facilities, the nature of psychiatric illness and substance abuse, treatment approaches, and the prevention and reduction of stress as well as teaching anger management techniques and discharge planning procedures.

Communication skills are sought in many jobs.

As a **Charge Nurse**, it is my responsibility to communicate to the staff what their duties, assignments, and responsibilities are. Assignments are made each day, and they must be orally communicated as well. I must inform not only my immediate staff of patient needs, but also I must contact various hospital staffs to arrange for tests, consults, and other needs that the patient might have. Throughout the day I am constantly communicating with the patient while simultaneously collecting data on their mental status. This is sometimes a difficult task due to the fact that some of my patients may be psychotic and sometimes quite paranoid. I must inform the doctor by telephone or in person of any changes in the patient's status that might suggest the need for immediate attention or intervention. It is my responsibility as a nurse to make sure the doctor has not overlooked or disregarded a problem, and this area of my oral communications responsibilities requires that I utilize the utmost tact, diplomacy, and delicacy so that the information I relay orally will be received in a positive and professional manner and so that all medical professionals remain firmly focused on quality patient care above all else.

As a **Charge Nurse** in my current position as a Psychiatric Nurse, my duties include ER admission assessments/screening. This requires me to collect data from and about the patient. I speak with not only the patient but quite often also with the family, staff, and other facilities such as nursing homes. After gathering the information, I must call the doctor and communicate a clear synopsis of the patient's problem so that the doctor can decide whether to admit the patient or not.

Another of my duties as a **Charge Nurse** which involves oral communications involves teaching nursing education classes. I utilize a lecture and discussion format and vary my style according to what is being taught and also according to the skills level of my students. Indeed, in an informal manner, I am constantly involved in teaching other nurses many concepts and skills. I am responsible for following up with patients, with the patient's family, and with the facility the patient will be assigned to.

Nurse/Patient
Advocate, GS-09
Announcement
#XYZ123
Page Two of
KSA #2

I serve as a patient advocate, liaison, and communicator for the delivery of individualized, safe, quality care. I communicate on a regular basis with the unit manager to keep informed and up to date on information concerning the condition of patients, their problems, and any other issues which come up that directly affect a patient's care. I perform one-on-one counseling and group sessions with patients to facilitate a useful change in their life, and I focus on motivating and redirecting the behavior of psychiatric patients. I initiate trust building and establish rapport with the patient. Using the nursing process, I perform initial nursing history and assessment and I address the client's resistance if it becomes apparent due to care initiated at someone else's request or insistence, fears and misconceptions about therapy, or an unsatisfactory past therapeutic experience. I involve the patient as a full partner in the therapeutic process, identify and perform patient teaching specific to each patient's needs, teach patients about and prepare them for diagnostic procedures, and I participate in group therapy sessions and teach patient groups on anger management, discharge planning, medications, the nature of psychiatric illness and substance abuse, and social skills.

In jobs prior to nursing, I greatly refined my communication skills. As a **Drug and Alcohol Abuse Counselor** from 1993-94, I was continuously using my oral communication skills while working with patients as well as with their families and with medical professionals and referral sources. In my job prior to my current position as a Staff Registered Nurse, I also utilized my communication skills in order to communicate about highly technical matters in a nursing environment. I also used my oral communication skills as a Mental Health Nurse from 1992-93 while working with emotionally and mentally disturbed patients, and that job required extensive interviewing of patients as well as subsequent extensive consulting with medical professionals and others.

Education and Training related to this KSA:
- Hold an Associate of Science in Nursing degree from Davidson State College, Austin, TX, 1992.
- Graduated **magna cum laude** and was recognized as one of the class's top four students.
- Have completed professional development training related to providing nursing care in medical/surgical, oncology, and the mental health field.
- Am **Certified in Psychiatric Nursing**.
- Am a licensed Registered Nurse in FL, TX, and AZ.

KSAs of Penny Guillard

PENNY C. GUILLARD

SSN: 000-00-0000

PSYCHIATRIC CHARGE NURSE, GS-13 ANNOUNCEMENT #XYZ123

KSA #1: Ability to Assign the Work of Other Nursing Personnel

In my current position as the day Charge Nurse for the Adult Geriatric Unit, it my job to address the needs of the unit and make daily assignments to RNs, LPNs, and MHTs. The assignments are determined by acuity of unit, the needs of each patient, and the staff scope of practice. The duties are assigned orally first thing in the morning; they are also written on an assignment board to avoid any confusion. Throughout the day, it is not only my job to take care of patients and their records but also to oversee all staff to make sure all assigned tasks are completed in a timely manner.

As a Psychiatric Nurse and Charge Nurse, I direct other nursing professionals in providing patient and family care using the nursing process and work in close cooperation with other members of the total treatment team in the formulation, implementation, and evaluation of the total care plans for patients. I direct other nursing professions in establishing cooperative interpersonal relationships with hospital and medical staff members in order to coordinate patient care, and I have responsibility for the milieu and contact with patients at all stages of daily life. I train, supervise, and monitor other nursing professionals in teaching self care — medications, health care, and hygiene, and I also teach residents how to relate to others, solve problems, communicate clearly, and try out new ways of coping while helping clients progress toward less restricted living situations and less restrictive environments. I oversee other nursing professionals as they inform patients and families about available mental health facilities, the nature of psychiatric illness and substance abuse, treatment approaches, and the prevention and reduction of stress as well as teaching anger management techniques and discharge planning procedures.

As a Charge Nurse I am responsible for coordinating and supervising day-to-day nursing activities in the psychiatric nursing unit while ensuring the quality of patient care through close observation of all unit activities. I routinely assist emergency room staff in evaluating patients to determine whether they meet Psychiatric admission criteria and provide a complete nurse assessment upon admission. I provide outstanding case management for adult and geriatric patients while ensuring that all standards of care were met and proper procedures followed. I continuously remain alert to potential emergency or high-risk situations so that appropriate actions can be taken. I keep up-to-date in areas including equipment familiarity as well as safety and procedural issues. I have earned the respect of physicians and other nursing staff for my skills, attitude, concern for patients, willingness to work long hours, and respect for confidentiality.

Education and Training related to this KSA:

Hold an Associate of Science in Nursing degree from Butler University, Indianapolis, IN 1997.
Graduated magna cum laude and was recognized as one of the class's top four students.
Have completed professional development training related to providing nursing care in medical/surgical, oncology, and the mental health field.
Am Certified in Psychiatric Nursing by National Association of Nursing Professionals.
Am a licensed Registered Nurse in IN and MI.

PENNY C. GUILLARD

SSN: 000-00-0000

PSYCHIATRIC CHARGE NURSE, GS-13 ANNOUNCEMENT #XYZ123

KSA #2: Ability to communicate orally.

As a Psychiatric Nurse and Charge Nurse, I provide direct patient and family care using the nursing process and work in close cooperation with other members of the total treatment team in the formulation, implementation, and evaluation of the total care plans for patients. I establish cooperative interpersonal relationships with hospital and medical staff members in order to coordinate patient care, and I have responsibility for the milieu and contact with patients at all stages of daily life. I teach self care — medications, health care, and hygiene, and I also teach residents how to relate to others, solve problems, communicate clearly, and try out new ways of coping while helping clients progress toward less restricted living situations and less restrictive environments. I am responsible for informing patients and families about available mental health facilities, the nature of psychiatric illness and substance abuse, treatment approaches, and the prevention and reduction of stress as well as teaching anger management techniques and discharge planning procedures.

As a Charge Nurse, it is my responsibility to communicate to the staff what their duties, assignments, and responsibilities are. Assignments are made each day, and they must be orally communicated as well. I must inform not only my immediate staff of patient needs, but also I must contact various hospital staffs to arrange for tests, consults, and other needs that the patient might have. Throughout the day I am constantly communicating with the patient while simultaneously collecting data on their mental status. This is sometimes a difficult task due to the fact that some of my patients may be psychotic and sometimes quite paranoid. I must inform the doctor by telephone or in person of any changes in the patient's status that might suggest the need for immediate attention or intervention. It is my responsibility as a nurse to make sure the doctor has not overlooked or disregarded a problem, and this area of my oral communications responsibilities requires that I utilize the utmost tact, diplomacy, and delicacy so that the information I relay orally will be received in a positive and professional manner and so that all medical professionals remain firmly focused on quality patient care above all else. As a Charge Nurse in my current position as a Psychiatric Nurse, my duties include ER admission assessments/screening. This requires me to collect data from and about the patient. I speak with not only the patient but quite often also with the family, staff, and other facilities such as nursing homes. After gathering the information, I must call the doctor and communicate a clear synopsis of the patient's problem so that the doctor can decide whether to admit the patient or not.

Another of my duties as a Charge Nurse which involves oral communications involves teaching nursing education classes. I utilize a lecture and discussion format and vary my style according to what is being taught and also according to the skills level of my students. Indeed, in an informal manner, I am constantly involved in teaching other nurses many concepts and skills. I am responsible for following up with patients, with the patient's family, and with the facility the patient will be assigned to.

Education and Training related to this KSA:
Hold an Associate of Science in Nursing degree from Butler University, Indianapolis, IN 1997. Graduated magna cum laude. Recognized as one of the class's top four students.

KSA #3: Knowledge of Professional Nursing Care Principles, Practice, and Procedures.

In my current position as a Psychiatric Charge Nurse, I am expected to be a patient advocate and to provide care for the patient with mental and emotional disorders, sometimes in conjunction with physical disorders. I contribute to the effectiveness of patient care for emotionally and mentally disturbed patients by handling patient assessment interviews, collecting and evaluating psychological and health histories, monitoring behaviors, and documenting instances of ill health and inappropriate behaviors while supervising other RNs, LPNs, and MHT. As a Staff Nurse in medical/ surgical and oncology, I provided the same type of assessment and care; only the disorders and ailments were mostly of a physical nature and required more technical skill with IV pumps, chest tubes, wound care, etc.

My positions which have helped me acquire expert knowledge of professional nursing care principles, practice, and procedures are these:
- **Psychiatric Charge Nurse**, Xavier Hospital, Lansing, MI (2003-present)
- **Staff Registered Nurse**, Langston Regional Medical Center, Lansing, MI (2003) and Memorial Hospital, Indianapolis, IN (1999-03)
- **Psychiatric Staff Nurse/Mental Health Technician**, Battle Creek Regional Hospital, Battle Creek, MI (1997-99)

In all of the above positions, I used my initiative and independent judgment to plan and implement professional nursing care for patients in accordance with hospital policies and regulations. I established cooperative interpersonal relationships with other hospital staff and medical staff members. Among my responsibilities, I used the nursing process and performed the initial nursing history and assessment, developed a nursing care plan, and also developed and implemented nursing orders. I evaluated patient care depending on the patient's response to that care and revised the nursing care plan accordingly. I recognized and informed appropriate personnel of changes in a patient's condition. For psychiatric patients, I followed established protocols, and I worked closely with other members of the total treatment team in the formulation of the total care plan for patients. I focused on motivating and redirecting the behavior of psychiatric patients, and I participated in group therapy sessions while also providing one-to-one counseling sessions with patients. I administered prescribed medications by oral, intramuscular, subcutaneous and topical routes, and I also prepared patients for diagnostic examinations. I identified and performed patient teaching specific to each patient's needs and initiated and completed patient discharge plan. I followed infection control procedures and practiced proper aseptic techniques at all times while also maintaining appropriate records and documents.

In my most recent position as a Psychiatric Registered Nurse, I have functioned as a Charge Nurse and am responsible for coordinating and supervising day-to-day nursing activities in the psychiatric nursing unit while ensuring the quality of patient care through close observation of all unit activities. I routinely assist emergency room staff in evaluating patients to determine whether they meet Psychiatric admission criteria and provide a complete nurse assessment upon admission. I have provided outstanding case management for adult and geriatric patients while ensuring that all standards of care were met and proper procedures followed. I continuously remain alert to potential emergency or high-risk situations so that appropriate actions can be taken to keep up-to-date in areas including equipment familiarity as well as safety and procedural issues. I have earned the respect of physicians and other nursing staff for my skills, attitude, concern for patients, willingness to work long hours, and respect for confidentiality.

Overview of skills and knowledge:

Through education, training, and experience, have acquired expert skills related to the following areas:

physical assessment	mental-spiritual assessment
intravenous therapy and management	observing signs/symptoms of illness
blood transfusion	water-seal drainage system
tracheostomy care	suctioning
bladder irrigation	colostomy care
wound care	crisis intervention
patient instruction	documentation of nursing care
supervising and coordinating health teams	blood glucose testing
Hemocults	reviewing lab tests
obtaining cultures: throat, wound, IV cannula	catheter insertion, male and female
catheter care	suprapubic catheter
oxygen therapies	volume spirometer
CPR	Hickman and Groshong catheters
subcutaneous infusion port	cast care
Medications	

medication administration observing reaction/response
preparing patients for surgery, X-ray, and various tests

Education and Training related to this KSA:

Hold an Associate of Science in Nursing degree from Butler University, Indianapolis, IN 1997.

Graduated magna cum laude and was recognized as one of the class's top four students.

Have completed professional development training related to providing nursing care in medical/surgical, onology, and the mental health field.

Am Certified in Psychiatric Nursing by National Association of Nursing Professionals.

Am a licensed Registered Nurse in IN and MI.

KSAs of Yolanda Marin

YOLANDA M. MARIN

SSN: 000-00-0000

PSYCHIATRIC NURSE, GS-09 ANNOUNCEMENT #XYZ123

KSA #1: Ability to plan, assign, and direct the work of other nursing personnel

Perform Charge Nurse duties on a regular basis while supervising two or three Residential Care Specialists on the evening shift at the Residential Treatment Center. Use my initiative and independent judgment to plan and implement professional nursing care for patients in accordance with hospital policies. Am familiar with hospital policies regarding patient care. Also am responsible for knowing and following the chain of command. Am familiar with the resources available to me so that I can fill the role of Charge Nurse. Have established cooperative interpersonal relationships with other hospital staff and medical staff members. Among my responsibilities is knowing the position descriptions of nursing personnel supervised. In order to effectively delegate tasks I determine what needs to be done and what can be delegated to others. Evaluate the job performance of team members in order to determine who can best take care of each delegated task.

Describe the tasks and assignments to the team members and make sure each member understands the tasks and assignments given to them and to test their listening skills. Provide the guidelines for them to report back and on how and when the assignments will be evaluated. Ensure that follow up and evaluation is as previously stated to each team member. Provide the authority, responsibility, and support needed to complete the assignment. I recognize and appreciate a job well done by giving praise that is specific, honest, sincere, and succinct. Acknowledge improvement in performance of a task and promote team synergy and cooperation. Am familiar with disruptive behaviors that may prevent coworkers from functioning well and effective in redirecting those behaviors. Endeavor to build and maintain morale to help coworkers work together smoothly. Attended and participated in the Taking Charge Workshop presented by the Education Department of Northwestern Medical Center.

Performed as a Charge Nurse as assigned at Rockefeller Regional Medical Center, supervising three or four Registered Nurses, one LPN or occasion, two Nursing Assistants, and a Unit Secretary. Became familiar with hospital policies governing patient care, the chain of command, available hospital resources, and position descriptions of nursing staff members supervised. Planned, assigned, and implemented nursing care for patients on the acute psychiatric unit, which treated adult patients and with substance and mental illness. Accompanied physicians on rounds, assisting them with planning, evaluating, and implementing patient care, based on the physician's medical care plans.

YOLANDA M. MARIN

SSN: 000-00-0000

PSYCHIATRIC NURSE, GS-09 ANNOUNCEMENT #XYZ123

KSA #2: Ability to communicate orally

As a Psychiatric Nurse, provide direct patient and family care using the nursing process. Work in close cooperation with other members of the total treatment team in the formulation, implementation, and evaluation of the total care plans for patients. Establish cooperative interpersonal relationships with hospital and medical staff members in order to coordinate patient care. As a Psychiatric Nurse, have responsibility for the milieu and contact with patients at all stages of daily life. Teach self care: medications, health care, and hygiene.

Also teach residents how to relate to others, solve problems, communicate clearly, and try out new ways of being. Help clients progress toward less restricted living situations and less restrictive environments. Am also responsible for informing patients and families about available mental health facilities, the nature of psychiatric illness and substance abuse, treatment approaches, and the prevention and reduction of stress as well as teaching anger management techniques and discharge planning procedures.

Perform one-on-one counseling sessions with patients to facilitate a useful change in their life. Focus on motivating and redirecting the behavior of psychiatric patients. Initiate trust building and establish rapport with the patient. Using the nursing process, perform initial nursing history and assessment. Address the client's resistance if it becomes apparent due to care initiated at someone else's request or insistence, fears and misconceptions about therapy, or an unsatisfactory past therapeutic experience. Involve the patient as a full partner in the therapeutic process. Identify and perform patient teaching specific to each patient's needs. Teach patients about and prepare them for diagnostic procedures. Participate in group therapy sessions and teach patient groups on anger management, discharge planning, medications, the nature of psychiatric illness and substance abuse, and social skills.

Also serve as a patient advocate, liaison, and communicator for the delivery of individualized, safe, quality care.

Communicate on a regular basis with the unit manager to keep informed and up to date on information concerning the condition of patients, their problems, and any other issues which come up that directly affect a patient's care.

Psychiatric Nurse,
GS-09 Announcement
#XYZ123 KSA #3

KSA #3: Knowledge of pharmaceuticals and their desired effects

Am responsible for daily administration of prescribed medications by oral, intramuscular, subcutaneous, and topical routes. Use the "five rights" as a guide while preparing and administering medications: the right drug, right dose, right route, right patient, and the right time.

Anti-anxiety and sedative-hypnotic drugs are divided into the two categories of benzodiazepines and nonbenzodiazepines. The former exert anti-anxiety effects through potentiation of inhibitory neurotransmitter gamma-aminobutyric acid (GABA). They are prescribed for the management of anxiety, insomnia, and stress-related conditions. Other indications for their use are sleep disorders, anxiety associated with phobic disorders, posttraumatic stress disorder, alcohol and drug withdrawal, seizure disorders, and postoperative anxiety. Side effects to watch for are sedation, ataxia, irritability, and memory problems.

Transcribed medical orders and treatments to the MAR (Medication Administration Record) with responsibility for ensuring that the medication order is complete, correct, and appropriate. Read labels, check and compare them with the MAR. Am familiar with the basic action and use of each drug given as well as with the possible side effects of each drug given. Know the usual route of administration for each drug given. Ensure that medications are swallowed if given orally. Record each medication given accurately on the MAR. Must be aware of any allergies. Ensure that patients know the name and the action of the drug they are taking, the dosages, and the times to be taken. Evaluate the effectiveness of a medication given a suitable time after its administration. Also evaluate the duration of effectiveness.

Check the spelling of all names of products etc.!

Nonbenzodiazepines are barbiturates. Tolerances can develop to the anti-anxiety effects of barbiturates. These medications are more addictive and can cause serious withdrawal reactions. Benzodiazepines are generally not strongly addictive if their discontinuation is accomplished by gradual tapering, if they have been used for appropriate purposes, and if their use has not been complicated by the use of other substances.

Antidepressant drugs are tricyclic antidepressants, selective serotonin reuptake inhibitors, and monoamine oxidase inhibitors (MAOIs). They are prescribed for major depressive illnesses and are also used in the treatment of panic disorders and enuresis in children. Tricyclic antidepressants appear to regulate the brain's reaction to neurotransmitters norepinephrines and serotonin. With an acceptable cardiac history and ECG within normal limits, particularly if over age 40, are safe and effective for acute and long-term depressive illness. These drugs cause sedation and anticholinergic side effects such as dry mouth, blurred vision, constipation, urinary retention, orthostatic hypertension, tachycardia, and photosensitivity. Most of these are common, short-term side effects which can be minimized with a decrease in dose.

KSAs of Bernice McLaughlin

BERNICE MCLAUGHLIN

SSN: 000-00-0000

REGISTERED NURSE, GS-07 ANNOUNCEMENT #XYZ123

KSA #1: KNOWLEDGE OF VARIOUS NURSING CARE PRINCIPLES, PRACTICES, AND PROCEDURES REQUIRED TO ASSESS AND PROVIDE NURSING CARE TO PATIENTS IN AND OUT OF THE HOSPITAL.

Throughout my career as a Registered Nurse, I have been required to demonstrate my knowledge of nursing care principles, practices, and procedures on a daily basis. Currently, as Dependent Care Program (DCP) Nurse and Program Administrative Assistant, Winn Army Medical Center (2002-present), I provide professional nursing support for the DCP and apply professional nursing and related medical knowledge while evaluating the medical, psychological, and social needs of patient and family.

In Clinical Nurse positions in pediatric and medical-surgical environments, provided care for pediatric and adult medical and surgical patients ranging from those who were ambulatory to those receiving complex new or nonstandard treatments. Prepared patients for surgical or diagnostic procedures; observed post-operative patients and those receiving medical therapy for adverse reactions; took immediate action in response to medical emergencies. Cared for patients requiring intensive care such as post-operative and burn patients, accident victims, etc. Administered medications orally, intravenously, subcutaneously, and through inhalation to patients of all ages. Initiated emergency resuscitative measures and assisted physicians with further emergency responses. Operated specialized medical equipment such as cardiac monitoring devices.

KSA #2: KNOWLEDGE OF NURSING AND UTILIZATION REVIEW PRACTICES AND DISCHARGE PLANNING PROCESS TO DEVELOP APPROPRIATE TREATMENT PLANS.

As a Clinical Nurse on the Pediatric floor at Winn Army Medical Center (2000-02), I recorded initial histories, performed patient assessments, and developed nursing care plans. Provided comprehensive patient care based on the needs of the patient, the nursing care plan, and the physician's medical plan. Evaluated the patient's response to treatment and revised the nursing care plan, as necessary. Verified and annotated physician's orders and advised the attending physician of any significant changes in a patient's condition.

Earlier as Admission Coordinator Nurse at Tuttle Army Health Clinic in Fort Stewart, GA (September 1999 - April 2000), was given additional responsibilities and placed in charge of the patient pre-admission process to include:
- education, pre-admission, and assessment of surgical and nonsurgical patients
- preparation of admissions forms, standardized care plans, teaching materials and other documentation
- coordination of services with laboratory, x-ray, EKG, anesthesia, the emergency room for unscheduled emergency response, and the Rehabilitation Program.

KSA #3: ABILITY TO COMMUNICATE EFFECTIVELY ORALLY AND IN WRITING.

Throughout my career as a Registered Nurse, I have demonstrated my ability to communicate effectively orally and in writing. Communicated orally with physicians and nurses while delivering reports at the end of shift to physicians and nurses coming on-shift; give a detailed verbal account of the condition and progress of treatment for each patient under my care. Taught on-the-job and in-service training for staff personnel and assisted with new-employee orientations. Provided verbal instruction in aftercare and home care procedures, as well as in proper administration of medications and possible interactions to patients and family members.

My strong written communication skills are exhibited in the clarity and precision with which I compose the various types of reports which I am required to prepare. These include but are not limited to care plans, incident and accident reports, customer complaints, and discharge plans.

A native of Guatemala, I am bilingual and fluent in both Spanish and English.

Education and Training Related to these KSAs:

Diploma awarded upon completion of a three-year program from the School of Nursing, Georgia Southern University, Statesboro, GA; awarded Registered Nursing license #9999, valid through 02/28/05.

Completed training and was certified as a Basic Cardiac Life Support provider by the American Heart Association, certification renewed 01/21/03.

Complete an additional 38 hours of Continuing Medical Education every two years, in order to update and maintain my nursing skills and certifications.

PART SIX: The Optional Form (OF) 612, Used to Apply for Federal Government Jobs

On the pages that follow, you will see an example of the Optional Form 612, which is sometimes used to apply for federal government jobs. You will usually have a choice of applying with an OF 612, a federal resume or resumix, or even a standard form 171 (which is not illustrated in this book). You will submit either a resumix or a 612, but not both.

612 used to apply for federal positions

DANIELLE M. RIVERA

SSN: 000-00-0000

CONTINUATION SHEET FOR 612 ITEM 8 (1)

This 612 is for a
Psychiatric Nurse.

Job Title: Psychiatric Nurse
From (MM/YY): 01/2002
To (MM/YY): present
Salary: $16.39 per hour
Hours per week: 40
Employer's name and address: Wendover Hospital of Merrick Bluffs Medical Center, 1110 Hay Street, Riverdale, NY 28305
Supervisor's name and phone number: Francis Sweeney, (910) 483-6611

As the Charge Nurse on the evening shift, I am responsible for providing long-term care to adolescents living at the Residential Treatment Center (RTC) which provides intermediate care to residents with a history of legal problems, placement problems, family and/or school difficulties, and on occasion sexually deviant behavior. Handle the admissions process on the arrival of scheduled new residents when they are admitted on my shift. Supervise three Residential Care Specialists. Provide direct patient care, administer medications (by oral, intramuscular, subcutaneous, and topical routes), and educate residents and their parents on prescribed medications.

This psychiatric nurse had
to relocate with
her spouse
but wanted to remain
in her field.

Provide one-on-one counseling with clients and with groups on social skills, anger management, substance abuse, and hygiene. Counsel parents or other responsible parties on the patient's treatment and progress. Assist patients with behavior modification. Perform high-risk intervention charting on clients with a history of legal problems, placement problems, family and/or school difficulties, aggressive and sexually deviant problems. Conduct rounds with physicians.

Am cross-trained on the Acute Adolescent Unit as Charge Nurse supervising two Mental Health Specialists. Remain alert at all times in order to observe any changes in any patient's condition and inform the appropriate personnel. Focus on motivating and redirecting the behavior of psychiatric patients.

Job Title: Psychiatric Staff Nurse
From (MM/YY): 04/95
To (MM/YY): 12/2001
Salary: $16.15 per hour
Hours per week: 40
Employer's name and address: Valley Oaks Medical Center, Albany, NY 28305
Supervisor's name and phone number: Frances Sweeney, (910) 483-6611

Continuation Sheet
For 612 Item 8 (2)

As the Staff Nurse on 3 East, the Psychiatric Unit at Valley Oaks, provided direct patient care to from five to 12 patients on an acute psychiatric unit. This unit consisted of adult patients with substance abuse and mental illness. As the Charge Nurse responsible for supervising three or four Registered Nurses, male and female Nursing Assistants, and a Unit Secretary, was responsible for administering medications (by oral, intramuscular, subcutaneous, and topical routes) and completing charting on each patient. *Her duties in this job were similar to her duties in Job (1).*

Conducted patient groups on medications, anger management, discharge planning, and hygiene. Educated patients on diagnosis, medications, and community resources. Coordinated care with other interdisciplinary team members. Admitted both voluntary and involuntary patients with commitment papers. Performed rounds with physicians.

Used the nursing process and was involved in performing initial nursing histories and assessments and in the development of nursing care plans. Evaluated nursing care provided based on the patient's response and made revisions to the nursing care plan as needed. Worked closely with other members of the total treatment team in order to formulate total care plans for each patient. Participated in group therapy sessions and performed one-on-one counseling.

612 used to apply for federal positions

DANIELLE M. RIVERA

SSN: 000-00-0000

CONTINUATION SHEET FOR 612 ITEM 8 (3)

**Continuation Sheet
For 612 Item 8 (3)**

Job Title: Staff Nurse
From (MM/YY): 01/95
To (MM/YY): 04/95
Salary: $14.25 per hour
Hours per week: 40
Employer's name and address: Convalescent Center of Harper County, Des Moines, IA
Supervisor's name and phone number: Ms. Frances Sweeney, (910) 483-6611

Was a Staff Nurse on Hall 1 which provided intermediate nursing care to nursing home residents. Worked as the primary nurse on the hall, along with one other RN or LPN, to provide direct patient care to the 33 residents (on my hall).

Sometimes the military spouse must move frequently, so the durations of work are often brief.

Care included dependent nursing functions delegated by physicians and independent nursing functions which included patient assessments, evaluation of patient responses, and the education of patients and their families. Ensured that a safe environment was provided. Administered medications as ordered by physicians using the oral, intramuscular, subcutaneous, and topical routes. Recognized life-threatening situations and responded appropriately. Coordinated the transfer of patients to the local hospital emergency room (ER) when necessary.

Maintained an accurate and relevant record of resident care. Established cooperative interpersonal relationships with other nursing home staff members and physicians.

Job Title: Staff Nurse
From (MM/YY): 09/94
To (MM/YY): 12/94
Salary: $13.30 per hour (part time)
Hours per week: 20
Employer's name and address: Hope Medical Center, San Francisco, CA 28305
Supervisor's name and phone number: Frances Sweeney, number unknown

**Continuation Sheet
For 612 Item 8 (4)**

Was the primary nurse providing direct patient care, including personal hygiene, dependent nursing functions delegated by physicians, and independent nursing functions which included patient assessments, teaching patients and families, evaluating patient responses, and coordinating care between interdisciplinary team members.

Notice how a part-time job is shown.

Assessed patients and identified nursing diagnoses. Planned, organized, implemented, and evaluated patient care. Provided a safe environment. Maintained an accurate and relevant record of patient care. Safely administered medications as ordered by physicians by the oral, intravenous, intramuscular, subcutaneous, and topical routes. Recognized life-threatening situations and responded appropriately. Established cooperative interpersonal relationships with other hospital staff and medical staff.

612 used to apply for federal positions

DANIELLE M. RIVERA

SSN: 000-00-0000

CONTINUATION SHEET FOR 612 ITEM 8 (5)

**Continuation Sheet
For 612 Item 8 (5)**

Job Title: Homemaker and Student
From (MM/YY): 12/85
To (MM/YY): 09/94
Salary: N/A
Hours per week: N/A
Employer's name and address: N/A
Supervisor's name and phone number: N/A

A period of extensive at-home work, often involving raising children, may be accounted for in this way. If she had been involved in **volunteer** work, such as PTA or military support activities, she could have written about that, too.

Was a housewife and mother from 12/85 to 8/90 and from 8/90 to 9/94 was a part-time and full-time student (see education section).

DANIELLE M. RIVERA

SSN: 000-00-0000

CONTINUATION SHEET FOR 612 ITEM 13

Job-Related Training Courses:

- Taking Charge Workshop, given by the Education Department of Merrick Bluffs Medical Center, Jan. 28-29, 1997
- Pediatric Asthma Update, given by the Riverdale Health Education Center, Feb. 19, 1997
- Child Abuse Workshop, given by the Riverdale Health Education Center, Feb. 19, 1997
- Volunteer Training for Rape Crisis Intervention, Jan. 1994
- CPR Certified, Merrick Bluffs Medical Center, Nov. 1996
- PIC Training, Nov. 1996

Computer Skills:

Use SMS Invision industry-specific software for checking patient census information, confirming doctors' orders, retrieving the results of laboratory work, and for completing paperwork related to the discharging or transfer of patients.

Since she is applying for Psychiatric Nurse jobs, her readers will understand what PLC and CPR stand for.

Job-Related Skills:

- Employee supervision, training, evaluations, and analysis
- Counseling, interviewing, screening
- Public relations and customer service
- Safety, security, and emergency procedures
- Scheduling, planning, and coordination
- Program development and administration
- Charge nurse
- CPR certified
- Protective Intervention Course (PIC)
- Projecting time/labor/material requirements
- Procurement, supply, and inventory control
- Verification, documentation, and reporting
- Problem identification and decision-making skills
- Negotiation and mediation
- Skilled in counseling on alcohol and drug abuse prevention
- Attended child abuse and pediatric asthma workshops

ABOUT THE EDITOR

Anne McKinney holds an MBA from the Harvard Business School and a BA in English from the University of North Carolina at Chapel Hill. A noted public speaker, writer, and teacher, she is the senior editor for PREP's business and career imprint, which bears her name. Early titles in the Anne McKinney Career Series (now called the Real-Resumes Series) published by PREP include: *Resumes and Cover Letters That Have Worked, Resumes and Cover Letters That Have Worked for Military Professionals, Government Job Applications and Federal Resumes, Cover Letters That Blow Doors Open,* and *Letters for Special Situations.* Her career titles and how-to resume-and-cover-letter books are based on the expertise she has acquired in 20 years of working with job hunters. Her valuable career insights have appeared in publications of the "Wall Street Journal" and other prominent newspapers and magazines.

PREP Publishing Order Form

You may purchase any of our titles from your favorite bookseller! Or send a check or money order or your credit card number for the total amount*, plus $4.00 postage and handling, to PREP, 1110 1/2 Hay Street, Fayetteville, NC 28305. You may also order our titles on our website at www.prep-pub.com and feel free to e-mail us at preppub@aol.com or call 910-483-6611 with your questions or concerns.

Name: _____

Phone #:_____

Address: _____

E-mail address:_____

Payment Type: ☐ Check/Money Order   ☐ Visa   ☐ MasterCard

Credit Card Number: _____ Expiration Date: _____

Put a check beside the items you are ordering:

☐ Free—Packet describing PREP's professional writing and editing services

☐ $16.95—REAL-RESUMES FOR RESTAURANT, FOOD SERVICE & HOTEL JOBS. Anne McKinney, Editor

☐ $16.95—REAL-RESUMES FOR MEDIA, NEWSPAPER, BROADCASTING & PUBLIC AFFAIRS JOBS. Anne McKinney, Editor

☐ $16.95—REAL-RESUMES FOR RETAILING, MODELING, FASHION & BEAUTY JOBS. Anne McKinney, Editor

☐ $16.95—REAL-RESUMES FOR HUMAN RESOURCES & PERSONNEL JOBS. Anne McKinney, Editor

☐ $16.95—REAL-RESUMES FOR MANUFACTURING JOBS. Anne McKinney, Editor

☐ $16.95—REAL-RESUMES FOR AVIATION & TRAVEL JOBS. Anne McKinney, Editor

☐ $16.95—REAL-RESUMES FOR POLICE, LAW ENFORCEMENT & SECURITY JOBS. Anne McKinney, Editor

☐ $16.95—REAL-RESUMES FOR SOCIAL WORK & COUNSELING JOBS. Anne McKinney, Editor

☐ $16.95—REAL-RESUMES FOR CONSTRUCTION JOBS. Anne McKinney, Editor

☐ $16.95—REAL-RESUMES FOR FINANCIAL JOBS. Anne McKinney, Editor

☐ $16.95—REAL-RESUMES FOR COMPUTER JOBS. Anne McKinney, Editor

☐ $16.95—REAL-RESUMES FOR MEDICAL JOBS. Anne McKinney, Editor

☐ $16.95—REAL-RESUMES FOR TEACHERS. Anne McKinney, Editor

☐ $16.95—REAL-RESUMES FOR CAREER CHANGERS. Anne McKinney, Editor

☐ $16.95—REAL-RESUMES FOR STUDENTS. Anne McKinney, Editor

☐ $16.95—REAL-RESUMES FOR SALES. Anne McKinney, Editor

☐ $16.95—REAL ESSAYS FOR COLLEGE AND GRAD SCHOOL. Anne McKinney, Editor

☐ $25.00—RESUMES AND COVER LETTERS THAT HAVE WORKED. McKinney. Editor

☐ $25.00—RESUMES AND COVER LETTERS THAT HAVE WORKED FOR MILITARY PROFESSIONALS. McKinney, Ed.

☐ $25.00—RESUMES AND COVER LETTERS FOR MANAGERS. McKinney, Editor

☐ $25.00—GOVERNMENT JOB APPLICATIONS AND FEDERAL RESUMES: Federal Resumes, KSAs, Forms 171 and 612, and Postal Applications. McKinney, Editor

☐ $25.00—COVER LETTERS THAT BLOW DOORS OPEN. McKinney, Editor

☐ $25.00—LETTERS FOR SPECIAL SITUATIONS. McKinney, Editor

☐ $16.95—REAL-RESUMES FOR NURSING JOBS. McKinney, Editor

☐ $16.95—REAL-RESUMES FOR AUTO INDUSTRY JOBS. Patty Sleem

☐ $24.95—REAL KSAS--KNOWLEDGE, SKILLS & ABILITIES--FOR GOVERNMENT JOBS. McKinney, Editor

☐ $24.95—REAL RESUMIX AND OTHER RESUMES FOR FEDERAL GOVERNMENT JOBS. McKinney, Editor

☐ $24.95—REAL BUSINESS PLANS AND MARKETING TOOLS ... Samples to use in starting, growing, marketing, and selling your business

_____ **TOTAL ORDERED**

_____ **(add $4.00 for shipping and handling)**

_____ **TOTAL INCLUDING SHIPPING**

PREP offers volume discounts on large orders. Call us at (910) 483-6611 for more information.

THE MISSION OF PREP PUBLISHING IS TO PUBLISH
BOOKS AND OTHER PRODUCTS WHICH ENRICH
PEOPLE'S LIVES AND HELP THEM OPTIMIZE THE
HUMAN EXPERIENCE. OUR STRONGEST LINES ARE
OUR JUDEO-CHRISTIAN ETHICS SERIES AND OUR
REAL-RESUMES SERIES.

Would you like to explore the possibility of having PREP's writing
team create a resume for you similar to the ones in this book?

For a brief free consultation, call 910-483-6611
or send $4.00 to receive our Job Change Packet to
PREP, 1110 1/2 Hay Street, Fayetteville, NC 28305. Visit our
website to find valuable career resources: www.prep-pub.com!

QUESTIONS OR COMMENTS? E-MAIL US AT PREPPUB@AOL.COM

CPSIA information can be obtained at www.ICGtesting.com
Printed in the USA
BVOW05s1322261113

337389BV00004BA/5/P